John Pearson, Thomas Heywood

The Dramatic Works of Thomas Heywood

Vol. 4

John Pearson, Thomas Heywood

The Dramatic Works of Thomas Heywood
Vol. 4

ISBN/EAN: 9783337341343

Printed in Europe, USA, Canada, Australia, Japan

Cover: Foto ©Thomas Meinert / pixelio.de

More available books at **www.hansebooks.com**

THE DRAMATIC WORKS OF
THOMAS HEYWOOD NOW
FIRST COLLECTED WITH
ILLUSTRATIVE NOTES AND
A MEMOIR OF THE AUTHOR
IN SIX VOLUMES

Aut prodesse solent, aut Delectare—

VOLUME THE FOURTH

LONDON
JOHN PEARSON YORK STREET COVENT GARDEN
1874

THE
ENGLISH
TRAVELLER.
AS IT HATH BEENE

Publikely acted at the Cock-pit

in Drury-lane:

By Her Maiesties seruants.

Written by Thomas Heyvvood.

Aut prodesse solent, aut delectare———

LONDON,
Printed by *Robert Raworth*: dwelling in Old Fish-street,
neere Saint *Mary Maudlins* Church. 1633.

Dramatis Personæ.

Geraldine. } *Dalauill.* }	Two yong Gentlemen.
Olde Wincott	The husband.
His Wife	A yong Gentlewoman.
Prudentilla	Sister to the wife.
Reignald	A parasiticall seruing-man.
Robin	A countrey seruing-man.
Lionell	A riotous Citizen.
Blanda	A Whore.
Scapha	A Bawde.
Rioter	A Spend-thrift.
Two Gallants	His Companions.
Roger the Clowne	Seruant to Olde Wincott.
Two prostitutes	Companions with Blanda.
Olde Lionell	A Merchant father to yong Lionell.
A Seruant	To Olde Lionell. .
Olde Mr. Geraldine	Father to yong Geraldine.
An Vsurer and his man.	
A Gentleman	Companion with Dalauill.
Besse	Chambermaid to Mistris Wincott.
A Tauerne Drawer	
Master Ricott	A Merchant.

The *Owner* of the house, supposed to be possest.

To the Right
WORSHIPFVLL
Sir HENRY APPLETON,
Knight Barronet, &c.

NOBLE SIR,

Or many reasons I am induced, to present this Poem, to your fauourable acceptance ; and not the least of them that alternate Loue, and those frequent curtesies which interchangably past, betwixt your selfe and that good old Gentleman, mine vnkle (Master *Edmund Heywood*) whom you pleased to grace by the Title of Father : I must confesse, I had altogether slept (my weaklines and bashfullnesse discouraging mee) had they not bin waken'd and animated, by that worthy Gentleman your friend, and my countreyman, Sir *William Eluish*, whom (who for his vnmerited loue many wayes extended towards me,) I much honour ; Neither Sir, neede you to thinke it any vnderualuing of your worth, to vndertake the patronage of a Poem in this nature, since the like hath beene done by Roman *Lælius*, *Scipio*, *Mecænas*, and many other mighty Princes and Captaines, Nay, euen by *Augustus Cæsar* himselfe, concerning whom *Ouid* is thus read, *De tristi* : *lib.* 2.

The Epistle Dedicatorie.

Inspice ludorum sumptus Auguste tuorum
Empta tibi magno, talia multa leges
Hæc tu spectasti, spectandaque sæpe de desti
Maiestas adeo comis vbique tua est.

So highly were they respected in the most flourishing estate of the Roman Empire; and if they haue beene vilefied of late by any Separisticall humorist, (as in the now questioned *Histrio-mastix*) I hope by the next Terme, (*Minerua afsistente*) to giue such satisfaction to the world, by vindicating many particulars in that worke maliciously exploded and condemned, as that no Gentleman of qualitie and iudgement, but shall therein receiue a reasonable satisfaction; I am loth by tediousnesse to grow troublesome, therefore conclude with a gratefull remembrance of my seruice intermixt with Miriads of zealous wishes for your health of body, and peace of minde, with superabundance of Earths blessings, and Heauens graces, euer remaining;

Yours most obseruant,

Thomas Heywood.

To the Reader.

F Reader thou haſt of this Play beene an auditour? there is leſſe apology to be vſed by intreating thy patience. This Tragi-Comedy (being one reſerued amongſt two hundred and twenty, in which I haue had either an entire hand, or at the leaſt a maine finger, comming accidentally to the Preſſe, and I hauing Intelligence thereof, thought it not fit that it ſhould paſſe as filius populi, a Baſtard without a Father to acknowledge it: True it is, that my Playes are not expoſed vnto the world in Volumes, to beare the title of Workes, (as others) one reaſon is, That many of them by ſhifting and change of Companies, haue beene negligently lost, Others of them are ſtill retained in the hands of ſome Actors, who thinke it againſt their peculiar profit to haue them come in Print, and a third, That it neuer was any great ambition in me, to bee in this kind Volumniouſly read. All that I haue further to ſay at this time is onely this: Cenſure I intreat as fauourably, as it is expoſed to thy view freely, euer

Studious of thy Pleaſure and Profit,

Thomas Heywood.

The Prologue.

 *Strange Play you are like to haue, for know,*
We vse no Drum, nor Trumpet, nor Dumbe
  show ;
No Combate, Marriage, not so much to day,
As Song, Dance, Masque, to bumbaste out a
  Play ;
Yet these all good, and still in frequent vse
With our best Poets ; *nor is this excuse*
Made by our Author, *as if want of skill*
Caus'd this defect ; it's rather his selfe will:
Will you the reason know ?   There haue so many
Beene in that kind, that Hee desires not any
At this time in His Sceane, no helpe, no straine,
Or flash that's borrowed from an others braine ;
Nor speakes Hee this that Hee would haue you feare it,
He onely tries if once bare Lines will beare it ;
Yet may't afford, so please you silent sit,
Some Mirth, some Matter, and perhaps some Wit.

THE
ENGLISH
TRAVELLER.

Actus primus. Scena prima,

Enter young Geraldine and master Dalauill.

Dal. H friend, that I to mine owne Notion
Had ioyned but your experience ; I
haue the Theoricke, But you the
Practicke.

  Y. Ger.   I perhaps, haue feene what you haue onely read of.

  Dal.   There's your happineffe.
A Scholler in his ftudy knowes the ftarres,
Their motion and their influence, which are fixt,
And which are wandering, can decipher Seas,
And giue each feuerall Land his proper bounds ;
But fet him to the Compaffe, hee's to feeke,
When a plaine Pilot can, direct his courfe
From hence vnto both th' Indies ; can bring backe
His fhip and charge, with profits quintuple.

I haue read Ierufalem, and ftudied Rome,
Can tell in what degree each City ftands,
Defcribe the diftance of this place from that,
All this the Scale in euery Map can teach,
Nay, for a neede could punctually recite
The Monuments in either; but what I
Haue by relation only, knowledge by trauell
Which ftill makes vp a compleat Gentleman,
Prooues eminent in you.

Y. Ger. I muft confeffe,
I haue feene Ierufalem and Rome, haue brought
Marke from th' one, from th' other Teftimony,
Know Spaine, and France, and from their ayres haue fuckt
A breath of euery language: but no more
Of this difcourfe fince wee draw neere the place
Of them we goe to vifit.

Enter Clowne.

Clo. Noble mafter Geraldine, worfhipfull mafter Dalauill.

Dal. I fee thou ftill remember'ft vs.

Clo. Remember you, I haue had fo many memorandomes from the multiplicities of your bounties, that not to remember you were to forget my felfe, you are both moft ingenioufly and nobly welcome.

Y. Ger. And why ingenioufly and nobly?

Clo. Becaufe had I giuen your welcomes other attributes then I haue done, the one being a Souldier, and the other feeming a Scholler, I fhould haue lied in the firft, and fhewed my felfe a kind of blockhead in the laft.

Y. Ger. I fee your wit is nimble as your tongue, But how doth all at home?

Clo. Small doings at home fir, in regard that the age of my Mafter correfponds not with the youth of my Miftris, and you know cold Ianuary and lufty May feldome meet in coniunction.

Dal. I doe not thinke but this fellow in time may for his wit and vnderstanding make Almanackes?

Clo. Not so sir, you being more iudicious then I, ile giue you the preeminence in that, because I see by proofe you haue such iudgement in times and seasons.

Dal. And why in times and seasons?

Clo. Because you haue so seasonably made choise, to come so iust at dinner time; you are welcome Gentlemen, ile goe tell my Master of your comming.

Exit Clowne.

Dal. A pleasant knaue.

Y. Ger. This fellow I perceiue
Is well acquainted with his Masters mind,
Oh tis a good old man.

Dal. And shee a Lady
For Beauty and for Vertue vnparraleld,
Nor can you name that thing to grace a woman
Shee has not in a full perfection,
Though in their yeeres might seeme disparity
And therefore at the first, a match vnfit;
Imagine but his age and gouernement,
Withall, her modesty, and chaste respect;
Betwixt them, there's so sweet a simpathie,
As crownes a noble marriage.

Y. Ger. 'Tis acknowledged,
But to the worthy gentleman himselfe,
I am so bound in many courtesies,
That not the least, by all th' expression
My Labour, or my Industry can shew,
I will know how to cancell.

Dal. Oh you are modest.

Y. Ger. Hee studies to engrosse mee to himselfe,
And is so wedded to my company,
Hee makes mee stranger to my Fathers house,
Although so neere a neighbour.

Dal. This approues you,
To be most nobly propertied, that from one
So exquisite in Iudgement, can Attract
So affectionate an eye.

Y. Ger.   Your Carracter,
I muſt beſtow on his vnmerrited loue,
As one that know I haue it, and yet ignorant
Which way I ſhould deſerue it : Heere both come.

Enter old Mr. Wincott, Wife, Prudentilla *the ſiſter, and the* Clowne.

Winc.   Gentlemen, welcome, but what neede I vſe
A word ſo common, vnto ſuch to whom
My houſe was neuer priuate ; I expect
You ſhould not looke for ſuch a needles phraſe,
Eſpecially you Maſter Geraldine,
Your Father is my neighbour, and I know you,
Euen from the Cradle, then I loued your Infancy,
And ſince your riper growth better'd by trauell ;
My wife and you, in youth were play-fellowes,
And nor now be ſtrangers ; as I take it,
Not aboue two yeeres different in your Age.
Wife.   So much hee hath out ſtript mee.
Winc.   I would haue you
Thinke this your home, free as your Fathers houſe,
And to command it, as the Maſter on't ;
Call bouldly heere, and entertaine your friends,
As in your owne poſſeſsions, when I ſee't,
Ile ſay you loue me truely, not till then ;
Oh what a happineſſe your Father hath,
Farre aboue mee, one to inherit after him,
Where I (Heauen knowes) am childleſſe.
Y. Ger.   That defect
Heauen hath ſupplied in this your vertuous Wife,
Both faire, and full of all accompliſhments,
My Father is a Widower, and heerein
Your happineſſe tranſcends him.
Wife.   Oh Maſter Geraldine,
Flattery in Men's an adiunct of their ſex,
This Countrie breeds it, and for that, ſo farre
You needed not to haue trauell'd.
Y. Ger.   Trueth's a word,

That fhould in euery language relifh well,
Nor haue I that exceeded.
 Wife. Sir, my Husband
Hath tooke much pleafure in your ftrange difcourfe
About Ierufalem and the Holy Land ;
How the new Citie differs from the old,
What ruines of the Temple yet remayne,
And whether Sion, and thofe hills about,
With thefe Adiacent Townes and Villages,
Keepe that proportioned diftance as wee read :
And then in Rome, of that great Piramis
Reared in the Front, on foure Lyons Mounted,
How many of thofe Idoll Temples ftand,
Firft dedicated to their Heathen gods,
Which ruined, which to better vfe repayred,
Of their Panthæon, and their Capitoll,
What Structures are demolifh't, what remaine.
 Winc. And what more pleafure to an old mans eare,
That neuer drew, faue his owne Countries aire,
Then heare fuch things related. I doe exceed him
In yeeres, I muft confeffe, Yet he much older
Then I in his experience.
 Prud. Mafter Geraldine,
May I bee bould to aske you but one queftion,
The which I'de be refolued in.
 Y. Ger. Any thing, that lies within my knowledge.
 Winc. Put him too't,
Doe Sifter, you fhall finde him (make no doubt)
Moft pregnant in his anfwere.
 Prud. In your trauells
Through France, through Sauoye, and through Italy,
Spaine, and the Empire, Greece and Paleftine,
Which breedes the choyceft beauties.
 Y. Ger. Introath Lady,
I neuer caft on any in thofe parts
A curious eye of cenfure, fince my Trauell
Was onely aymed at Language, and to know ; ·

Thefe paſt me but as common obiects did.
Seene, but not much regarded.

 Prud. Oh you ſtriue
To expreſſe a moſt vnheard of modeſtie,
And feldome found in any Traueller,
Eſpecially of our Countrey, thereby feeking
To make your felfe peculiar.

 Y. Ger. I ſhould be loath
Profeſſe in outward ſhew to be one Man.
And prooue my felfe another.

 Prud. One thing more,
Were you to marry, You that know thefe clymes,
Their ſtates and their conditions, out of which
Of all thefe countries would you chufe your wife.

 Y. Ger. Ile anfwere you in briefe, (as I obſerue)
Each feuerall clime for obiect, fare, or vfe,
Affords within it felfe, for all of thefe
What is moſt pleaſing to the man there borne ;
Spaine, that yeelds ſcant of food, affords the Nation
A parſimonious ſtomach, where our appetites
Are not content but with the large exceſſe
Of a full table ; where the pleaſing'ſt fruits
Are found moſt frequent, there they beſt content ;
Where plenty flowes, it askes abundant Feaſts ;
For fo hath prouident Nature dealt with all ;
So in the choyce of Women, the Greeke wantons
Compel'd beneath the Tnrkiſh ſlauery,
Vaſſaile themfelues to all men, and fuch beſt
Pleaſe the voluptious, that delight in change ;
The French is of one humor, Spaine another,
The hot Italian hee 's a ſtraine from both,
All pleafed with their owne nations, euen the Moore.
Hee thinks the blackeſt the moſt beautifull ;
And Lady, ſince you fo farre taxe my choyce,
Ile thus refolue you ; Being an Engliſh man,
Mong'ſt all thefe Nations I haue feene or tri'd,
To pleafe me beſt, heere would I chufe my bride.

Pru. And happy were that Lady, in my thoughts,
Whom you would deine that grace too.
 Wife. How now Sifter,
This is a fashion that's but late come vp,
For maids to court their husbands.
 Winc. I would wife
It were no worfe, vpon condition,
They had my helping hand and purfe to boote,
With both in ample meafure ; oh this Gentleman,
I loue, nay almoft doate on.
 Wife. Ya'ue my leaue,
To giue it full exprefsion.
 Winc. In thefe armes then,
Oh had my youth bin bleft with fuch a fonne,
To haue made my eftate to my name hereditary,
I fhould haue gone contented to my graue,
As to my bed ; to death, as to my fleepe ;
But Heauen hath will in all things, once more welcome,
And you fir, for your friends fake.
 Dal. Would I had in mee,
That which he hath, to haue clam'd it for mine owne,
How euer, I much thanke you.

Enter *Clowne.*

 Winc. Now fir, the newes with you.
 Clo. Dancing newes fir,
For the meat ftands piping hot vpon the dreffer,
The kitchin's in a heat, and the Cooke hath fo beftir'd himfelfe,
That hee's in a fweat. The Iacke plaies Muficke, and the Spits
Turne round too't.
 Winc. This fellowes my beft clocke,
Hee ftill ftrikes trew to dinner.
 Clo. And to fupper too fir, I know not how the day goes with you, but my ftomacke hath ftrucke twelue,
I can affure you that.

Winc. You take vs vnprouided Gentlemen,
Yet fomething you fhall finde, and wee would rather
Giue you the entertaine of houfhold guefts,
Then complement of ftrangers, I pray enter.
Exeunt. Manet Clo.

Clo. Ile ftand too't, that in good hofpitality, there can be nothing found that's ill, he that's a good houfe-keeper, keepes a good table, a good table, is neuer without good ftooles, good ftooles, feldome without good guefts, good guefts, neuer without good cheere, good cheere, cannot bee without good ftomackes, good ftomackes, without good digeftion, good digeftion, keepes men in good health, and therefore all good people, that beare good minds, as you loue goodneffe, be fure to keepe good meat and drinke in your houfes, and fo you fhall be called good men, and nothing can come on't but good, I warrant you.
Exit.

Actus Primus. Scena Secundus.

Enter two feruing-men Reignald *and* Robin.

Reig. Away you Corridon.

Rob. Shall I bee beate out of my Mafters houfe thus?

Reig. Thy Mafter, wee are Lords amongft our felues,
And heere we Liue and Reigne, Two yeeres already
Are paft of our great Empire, and wee now
Write, Anno Tertio.

Rob. But the old man liues,
That fhortly will depofe you.

Reig. Ith' meane time,
I, as the mighty Lord and Senefhcall
Of this great houfe and caftle, banifh thee,

The very smell ath' kitchin, bee it death,
To appeare before the dresser.
   Rob. And why so?
   Reig. Becaufe thou stink'st of garlike, is that breath
Agreeing with our Pallace, where each Roome,
Smells with Muske, Ciuit, and rich Amber-greece,
Alloes, Cafsia, Aromaticke-gummes,
Perfumes, and Pouders, one whofe very garments
Scent of the fowlds and stables, oh fie, fie,
What a bafe naftie rogue tis.
   Rob. Yet your fellow.
   Reig. Then let vs put a Cart-Horfe in rich
     trappings,
And bring him to the Tilt-yard.
   Rob. Prancke it, doe,
Wafte, Ryot, and Confume, Mifpend your Howres
In drunken Surfets, lofe your dayes in sleepe,
And burne the nights in Reuells, Drinke and Drab,
Keepe Chriftmaffe all yeere long, and blot leane
     Lent
Out of the Calender; all that maffe of wealth
Got by my Mafters fweat and thrifty care,
Hauocke in prodigall vfes; Make all flie,
Powr't downe your oylie throats, or fend it fmoaking
Out at the tops of chimnies: At his departure,
Was it the old mans charge to haue his windowes
Glifter all night with Starres? his modeft Houfe
Turn'd to a common Stewes? his Beds to pallats
Of Lufts and Proftitutions? his Buttrey hatch
Now made more common then a Tauernes barre,
His Stooles that welcom'd none but ciuill guefts,
Now onely free for Pandars, Whores and Bawdes,
Strumpets, and fuch.
   Reig. I fuffer thee too long,
What is to me thy countrey; or to thee
The pleafure of our Citie? thou haft Cowes,
Cattell, and Beeues to feed, Oues and Boues,
Thefe that I keepe, and in this pafture graze,
Are dainty Damofellaes, bonny Girles;

If thou be'ft borne to Hedge, Ditch, Thrafh and
  Plough
And I to Reuell, Banquet and Carrowfe ;
Thou Peffant, to the Spade and Pickaxe, I
The Battoone and Steeletto, thinke it onely
Thy ill, my good, our feuerall lots are caft,
And both muft be contented.
 Rob. But when both our feruices are queftioned.
 Reig. Looke thou to one,
My anfwere is prouided.

Enter *Y. Lionell.*

 Rob. Farewell Musk-Cat.   *Exit.*
 Reig. Adue good Cheefe and Oynons, ftuffe thy
  guts
With Specke and Barley-pudding for difgeftion,
Drinke Whig and fowre Milke, whileft I rince my
  Throat,
With Burdeaux and Canarie.
 Y. Lio. What was hee ?
 Reig. A Spie Sir,
One of their Hindes oth' countrey, that came prying
To fee what dainty fare our kitchin yeelds,
What Guefts we harbour, and what rule we keepe,
And threats to tell the old man when he comes ;
I thinke I fent him packing.
 Y. Lio. It was well done.
 Reig. A whorefon-Iack-an-apes, a bafe Baboone,
To infinuate in our fecrets.
 Y. Lio. Let fuch keepe, the Countrey where their
charge is.
 Reig. So I faid Sir.
 Y. Lio. And vifit vs when we command them
  thence,
Not fearch into our counfels.
 Reig. 'Twere not fit.
 Y. Lio. Who in my fathers abfence fhould com-
  mand,
Saue I his only fonne ?

Reig. It is but iuſtice.

Y. Lio. For am not I now Lord?

Reig. Dominus fac totum.
And am not I your Steward?

Y. Lio. Well remembred,
This night I have a purpoſe to bee Merry,
Iouiall and Frollicke, how doth our caſh hold out?

Reig. The bag's ſtill heauy.

Y. Lio. Then my heart's ſtill light.

Reig. I can aſſure you, yet tis pritty deepe,
Tho ſcarce a mile to th' bottome.

Y. Lio. Let mee haue
to Supper, Let mee ſee, a Ducke——

Reig. Sweet Rogue.

Y. Lio. A Capon——

Reig. Geld the Raſcall.

Y. Lio. Then a Turkey——

Reig. Now ſpit him for an Infidell.

Y. Lio. Greene Plouer, Snite,
Partridge, Larke, Cocke, and Pheſſant.

Reig. Nere a Widgin?

Y. Lio. Yes, wait thy ſelfe at Table.

Reig. Where I hope your ſelfe will not be abſent.

Y. Lio. Nor my friends.

Reig. Weele haue them then in plenty.

Y. Lio. Cauiare, Sturgeon, Anchoues, pickle Oyſters: Yes.
And a Potato Pie; beſides all theſe,
What thou think'ſt rare and coſtly.

Reig. Sir, I know
What's to be done; the ſtocke that muſt be ſpent,
Is in my hands, and what I haue to doe,
I will doe ſuddenly.

Y. Lie. No Butchers meat,
Of that, beware in any caſe.

Reig. I ſtill remember,
Your father was no Graſier, if he were,
This were a way to eate vp all his Fields,
Hedges and all.

Y. Lio. You will be gone fir.
Reig. Yes, and you are ith' way going.   *Exit.*
Y. Lia. To what may young men beſt compare themſelues?
Better to what, then to a houſe new built?
The Fabricke ſtrong, the Chambers well contriu'd,
Poliſht within, without, well beautifi'd;
When all that gaze vpon the Edifice,
Doe not alone commend the workemans craft,
But either make it their faire preſident
By which to build another, or at leaſt,
Wiſh there to inhabite: Being ſet to ſale,
In comes a ſlothfull Tenant, with a Family
As laſie and deboſht; Rough tempeſts riſe,
Vntile the roofe, which by their idleneſſe,
Left vnrepaired, the ſtormy ſhowres beat in,
Rot the maine Poſtes and Rafters, ſpoile the Roomes,
Deface the Seelings, and in little ſpace,
Bring it to utter Ruine, yet the fault,
Not in the Architector that firſt reared it,
But him that ſhould repaire it: So it fares
With vs yong men; Wee are thoſe houſes made,
Our Parents raiſe theſe Structures, the foundation
Laid in our Infancy; and as wee grow
In yeeres, they ſtriue to build vs by degrees,
Story on ſtory higher; vp at height,
They cover vs with Councell, to defend vs
From ſtormes without: they poliſh vs within,
With Learnings, Knowledge, Arts and Diſciplines;
All that is nought and vicious, they ſweepe from vs,
Like Duſt and Cobwebs, and our Roomes concealed,
Hang with the coſtlieſt hangings; Bout the Walls,
Emblems and beautious Symbols pictured round;
But when that laſie Tenant, Loue, ſteps in,
And in his Traine, brings Sloth and Negligence,
Luſt, Diſobedience, and profuſe Exceſſe;
The Thrift with which our fathers tiled our Roofes,
Submits to euery ſtorme and Winters blaſt.

Enter *Blanda* a Whore, and *Scapha* a Bawde.

And yeelding place to euery riotous finne,
Giues way without, to ruine what's within :
Such is the ſtate I ſtand in.
   Blan. And how doth this Tire become me?
   Sca. Rather aske, how your fweet carriage,
And Court behauiour, doth beſt grace you, for Louers regard,
Not fo much the outward habit, as that which the garment couers.
   Y. Lio. Oh heer's that Haile, Shower, Tempeſt, Storme, and Guſt,
That ſhatter'd hath this building ; Let in Luſt,
Intemperance, appetite to Vice ; withall,
Neglect of euery Goodneſſe ; Thus I fee,
How I am fincking in mine owne difeafe,
Yet can I not abide it.
   Bla. And how this Gowne? I prethee view mee well,
And fpeake with thy beſt Iudgement.
   Sca. What doe you talke of Gownes, and Ornaments ;
That haue a Beautie, pretious in it felfe,
And becomes any thing.
   Y. Lio. Let me not liue, but ſhe fpeaks nought but truth,
And ile for that reward her.
   Bla. All's one to mee, become they mee, or not,
Or bee I faire, or fowle, in others eyes,
So I appeare fo to my Lionell,
Hee is the glaſſe, in whom I iudge my face,
By whom in order, I will dreſſe thefe curles,
And place thefe Iewels, onely to pleafe him,
Why do'ſt fmile.
   Sca. To heere a Woman, that thinks her felfe fo wife, fpeake fo foolifhlie, that knowes well, and does ill.
   Bla. Teach me wherein I erre.

Sca. Ile tell thee Daughter; In that thou knoweſt thy ſelfe to bee beloued of ſo many, and ſetleſt thy affection, only vpon one; Doth the Mill grinde onely, when the Wind ſits in one corner? Or Shipps onely Saile, when it's in this, or that quarter? Is hee a cunning Fencer, that lies but at one Guard? Or he a Skilfull Muſician, that plaies but on one String? Is there but one way to the Wood? And but one Bucket that belongs to the Well? To affect one, and deſpiſe all other, becomes the preciſe Matron, not the Proſtitute; the loyall Wife, not the looſe Wanton: Such haue I beene, as you are now, and ſhould learne, to Saile with all Windes, defend all Blowes, make Muſicke with all Strings, know all the wayes, to the Wood, and like a good trauelling Hackney, learne to drinke of all Waters.

Y. Lio. May I miſcarry in my Blandaes loue;
If I that old damnation, doe not ſend
To Hell, before her time.

Bla. I would not haue you Mother, teach me ought,
That tends to injure him.

Sca. Well looke too 't when 'tis too late, and then repent at leaſure, as I haue done: Thou ſee'ſt, heeres nothing but Prodigallity and Pride, Wantoning, and Waſting, Rioting, and Reuelling, Spoyling, and Spending, Gluttony, and Gormondiſing, all goes to Hauocke, and can this hold out? When he hath nothing left, to helpe himſelfe, how can he Harbour thee? Looke at length, to Drinke from a dry Bottle, and feed from an emptie Knap-ſacke, looke too 't, 'twill come to that.

Y. Lio. My parſemony ſhall begin in thee,
And inſtantly, for from this houre, I vow,
That thou no more ſhalt Drinke vpon my coſt,
Nor taſte the ſmalleſt Fragment from my Board;
Ile ſee thee ſtarue ith' ſtreet firſt.

Sca. Liue to one man? a ieaſt, thou may'ſt aſwell, tie thy ſelfe to one Gowne; and what Foole, but will

change with the Fashion, Yes, doe, Confine thy selfe
to one Garment, and vse no Varietie, and see how
soone it will Rot, and turne to Raggs.

Y. Lio. Those Raggs, be thy Reward; Oh my
  sweet Blanda,
Onely for Thee, I wish my Father dead,
And neere to Rouse vs from our Sweet delight;
But for this Hag, this Beldam, shee whose backe,
Hath made her Items, in my Mercers Bookes,
Whose rauenous Guts, I haue Stuft with Delicates,
Nay euen to Surfit; and whose frozen Blood,
I haue Warmed with Aquauitæ; Be this day
My last of Bounty, to a Wretch Ingrate,
But vnto Thee, a new Indenture Sealed,
Of an affection fixt, and Permanent,
Ile loue thee still, bee 't but to giue the lye,
To this old Cancker'd Worme.

Bla. Nay, be not angrie.

Y. Lio. With thee, my Soule shall euer be at peace,
But with this loue seducer, still at Warre.

Enter Rioter *and two* Gallants.

Sca. Heere me but speake.

Y. Lio. Ope but thy lips againe, it makes a way,
To haue thy Tongue pluck'd out.

Rio. What all in Tempest?

Y. Lio. Yes, and the Storme, raised by that
  Witches Spells,
Oh 'tis a Damn'd Inchantresse.

Rio. What's the businesse?

Bla. Onely some few words, slipt her vnawares,
For my Sake, make her peace.

Rio. You charge me deepely,
Come Friend, will you be Moou'd at womens Words,
A man of your knowne iudgement?

Y. Lio. Had you but heard,
The damn'd Erronious Doctrine that shee taught,
You would haue iudg'd her to the Stake.

Bla. But Sweet heart,
Shee now Recants thofe Errours, once more Number her
Amongft your Houfhold feruants.
 Rio. Shall fhe beg, and be denyed ought from you?
 Bla. Come this Kiffe, Shall end all former quarells.
 Rio. 'Tis not pofsible,
Thofe Lippes fhould mooue in vaine, that two wayes plead;
Both in their Speech, and Silence.
 Y. Lio. You haue preuail'd,
But vpon this Condition, noway elfe,
Ile Senfure her, as fhee hath Sentenc'd thee;
But with fome fmall Inuerfion.
 Rio. Speake, how's that?
 Bla. Not too feuere, I prethee, fee poore wretch,
Shee at the barre, ftands quaking.
 Y. Lio. Now, hold vp?
 Rio. How man, how?
 Y. Lio. Her hand, I meane; And now il'e fentence thee,
According to thy Councell giuen to her:
Saile by one Winde; Thou fhalt, to one tune Sing,
Lie at one Guard, and Play but on one String,
Hencefoorth, I will Confine thee to one Garment,
And that fhall be a caft one, Like thy felfe
Iuft, paft all Wearing, as thou paft all Vfe,
And not to be renewed, til't be as Ragged,
As thou art Rotten.
 Bla. Nay fweet.
 Y. Lio. That for her Habbit.
 Sca. A cold Sute, I haue on't.
 Y. Lio. To preuent Surfit,
Thy Diet, fhall bee to one Difh confin'd,
And that too Rifled, with as vncleane hands,
As ere were laid on thee.
 Sca. What hee fcants me in Victuals, would he but alow mee in Drinke.

Y. Lio. That shall be the refuse of the Flagons, Iacks,
And Snuffes, such as the nastiest Breathes shall leaue;
Of Wine, and Strong-water, neuer hope,
Hencefoorth to Smell.
   Sca. Oh me, I Faint already.
   Y. Lio. If I sincke in my State, of all the rest,
Be thou excused, what thou proposed to her,
Beldam, is now against thy selfe decreed,
Drinke from drie springs, from empty Knap-sacks feede.
   Sca. No burnt Wine, nor Hot-waters.
                                She Swounds.
   Y. Lio. Take her hence.
   Bla. Indeede you are too cruell.
   Y. Lio. Yes to her,
Onely of purpose, to be kind to thee;
Are any of my Guests come?
   Rio. Feare not Sir,
You will haue a full Table.
   Y. Lio. What, and Musicke?
   Rio. Best Consort in the Citie, for sixe parts.
   Y. Lio. Wee shall haue Songs then?
   Rio. Bith' eare.   *Whispers.*
   Y. Lio. And Wenches?
   Rio. Yes bith' eye.
   Bla. Ha, what was that you said?
   Rio. We shall haue such to beare you company,
As will no doubt content you.
   Y. Lio. Euer then:
In Youth there is a Fate, that swayes vs still,
To know what's Good, and yet pursue what's Ill.
                                     Exeunt omnes.

Actus Secundus. Scena Prima.

   Enter old Master Wincott, *and his* Wife.
   Winc. And what's this Dalauill?

Wife. My apprehenſion,
Can giue him no more true expreſsion,
Then that he firſt appeares, a Gentleman,
And well conditioned.
  Winc. That for outward ſhew;
But what in him haue you obſerued elſe,
To make him better knowne?
  Wife. I haue not Eyes,
To ſearch into the inward Thoughts of Men,
Nor euer was I ſtudied in that Art,
To iudge of Mens affection by the face;
But that which makes me beſt opinion'd of him,
Is, That he's the Companion, and the Friend
Beloued of him, whom you ſo much commend,
The Noble Maſter Geraldine.
  Winc. Thou haſt ſpoke,
That which not onely crownes his true deſert,
But now inſtates him in my better thoughts,
Making his Worth, vnqueſtioned.
  Wife. Hee pretends
Loue to my ſiſter Pru. I haue obſeru'd him,
Single her out, to priuate conference.
  Winc. But I could rather, for her owne ſake, wiſh
Young Geraldine would fixe his thoughts that way,
And ſhee towards him; In ſuch Affinity,
Truſt me, I would not vſe a ſparing hand.
  Wife. But Loue in theſe kindes, ſhould not be compel'd,
Forc'd, nor Perſwaded; When it freely Springs,
And of it ſelfe, takes voluntary Roote,
It Growes, it Spreads, it Ripens, and brings foorth,
Such an Vſurious Crop of timely Fruit,
As crownes a plentious Autume.

Enter *Clowne.*

  Winc. Such a Harueſt,
I ſhould not be th' vngladdeſt man to ſee,
Of all thy ſiſters friends: Now, whence come you?
  Clo. Who, I Sir, From a Lodging of Lardgeſſe, a

Houfe of Hofpitality, and a Pallace of Plenty; Where there's Feeding like Horfes, and Drinking like Fifhes; Where for Pints, w'are ferued in Pottles; and in ftead of Pottle-pots, in Pailes; in ftead of Siluer-tanckards, we drinke out of Water-tanckards; Clarret runs as freely, as the Cocks; and Canarie, like the Conduits of a Coronation day; Where there's nothing but Feeding and Frollicking; Caruing in Kifsing; Drinking, and Dauncing; Muficke and Madding; Fidling and Feafting.

Winc. And where, I pray thee, are all thefe Reuels kept?

Clo. They may be rather called Reakes then Reuells; As I came along by the doore, I was call'd vp amongft them; Hee-Gallants, and Shee-Gallants, I no fooner look'd out, but faw them out with their Kniues, Slafhing of Shoulders, Mangling of Legs, and Lanching of Loynes, till there was fcarce a whole Limbe left amongft them.

Winc. A fearefull Maffacre.

Clo. One was Hacking to cut off a Necke, this was Mangling a Breft, his Knife flip from the Shoulder, and onely cut of a Wing, one was picking the Braines out of a Head, another was Knuckle deepe in a Belly, one was Groping for a Liuer, another Searching for the Kidneyes; I faw one plucke the Sole from the Body (Goofe that fhe was to fuffer't) another prickt into the Breaft with his one Bill, Woodcocke to indure it.

Wife. How fell they out at firft?

Clo. I know not that, but it feemes, one had a Stomacke, and another had a Stomacke; But there was fuch biting and tearing with their teeths, that I am fure, I faw fome of their poore Carcafles pay for't.

Winc. Did they not fend for Surgeons?

Clo. Alas no, Surgeons helpe was too late; There was no ftitching vp of thofe Wounds, where Limbe was pluckt from Limbe; Nor any Salue for thofe Scarrs, which all the Plaifter of Paris cannot Cure.

Winc. Where grew the quarrell firſt ?

Clo. It ſeemes it was firſt Broacht in the Kitchin ; Certaine creatures being brought in thither, by ſome of the Houſe ; The Cooke being a Colloricke fellow, did ſo Towſe them and Toſſe them, ſo Plucke them and Pull them, till hee left them as naked as my Naile, Pinioned ſome of them like Fellons ; Cut the Spurres from others of their Heeles ; Then downe went his Spits, Some of them he ranne in at the Throat, and out at the Back-ſide : About went his Baſting-Ladle, where he did ſo beſawce them, that many a ſhrode turne they had amongſt them.

Wife. But in all this, How did the Women ſcape ?

Clo. They fared beſt, and did the leaſt hurt that I ſaw ; But for quietneſſe ſake, were forc'd to ſwallow what is not yet digeſted, yet euery one had their ſhare, and ſhee that had leaſt, I am ſure by this time, hath her belly full.

Winc. And where was all this hauocke kept ?

Clo. Marry Sir, at your next neighbours, Young Maſter Lionell, Where there is nothing but Drinking out of Dry-Fats, and Healthing in Halfe-Tubs, his Gueſts are fed by the Belly, and Beggers ſerued at his Gate in Baskets ; Hee's the Adamant of this Age, the Daffadill of theſe dayes, the Prince of Prodigallity, and the very Cæſar of all young Citizens.

Winc. Belike then, 'twas a Maſſacre of meat, not as I apprehended ?

Clo. Your grauity hath geſt aright ; The chiefeſt that fell in this Battell, were wild Fowle and tame Fowle ; Pheſſants were wounded in ſtead of Alfareſſe, and Capons for Captaines, Anchoues ſtood for Antiants, and Cauiare for Corporals, Diſhes were aſſaulted in ſtead of Ditches, and Rabbets were cut to pieces vpon the rebellings, ſome loſt their Legs, whil'ſt other of their wings were forc'd to flie ; The Pioner vndermind nothing but Pie-cruſt ; And——

Winc. Enough, enough, your wit hath plai'd too long vpon our patience ;

Wife, it grieues me much both for the yong and old man, the one,
Graces his head with care, endures the parching heat and biting cold,
The terrours of the Lands, and feares at Sea in trauell, onely to gaine
Some competent eſtate to leaue his ſonne;
Whiles all that Merchandiſe, through Gulfes, Croſſe-Tides,
Pirats and Stormes, he brings ſo farre, Th' other
Heere Shipwrackes in the Harbour.
    Wife. Tis the care of Fathers; and the weakeneſſe
Incident to youth, that wants experience.

    Enter Y. Geraldine, Dallauill, Prudentilla, *laughing*.

    Clo. I was at the beginning of the Battell,
But heere comes ſome, that it ſeemes
Were at the rifling of the dead Carcaſſes;
For by their mirth, they haue had part of the Spoile.
    Winc. You are pleaſant, Gentlemen, what I entreat,
Might be the Subiect of your pleaſant ſport,
It promiſeth ſome pleaſure?
    Prud. If their recreation
Bee, as I make no queſtion, on truth grounded,
'twill beget ſudden laughter.
    Wife. What's the Proiect?
    Dal. Who ſhall relate it.
    Winc. Maſter Geraldine, if there be any thing can pleaſe my Eare,
With pleaſant ſoundes, your Tongue muſt be the Inſtrument,
On which the String muſt ſtrike.
    Dal. Bee't his then.
    Prud. Nay heare it, 'tis a good one.
    Wife. Wee intreat you, Poſſeſſe vs oth' Nouell.
    Winc. Speake, good Sir.
    Y. Ger. I ſhall then, with a kind of Barbariſme,

Shaddow a Ieaſt, that askes a ſmoother Tongue,
For in my poore diſcourſe, I doe proteſt,
'twill but looſe his luſter.
    Wife. You are Modeſt.
    Winc. Howeuer, ſpeake, I pray; For my ſake doo't?
    Clo. This is like a haſtie Pudding, longer in eating,
then it was in making.
    Y. Ger. Then thus it was, this Gentleman and I,
Paſt but iuſt now, by your next Neighbours houſe,
Where as they ſay, dwels one Young Lionell.
    Clo. Where I was to night at Supper.
    Winc. An vnthrift Youth, his Father now at Sea.
    Y. Ger. Why that's the very Subiect. vpon which
It ſeemes, this Ieſt is grounded, there this Night,
Was a great feaſt.
    Clo. Why ſo I told you, Sir.
    Winc. Bee thou ſtill dumbe, 'tis hee that I would heare.
    Y. Ger. In the height of their Carowſing, all their braines,
Warm'd with the heat of Wine; Diſcourſe was offer'd,
Of Ships, and Stormes at Sea; when ſuddenly,
Out of his giddy wildneſſe, one conceiues
The Roome wherein they quafft, to be a Pinnace,
Moouing and Floating; and the confuſed Noiſe,
To be the murmuring Windes, Guſts, Marriners;
That their vnſtedfaſt Footing, did proceed
From rocking of the Veſſell: This conceiu'd,
Each one begins to apprehend the danger,
And to looke out for ſafety, flie faith one
Vp to the Maine-top, and diſcouer; Hee
Climbes by the bed poſt, to the Teaſter, there
Reports a Turbulent Sea and Tempeſt towards;
And wills them if they'le ſaue their Ship and liues,
To caſt their Lading ouer-board; At this
All fall to Worke, and Hoyſte into the Street,
As to the Sea, What next come to their hand,
Stooles, Tables, Treſſels, Trenchers, Bed-ſteds, Cups,

Pots, Plate, and Glaſſes; Heere a fellow Whiſtles,
They take him for the Boat-ſwaine, one lyes ſtrugling
Vpon the floore, as if he ſwome for life,
A third, takes the Baſe-violl for the Cock-boate,
Sits in the belly on't, labours and Rowes;
His Oare, the Sticke with which the Fidler plaid;
A fourth, beſtrides his Fellowes, thinking to ſcape
As did Arion, on the Dolphins backe,
Still fumbling on a gitterne.
   Clo. Excellent Sport.
   Winc. But what was the concluſion?
   Y. Ger. The rude multitude,
Watching without, and gaping for the ſpoyle
Caſt from the windowes, went bith' eares about it;
The Conſtable is called to Attone the broyle,
Which done, and hearing ſuch a noiſe within,
Of eminent Ship-racke; enters the houſe, and finds them
In this confuſion, They Adore his ſtaffe,
And thinke it Neptunes Trident, and that hee
Comes with his Tritons, (ſo they cal'd his watch)
To calme the Tempeſt, and appeaſe the Waues;
And at this point, wee left them.
   Clo. Come what will, ile ſteale out of Doores,
And ſee the end of it, that's certaine.   *Exit.*
   Winc. Thanks Maſter Geraldine, for this diſcourſe,
Introath it hath much pleaſed mee, but the night
Begins to grow faſte on vs, for your parts,
You are all young, and you may ſit vp late,
My eyes begin to ſummon mee to ſleepe,
And nothing's more offenſiue vnto Age,
Then to watch long and late.
   Y. Ger. Now good Reſt with you.
   Dal. What ſaies faire Prudentilla? Maids and Widdows,
And wee young Batchelors, ſuch as indeed
Are forc'd to lie in Solitary beds,
And ſleepe without diſturbance, wee methinks,
Should deſire later houres; when Married Wiues,

That in their amorous armes, hug their delights;
To often wakings fubiect; their more haft,
May better bee excufed.
    Prud. How can you,
That are as you confeffe, a fingle man,
Enter fo farre into thefe Mifticall fecrets
Of Mariage, which as yet you neuer prooued.
    Dal. There's Lady, an inftinct innate in man,
Which prompts vs to the apprehenfions
Of th' vfes wee were borne to; Such we are
Apteft to learne; Ambitious moft to know,
Of which our chiefe is Marriage.
    Prud. What you Men
Moft meditate, wee Women feldome dreame of.
    Dal. When dreame Maids moft?
    Prud. When thinke you?
    Dal. When you lie vpon your Backs, come come,
      your Eare.   *Exit* Dal. *and* Prud.
    Y. Ger. Wee now are left alone.
    Wife. Why fay wee be who fhould be iealous of vs?
This is not firft of many hundred Nights,
That wee two haue beene priuate, from the firft
Of our acquaintance, when our Tongues but clipt
Our Mothers-tongue, and could not fpeake it plaine,
Wee knew each other; As in ftature, fo
Increaft our fweet Societie; Since your trauell,
And my late Marriage, Through my Husbands loue,
Mid-night hath beene as Mid-day, and my Bed-chamber,
As free to you, as your owne Fathers houfe,
And you as welcome too't.
    Y. Ger. I muft confeffe,
It is in you, your Noble Courtefie,
In him, a more then common confidence,
And in this Age, can fcarce find prefident.
    Wife. Moft trew, it is withall an Argument,
That both our vertues are fo deepe impreft
In his good thoughts, hee knowes we cannot erre.

Y. Ger. A villaine were hee, to deceiue such trust,
Or (were there one) a much worse Carracter.
  Wife. And she no lesse, whom either Beauty, Youth,
Time, Place, or opportunity could tempt,
To iniure such a Husband.
  Y. Ger. You deserue, euen for his sake, to be for
    euer young;
And hee for yours, to haue his Youth renew'd;
So mutuall is your trew coniugall Loue;
Yet had the Fates so pleas'd
  Wife. I know your meaning.
It was once voyc'd, that wee two should haue Matcht,
The World so thought, and many Tongues so spake,
But Heauen hath now dispos'd vs otherwayes;
And being as it is, (a thing in me,
Which I protest, was neuer wisht, nor sought)
Now done, I not repent it.
  Y. Ger. In those times,
Of all the Treasures of my Hopes and Loue,
You were th' Exchequer, they were Stor'd in you;
And had not my vnfortunate Trauell croft them,
They had bin heere reserued still.
  Wife. Troath they had,
I should haue beene your trusty Treasurer.
  Y. Ger. Howeuer let vs Loue still, I intreat:
That, Neighbour-hood and breeding will allow;
So much the Lawes Diuine and Humaine both,
Twixt Brother and a Sister will approue;
Heauen then forbid, that they should limit vs
Wish well to one another.
  Wife. If they should not,
Wee might proclaime, they were not Charitable,
Which were a deadly sin but to conceiue.
  Y. Ger. Will you resolue me one thing?
  Wife. As to one,
That in my Bosome hath a second place,
Next my deere Husband.
  Y. Ger. That's the thing I craue,
And onely that, to haue a place next him.

Wife. Prefume on that already, but perhaps,
You meane to ftretch it further.
　Y. Ger. Onely thus farre,
Your Husbands old, to whom my Soule doth wifh,
A Neſters age, So much he merits from me ;
Yet if (as proofe and Nature daily teach)
Men cannot alwayes liue, efpecially
Such as are old and Crazed ; Hee be cal'd hence,
Fairely, in full maturity of time,
And we two be referu'd to after life,
Will you conferre your Widow-hood on mee ?
　Wife. You aske the thing, I was about to beg ;
Your tongue hath fpake mine owne thoughts.
　Y. Ger. Vow to that.
　Wife. As I hope Mercy.
　Y. Ger. 'Tis enough, that word
Alone, inflates me happy ; Now fo pleafe you,
Wee will diuide, you to your priuate Chamber,
I to find out my friend.
　Wife. Nay Mafter Geraldine,
One Ceremonie refts yet vnperform'd,
My Vow is paft, your oath muft next proceed,
And as you couet to be fure of me,
Of you I would be certaine.
　Y. Ger. Make ye doubt ?
　Wife. No doubt ; but Loue's ftill Iealous, and in that
To be excufed ; You then fhall fweare by Heauen,
And as in all your future Acts, you hope
To thriue and profper ; As the Day may yeeld
Comfort, or the Night reft, as you would keepe
Entire, the Honour of your Fathers houfe,
And free your Name from Scandall and Reproach,
By all the Goodneffe that you hope to enioy,
Or ill to fhun——
　Y. Ger. You charge me deeply Lady.
　Wife. Till that day come, you fhall referue your felfe

A fingle man; Conuerfe nor company
With any Woman, Contract nor Combine,
With Maid, or Widow; which expected houre,
As I doe wifh not hafte, fo when it happens,
It fhall not come vnwelcome; You heare all,
Vow this.

   Y. Ger. By all that you haue faid, I fweare,
And by this Kiffe Confirme.

   Wife. Y'are now my Brother,
But then, my fecond Husband.   *Exeunt.*

Enter Y. Lionell, Rioter, Blanda, Scapha, *two* Gallants, *and two* Wenches, *as newly wak'd from fleepe.*

   Y. Lio. Wee had a ftormy night on't.

   Bla. The Wine ftill workes,
And with the little reft they haue tooke to night,
They are fcarce come to themfelues.

   Y. Lio. Now 'tis a Calme,
Thankes to thofe gentle Sea-gods, that haue brought vs
To this fafe Harbour; Can you tell their names?

   Sca. He with the Painted-ftaffe, I heard you call
     Neptune.

   Y. Lio. The dreadfull god of Seas,
Vpon whofe backe neere ftucke March flees.

   1. *Gall.* One with the Bill, keepes Neptunes Porpofes,
So *Ouid* fayes in 's Metamorphofis.

   2. *Gall.* A third the learned Poets write on,
And as they fay, His name is Triton.

   Y. Lio. Thefe are the Marine gods, to whom my
     father
In his long voyage prayes too; Cannot they
That brought vs to our Hauen, bury him
In their Abiffe? For if he fafe ariue,
I with thefe Sailors, Syrens, and what not,
Am fure heere to be fhipwrackt.

   1. *Wen.* Stand vp ftiffe.

   Rio. But that the fhip fo totters: I fhall fall.

   1. *Wen.* If thou fall, Ile fall with thee.

Rio. Now I fincke,
And as I diue and drowne, Thus by degrees,
Ile plucke thee to the bottome. *They fall.*

Enter Reignald.

Y. Lio. Amaine for England, See, fee,
The Spaniard now ftrikes Saile.
Reig. So muft you all.
1. *Gall.* Whence is your fhip, from the *Bermoothes* ?
Reig. Worfe, I thinke from Hell :
We are all Loft, Split, Shipwrackt, and vndone,
This place is a meere quick-fands.
2. *Gall.* So we feared.
Reig. Wher's my young Mafter ?
Y. Sio. Heere man, fpeake, the Newes ?
Reig. The Newes is, I, and you——
Y. Lio. What ?
Reig. Shee, and all thefe——
Bla. I ?
Reig. We and all ours, are in one turbulent Sea
Of Feare, Difpaire, Difafter and mifchance fwallowed :
Your father, Sir——
Y. Lio. Why, what of him ?
Reig. He is, Oh I want breath.
Y. Lio. Where ?
Reig. Landed, and at hand.
Y. Lio. Vpon what coaft ? Who faw him ?
Reig. I, thefe eyes.
Y. Lio. Oh Heauen, what fhall I doe then ?
Reig. Aske ye me
What fhall become of you, that haue not yet
Had time of ftuddy to difpofe my felfe ;
I fay againe, I was vpon the Key,
I faw him land, and this way bend his courfe ;
What drunkard's this, that can out fleepe a ftorme
Which threatens all our ruines ? Wake him.
Bla. Ho, Rioter, awake.
Rio. Yes, I am wake ;

How dry hath this Salt-water made me ; Boy,
Giue me th' other Glaſſe.
   Y. Lio. Ariſe, I ſay,
My Fathers come from Sea.
   Rio. If he be come, Bid him be gone againe.
   Reig. Can you trifle
At ſuch a time, when your Inuentions, Braines,
Wits, Plots, Deuices, Stratagems, and all
Should be at one in action ? each of you
That loue your ſafeties, lend your helping hands,
Women and all, to take this drunkard hence,
And to beſtow him elſe where.
   Bla. Lift for Heauens ſake. *They carry him in.*
   Reig. But what am I the neerer, were all theſe
Conuey'd to ſundry places and vnſeene ;
The ſtaine of our diſorders ſtill remaine,
Of which, the houſe will witneſſe, and the old man
Muſt finde when he enters ; And for theſe

            Enter againe.

I am here left to anſwere : What is he gone ?
   Y. Lio. But whither ? But into th' ſelfe ſame houſe
That harbours him ; my Fathers, where we all
Attend from him ſurpriſeall.
   Reig. I will make
That Priſon of your feares, your Sanctuary ;
Goe get you in together.
   Y. Lio. To this houſe ?
   Reig. Your Fathers, with your Sweet-heart, theſe
      and all ;
Nay, no more words but doo 't.
   Bla. That were to betray vs to his fury.
   Reig. I haue 't heere,
To Baile you hence at pleaſure ; and in th' interim,
Ile make this ſuppoſed Goale, to you, as ſafe
From the iniur'd old mans iuſt incenſed ſpleene,
As were you now together ith' Low-Countreyes,

Virginia, or ith' Indies.
  Bla. Preſent feare,
Bids vs to yeeld vnto the faint beliefe
Of the leaſt hoped ſafety.
  Reig. Will you in ?
  Omn. By thee we will be counſell'd.
  Reig. Shut them faſt.
  Y. Lio. And thou and I to leaue them ?
  Reig. No ſuch thing,
For you ſhall beare your Sweet-heart company,
And helpe to cheere the reſt.
  Y. Lio. And ſo thou
Meaneſt to eſcape alone ?
  Reig. Rather without,
Ile ſtand a Champion for you all within ;
Will you be ſwai'd ? One thing in any caſe
I muſt aduiſe ; The gates boulted and lockt,
See that 'mongſt you no liuing voyce be heard ;
No not ſo much as a Dog to howle,
Or Cat to mewe, all ſilence, that I charge ;
As if this were a meere forſaken houſe,
And none did there inhabite.
  Y. Lio. Nothing elſe ?
  Reig. And though the old man thunder at the gates
As if he meant to ruine what he had rear'd,
None on their liues to anſwere.
  Y. Lio. 'Tis my charge ;
Remaines there nothing elſe ?
  Reig. Onely the Key ;
For I muſt play the goaler for your durance,
To bee the Mercurie in your releaſe,
  Y. Lio. Me and my hope, I in this Key deliuer
To thy ſafe truſt.
  Reig. When you are faſt you are ſafe,
And with this turne 'tis done : What fooles are theſe,
To truſt their ruin'd fortunes to his hands
That hath betrai'd his owne ; And make themſelues

Prifoner to one deferues to lie for all,
As being caufe of all ; And yet fomething prompts me,
Ile ftand it at all dangers ; And to recompence
The many wrongs vnto the yong man done :
Now, if I can doubly delude the old,
My braine, about it then ; All's hufht within,
The noife that fhall be, I muft make without ;
And he that part for gaine, and part for wit,
So farre hath trauell'd, ftriue to foole at home :
Which to effect, Art muft with Knauery ioyne,
And fmooth Diffembling meet with Impudence ;
Ile doe my beft, and howfoere it prooue,
My praife or fhame, 'tis but a feruants loue.

Enter old Lionell *like a ciuill Merchant, with Watermen, and two feruants with Burdens and Caskets.*

  Old Lio. Difcharge thefe honeft Sailors that haue brought
Our Chefts a fhore, and pray them haue a care,
Thofe merchandife be fafe we left aboord :
As Heauen hath bleft vs with a fortunate Voyage,
In which we bring home riches with our healthes,
So let not vs prooue niggards in our ftore ;
See them paid well, and to their full content.
  1. *Ser.* I fhall Sir.
  Old Lio. Then returne : Thefe fpeciall things,
And of moft value, weele not truft aboord ;
Meethinkes they are not fafe till they fee home,
And there repofe, where we will reft our felues,
And bid farewell to Trauell ; for I vow,
After this houre no more to truft the Seas,
Nor throw mee to fuch danger.
  Reig. I could wifh
You had tooke your leaue oth' Land too.
  Old Lio. And now it much reioyceth me, to thinke
What a moft fudden welcome I fhall bring,
Both to my Friends and priuate Family.

Reig. Oh, but how much more welcome had he beene,
That had brought certaine tidings of thy death.
  Old Lio. But foft, what's this? my owne gates fhut vpon me,
And barre their Mafter entrance? Whofe within there?
How, no man fpeake, are all afleepe or dead,
That no foule ftirres to open?   *Knocks aloud.*
  Reig. What madde man's that, who weary of his life,
Dares once lay hand on thefe accurfed gates?
  Old Lio. Whofe that? my feruant Reignald.
  Reig. My old Mafter,
Moft glad I am to fee you; Are you well Sir?
  Old Lio. Thou fee'ft I am.
  Reig. But are you fure you are?
Feele you no change about you? Pray you ftand off.
  Old Lio. What ftrange and vnexpected greetings this,
That thus a man may knocke at his owne gates,
Beat with his hands and feet, and call thus loud,
And no man giue him entrance?
  Reig. Said you Sir;
Did your hand touch that hammer?
  Old Lio. Why, whofe elfe?
  Reig. But are you fure you toucht it?
  Old Lio. How elfe, I prethee, could I haue made this noife?
  Reig. You toucht it then?
  Old Lio. I tell thee yet I did.
  Reig. Oh for the love I beare you,
Oh me moft miferable, you, for your owne fake,
Of all aliue moft wretched; Did you touch it?
  Old Lio. Why, fay I did?
  Reig. You haue then a finne committed,
No facrifice can expiate to the Dead;
But yet I hope you did not.
  Old Lio. 'Tis paft hope,

The deed is done, and I repent it not.
   Reig. You and all yours will doo't. In this one rafhnes,
You haue vndone vs all; Pray be not defperate,
But firft thanke Heauen that you haue efcapt thus well;
Come from the gate, yet further, further yet,
And tempt your fate no more; Command your feruants
Giue off and come no neerer, they are ignorant,
And doe not know the danger, therefore pity
That they fhould perifh in't; 'Tis full feuen moneths,
Since any of your houfe durft once fet foot
Ouer that threfhold.
   Old Lio. Preethee fpeake the caufe?
   Reig. Firft looke about, beware that no man heare,
Comnand thefe to remooue.
   Old Lio. Be gone. *Exit* Seruants. Now fpeake.
   Reig. Oh Sir, This houfe is growne Prodigious,
Fatall, Difafterous vnto you and yours.
   Old Lio. What Fatall? what Difafterous?
   Reig. Some Hoft that hath beene owner of this houfe,
In it hisGueft hath flaine; And we fufpect
'Twas he of whom you bought it.
   Old Lio. How came this
Difcouerd to you firft?
   Reig. Ile tell you Sir,
But further from the gate: Your fonne one night
Suppt late abroad, I within; Oh that night,
I neuer fhall forget; Being fafe got home,
I faw him in his chamber laid to reft;
And after went to mine, and being drowfie,
Forgot by chance, to put the Candle out;
Being dead afleepe; Your fonne affrighted, calls
So loud, that I foone waken'd; Brought in light,
And found him almoft drown'd in fearefull fweat;
Amaz'd to fee't, I did demand the caufe:
Who told me, that this murdered Ghoft appeared,

His body gasht, and all ore-stucke with wounds;
And spake to him as followes.

Old Lio. Oh proceed,
'Tis that I long to heare.

Reig. I am, quoth he,
A Transf-marine by birth, who came well stored
With Gold and Iewels, to this fatall house;
Where seeking safety, I encounter'd death:
The couetous Merchant, Land-lord of this rent,
To whom I gaue my life and wealth in charge;
Freely to enjoy the one, rob'd me of both:
Heere was my body buried, here my Ghost
Must euer walke, till that haue Christian right;
Till when, my habitation must be here:
Then flie yong man, Remooue thy family,
And seeke some safer dwelling: For my death,
This mansion is accurst; 'Tis my possesion,
Bought at the deere rate of my life and blood,
None enter here, that aymes at his owne good.
And with this charge he vanisht.

Old Lio. Oh my feare,
Whither wilt thou transport me?

Reig. I intreat keepe further from the gate, and flie.

Old Lio. Flie whither? Why doest not thou flie too?

Reig. What need I feare, the Ghost and I am friends.

Old Lio. But Reignald.

Reig. Tush, I nothing haue deserued,
Nor ought transgrest: I came not neere the gate.

Old Lio. To whom was that thou spakest?

Reig. Was't you Sir nam'd me?
Now as I liue, I thought the dead man call'd,
To enquire for him that thunder'd at the gate
Which he so dearely pai'd for: Are you mad,
To stand a fore-seene danger?

Old Lio. What shall I doe?

Reig. Couer your head and flie; Lest looking backe,

You fpie your owne confufion.
  Old Lio. Why doeft not thou flie too?
  Reig. I tell you Sir,
The Ghoft and I am friends.
  Old Lio. Why didft thou quake then?
  Reig. In feare left fome mifchance may fall on you,
That haue the dead offended; For my part,
The Ghoft and I am friends: Why flie you not,
Since here you are not fafe?
  Old Lio. Some bleft powers guard me.
  Reig. Nay Sir, ile not forfake you: I haue got the ftart;
But ere the goale, 'twill aske both Braine and Art.
                                  Exeunt.

Actus Tertius. Scena Prima.

Enter old Mafter Geraldine, Y. Geraldine, *Mafter* Wincott, *and* Wife, Dalauill, Prudentilla.

  Winc. We are bound to you, kind Mafter Geraldine,
For this great entertainement; Troath your coft
Hath much exceeded common neighbour-hood:
You haue feafted vs like Princes.
  Old Ger. This, and more
Many degrees, can neuer counteruaile
The oft and frequent welcomes giuen my fonne:
You haue tooke him from me quite, and haue I thinke,
Adopted him into your family,
He ftaies with me fo feldome.
  Win. And in this,
By trufting him to me, of whom your felfe
May haue both vfe and pleafure, y'are as kind
As money'd men, that might make benefit
Of what they are poffeft, yet to their friends

In need, will lend it gratis.
　Wife. And like fuch,
As are indebted more then they can pay ;
Wee more and more confeffe our felues engaged
To you, for your forbearance.
　Prud. Yet you fee,
Like Debtors, fuch as would not breake their day ;
The Treafure late receiued, wee tender backe,
The which, the longer you can fpare, you ftill
　The more fhall binde vs to you.
　Old Ger. Moft kind Ladies,
Worthy you are to borrow, that returne
The Principall, with fuch large vfe of thanks.
　Dal. What ftrange felicitie thefe Rich men take,
To talke of borrowing, lending, and of vfe ;
The vfurers language right.
　Winc. Y'aue Mafter Geraldine,
Faire walkes and gardens, I haue praifed them,
Both to my Wife and Sifter.
　Old Ger. You would fee them,
There's no pleafure that the Houfe can yeeld,
That can be debar'd from you ; prethee Sonne,
Be thou the Vfher to thofe Mounts and Profpects
May one day call thee Mafter.
　Y. Ger. Sir I fhall ;
Pleafe you to walke.
　Prud. What Mafter Dalauill,
Will you not beare vs company.
　Dal. 'Tis not fit
That wee fhould leaue our Noble hoft alone,
Be you my Friends charge, and this old man mine.
　Prud. Well, bee 't then at your pleafure.　*Exeunt.*

　　　Manet Dalauill *and* Old Geraldine.

　Dal. You to your Profpects, but there's proiect
　　heere
That's of another Nature ; Worthy Sir,
I cannot but approue your happineffe,
To be the Father of fo braue a Sonne,

So euery way accomplifh't and made vp,
In which my voice is leaft : For I alaffe,
Beare but a meane part in the common quier,
When with much lowder accents of his praife,
So all the world reports him.
   Old Ger.   Thanke my Starres,
They haue lent me one, who as he alwayes was,
And is my prefent ioy ; If their afpect
Be no wayes to our goods Maleuolent,
May be my Future comfort.
   Dal.   Yet muft I hold him happie aboue others,
As one that Solie to himfelfe inioyes
What many others aime at ; But in vaine.
   Old Ger.   How meane you that ?
   Dal.   So Beautifull a Miftreffe.
   Old Ger.   A Miftreffe, faid you ?
   Dal.   Yes Sir, or a Friend,
Whether you pleafe to ftile her.
   Old Ger.   Miftrefle ? Friend ?
Pray be more open languag'd.
   Dal.   And indeed,
Who can blame him to abfent himfelfe from home,
And make his Fathers houfe but as a grange,
For a Beautie fo Attractiue ? Or blame her,
Huging fo weake an old Man in her armes,
To make a new choice, of an equall youth,
Being in him fo Perfect ? yet introath,
I thinke they both are honeft.
   Old Ger.   You haue Sir,
Poffeft me with fuch ftrange fancies.
   Dal.   For my part,
How can I loue the perfon of your Sonne,
And not his reputation ?   His repaire
So often to the Houfe, is voyct by all,
And frequent in the mouthes of the whole Countrey,
Some equally addicted, praife his happineffe ;
But others, more Cenforious and Auftere,
Blame and reprooue a courfe fo difolute ;
Each one in generall, pittie the good man,

As one vnfriendly dealt with, yet in my confcience,
I thinke them truely Honeſt.

   Old Ger. 'Tis ſuſpitious.

   Dal. True Sir, at beſt; But what when ſcandalous tongues
Will make the worſt? and what good in it ſelfe,
Sullie and ſlaine by fabulous miſ-report;
For let men liue as charie as they can,
Their liues are often queſtioned; Then no wonder,
If ſuch as giue occaſion of ſuſpition,
Be ſubiect to this ſcandall: What I ſpeake,
Is as a Noble Friend vnto your Sonne;
And therefore, as I glory in his Fame,
I ſuffer in his wrong; for as I liue,
I thinke, they both are honeſt.

   Old Ger. Howſoeuer,
I wiſh them ſo.

   Dal. Some courſe might be deuiſ'd,
To ſtop this clamor ere it grow too wrancke;
Leſt that which yet but inconuenience ſeemes,
May turne to greater miſchiefe; This I ſpeake
In Zeale to both, in foueraine care of him
As of a Friend; And tender of her Honour,
As one to whom I hope to be allyed,
By Marriage with her Siſter.

   Old Ger. I much thanke you,
For you haue cleerely giuen me light of that,
Till now I neuer dreamt on.

   Dal. 'Tis my Loue,
And therefore I intreat you, make not mee
To be the firſt reporter.

   Old Ger. You haue done
The office of a Noble Gentleman,
And ſhall not be ſo iniur'd.

   Enter againe as from Walking Winc. Wife, Y. Ger.
                       Prud.

   Winc. See Maſter Geraldine,
How bold wee are, eſpecially theſe Ladies

Play little better then the theeues with you,
For they haue robb'd your Garden.
  Wife. You might Sir,
Better haue term'd it faucenes, then theft ;
You fee we blufh not, what we tooke in priuate,
To weare in publicke view.
  Prud. Befides, thefe cannot
Be mift out of fo many ; In full fields,
The gleanings are allow'd.
  Old Ger. Thefe and the reft,
Are Ladies, at your feruice.
  Winc. Now to horfe,
But one thing ere wee part, I muft intreat ;
In which my Wife will be ioynt futer with me,
My Sifter too.
  Old Ger. In what I pray.
  Winc. That hee
Which brought vs hither, may but bring vs home ;
Your much refpected Sonne.
  Old Ger. How men are borne,
To woe their owne difafters ?
  Wife. But to fee vs
From whence he brought vs Sir, that 's all.
  Old Ger. This fecond motion makes it Palpable :
To note a Womans cunning ; Make her husband
Bawde to her owne laciuious appetite,
And to Solicite his owne fhame.
  Prud. Nay Sir,
When all of vs ioyne in fo fmall a fuit,
It were fome iniurie to be deni'd.
  Old Ger. And worke her Sifter too ; What will
    not woman
To accomplifh her owne ends : But this difeafe,
Ile feeke to Phificke ere it grow too farre :
I am moft forrie to be vrg'd fweet Friends,
In what at this time I can no wayes grant ;
Moft, that thefe Ladies fhould be ought deni'd,
To whom I owe all Seruice, but occafions
Of weighty and important confeequence,

Such as concerne the beſt of my Eſtate,
Call him aſide ; excuſe vs both this once,
Preſume this buſineſſe is no ſooner ouer,
But hee's at his owne freedome.

   Winc. 'Twere no manners
In vs to vrge it further, wee will leaue you,
With promiſe Sir, that he ſhall in my will,
Not be the laſt remembred.

   Old Ger. Wee are bound to you ;
See them to Horſe, and inſtantly returne,
Wee haue Imployments for you.

   Y. Ger. Sir I ſhall.

   Dal. Remember your laſt promiſe.

   Old Ger. Not to doo 't,
I ſhould forget my ſelfe : If I finde him falſe
To ſuch a friend, be ſure he forfeits me ;
In which to be more punctually reſolu'd,
I haue a proiect how to ſift his ſoule,
How 'tis enclin'd ; whether to yonder place,

   Enter Y. Geraldine.

The cleare bright Pallace, or blacke Dungeon : See,
They are onward on the way, and hee return'd.

   Y. Ger. I now attend your pleaſure.

   Old Ger. You are growne perfect man, and now
     you float
Like to a well built Veſſell ; 'Tweene two Currents,
Vertue and Vice ; Take this, you ſteere to harbour
Take that, to eminent ſhipwracke.

   Y. Ger. Pray your meaning.

   Old Ger. What fathers cares are, you ſhall neuer
     know,
Till you your ſelfe haue children, Now my ſtuddy,
Is how to make you ſuch, that you in them
May haue a feeling of my loue to you.

   Y. Ger. Pray Sir expound your ſelfe ; for I proteſt
Of all the Languages I yet haue learn'd,
This is to me moſt forraine.

Old Ger. Then I fhall;
I haue liued to fee you in your prime of youth
And height of Fortune, fo you will but take
Occafion by the forehead; to be briefe,
And cut off all fuperfluous circumftance,
All the ambition that I ayme at now,
Is but to fee you married.
 Y. Ger. Married Sir.
 Old Ger. .And to that purpofe, I haue found out one,
Whofe Youth and Beauty may not onely pleafe
A curious eye; But her immediate meanes,
Able to ftrengthen a ftate competent,
Or raife a ruined Fortune.
 Y. Ger. Of all which,
I haue beleeue me, neither need nor vfe;
My competence beft pleafing as it is;
And this my fingularity of life,
Moft to my mind contenting.
 Od Ger. I fufpect, but yet muft proue him further;
Say to my care I adde a Fathers charge,
And couple with my counfell my command;
To that how can you anfwere?
 Y. Ger. That I hope:
My duty and obedience ftill vnblam'd,
Did neuer merit fuch aufterity;
And from a father neuer yet difpleas'd.
 Old Ger. Nay, then to come more neere vnto the point;
Either you muft refolue for prefent marriage,
Or forfeit all your intereft in my loue.
 Y. Ger. Vn-fay that language, I intreat you Sir,
And doe not fo oppreffe me; Or if needs
Your heauy impofition ftand in force,
Refolue me by your counfell; With more fafety
May I infringe a facred vow to heauen,
Or to oppofe me to your ftrict command?
Since one of thefe I muft.
 Old Ger. Now Dalauill,

I finde thy words too true.

Y. Ger. For marrie, Sir, I neither may, nor can.

Old Ger. Yet whore you may;
And that's no breach of any vow to Heauen:
Pollute the Nuptiall bed with Michall finne;
Afperfe the honour of a noble friend;
Forfeit thy reputation, here below,
And th' intereft that thy Soule might claime aboue,
In yon bleft City: Thefe you may, and can,
With vntoucht confcience: Oh, that I fhould liue
To fee the hopes that I haue ftor'd fo long,
Thus in a moment ruin'd: And the ftaffe,
On which my old decrepite age fhould leane;
Before my face thus broken: On which trufting,
I thus abortiuely, before my time,
Fall headlong to my Graue. *Falls on the earth.*

Y. Ger. It yet ftands ftrong;
Both to fupport you vnto future life,
And fairer comfort.

Old Ger. Neuer, neuer fonne:
For till thou canft acquit thy felfe of fcandall,
And me of my fufpition; Heere, euen heere,
Where I haue meafur'd out my length of earth;
I fhall expire my laft.

Y. Ger. Both thefe I can:
Then rife Sir, I intreat you; And that innocency,
Which poyfon'd by the breath of Calumnie,
Caft you thus low, fhall, thefe few ftaines wipt off,
With better thoughts erect you.

Old Ger. Well, Say on.

Y. Ger. There's but one fire from which this fmoake may grow:
Namely, the vnmatcht yoake of youth; And
In which, If euer I occafion was,
Of the fmalleft breach; the greateft implacable mifchiefe
Adultery can threaten, fall on me;
Of you may I be difauow'd a fonne;

And vnto Heauen a feruant: For that Lady,
As fhe is Beauties mirror, fo I hold her
For Chaftities examples: From her tongue,
Neuer came language, that ariued my eare,
That euen cenfurious *Cato*, liu'd he now,
Could mif-interpret; Neuer from her lips,
Came vnchafte kiffe; Or from her conftant eye,
Looke fauouring of the leaft immodefty:
Further——
   Old Ger. Enough; One onely thing remaines,
Which on thy part perform'd, affures firme credit
To thefe thy proteftations.
   Y. Ger. Name it then.
   Old Ger. Take hence th' occafion of this common fame;
Which hath already fpread it felfe fo farre,
To her difhonour and thy preiudice,
From this day forward, to forbeare the houfe:
This doe vpon my blefsing.
   Y. Ger. As I hope it,
I will not faile your charge.
   Old Ger. I am fatisfied. *Exeunt.*

Enter at one doore an Vfurer *and his Man, at the other,* Old Lionell *with his feruant: In the midft* Reignald.

   Reig. To which hand fhall I turne me; Here's my Mafter
Hath bin to enquire of him that fould the houfe,
Touching the murder; Here's an Vfuring-Rafcall,
Of whom we haue borrowed money to fupply
Our prodigall expences; Broke our day,
And owe him ftill the Principall and Vfe:
Were I to meet them fingle, I haue braine
To oppofe both, and to come off vnfcarr'd;
But if they doe affault me, and at once,
Not *Hercules* himfelfe could ftand that odds:
Therefore I muft encounter them by turnes;
And to my Mafter firft: Oh Sir, well met.
   Old Lio. What Reignald; I but now met with the man,

Of whom I bought yon houfe.

Reig. What, did you Sir?
But did you fpeake of ought concerning that
Which I laſt told you.

Old Lio. Yes, I told him all.

Reig. Then am I caſt: But I pray tell me Sir,
Did he confeſſe the murder?

Old Lio. No fuch thing;
Moſt ſtiffely he denies it.

Reig. Impudent wretch;
Then ferue him with awarrant, let the Officer
Bring him before a Iuſtice, you ſhall heare
What I can fay againſt him; Sfoot deni't:
But I pray Sir excufe me, yonder's one
With whom I haue fome bufineſſe; Stay you here,
And but determine what's beſt courfe to take,
And note how I will follow't.

Old Lio. Be briefe then.

Reig. Now, If I can afwell put off my Vfe-man,
This day, I ſhall be maſter of the field.

Vfu. That ſhould be Lionells man.

Man. The fame, I know him.

Vfu. After fo many friuolous delaies,
There's now fome hope. He that was wont to ſhun vs,
And to abfent himfelfe, accoaſts vs freely;
And with a pleafant countenance: Well met Reignald,
What's this money ready?

Reig. Neuer could you
Haue come in better time.

Vfu. Where's your maſter,
Yong Lionell, it fomething troubles me,
That hee ſhould breake his day.

Reig. A word in priuate.

Vfu. Tuſh, Priuate me no priuates, in a word,
Speake, are my moneys ready?

Reig. Not fo loud.

Vfu. I will be louder yet; Giue me my moneys,
Come, tender me my moneys.

Reig. We know you haue a throat, wide as your confcience;

You need not vſe it now——Come, get you home.
  Vſu. Home?
  Reig. Yes, home I ſay, returne by three a Clocke,
And I will ſee all cancell'd.
  Vſu. 'Tis now paſt two, and I can ſtay till three,
Ile make that now my buſineſſe, otherwayes,
With theſe lowd clamors, I will haunt thee ſtill;
Giue me my Vſe, giue me my Principall.
  Reig. This burre will ſtill cleaue to me; what, no
    meanes
To ſhake him off; I neere was caught till now:
Come come, y'are troubleſome.
  Vſu. Preuent that trouble,
And without trifling, pay me downe my caſh;
I will be fool'd no longer.
  Reig. So ſo ſo.
  Vſu. I haue beene ſtill put off, from time to time,
And day to day; theſe are but cheating tricks,
And this is the laſt minute ıle forbeare
Thee, or thy Maſter: Once againe, I ſay,
Giue me my Vſe, giue me my Principall.
  Reig. Pox a this vſe, that hath vndone ſo many;
And now will confound mee.
  Old Lio. Haſt thou heard this?
  Ser. Yes Sir, and to my griefe.
  Old Lio. Come hither Reignald.
  Reig. Heere Sir; Nay, now I am gone.
  Old Lio. What vſe is this?
What Principall hee talkes of? in which language
Hee names my Sonne; And thus vpbraideth thee,
What is't you owe this man?
  Reig. A trifle Sir,
Pray ſtop his mouth; And pay't him.
  Old Lio. I pay, what?
  Reig. If I ſay pay't him; Pay't him.
  Old Lio. What's the Summe?
  Reig. A toy, the maine about fiue hundred pounds;
And the vſe fiftie.
  Old Lio. Call you that a toy?

To what vfe was it borrowed? At my departure,
I left my Sonne fufficient in his charge,
With furplus, to defray a large expence,
Without this neede of borrowing.

Reig. 'Tis confeft,
Yet ftop his clamorous mouth; And onely fay,
That you will pay't to morrow.

Old Lio. I paffe my word.

Reig. Sir, if I bid you doo't; Nay, no more words,
But fay you'le pay't to morrow.

Old Lio. Ieaft indeed,
But tell me how thefe moneys were beftowed?

Reig. Safe Sir, I warrant you.

Old Lio. The Summe ftill fafe,
Why doe you not then tender it your felues?

Reig. Your eare fir; This fumme ioyn'd to the reft,
Your Sonne hath purchaft Land and Houfes.

Old Lio. Land, do'ft thou fay?

Reig. A goodly Houfe, and Gardens.

Old Lio. Now ioy on him,
That whil'ft his Father Merchandis'd abroad,
Had care to adde to his eftate at home:
But Reignald, wherefore Houfes?

Reig. Now Lord Sir,
How dull you are; This houfe poffeft with fpirits,
And there no longer ftay; Would you haue had
Him, vs, and all your other family,
To liue, and lie ith' ftreets; It had not Sir,
Beene for your reputation.

Old Lio. Blefsing on him,
That he is growne fo thriftie.

Vfu. 'Tis ftrooke three,
My money's not yet tender'd.

Reig. Pox vpon him,
See him difcharged, I pray Sir.

Old Lio. Call vpon me
To morrow Friend, as early as thou wilt;
Ile fee thy debt defraid.

Vsu. It is enough, I haue a true mans word.

Exit. Vsurer and man.

Old Lio. Now tell me Reignald,
For thou haft made me proud of my Sonnes thrift;
Where, in what Countrey, doth this faire Houfe ftand.

Reig. Neuer in all my time, fo much to feeke;
I know not what to anfwere.

Old Lio. Wherefore ftuddieft thou?
Vfe men to purchafe Lands at a deere rate,
And know not where they lie?

Reig. 'Tis not for that;
I onely had forgot his name that fould them,
'Twas let me fee, fee.

Old Lio. Call thy felfe to minde.

Reig. Non-pluft or neuer now; Where art thou
 braine?
O Sir, where was my memory; 'Tis this houfe
That next adioynes to yours.

Old Lio. My Neighbour Ricots.

Reig. The fame, the fame Sir; Wee had peni-
 worths in't;
And I can tell you, haue beene offer'd well
Since, to forfake our bargaine.

Old Lio. As I liue,
I much commend your choice.

Reig. Nay, 'tis well feated,
Rough-caft without, but brauely lined within;
You haue met with few fuch bargaines.

Old Lio. Prethee knocke,
And call the Mafter, or the feruant on't;
To let me take free view on't.

Reig. Puzzle againe on Puzzle; One word Sir,
The Houfe is full of Women, no man knowes,
How on the inftant, they may be imploy'd;
The Roomes may lie vnhanfome; and Maids ftand
Much on their cleanlineffe and hufwiferie;
To take them vnprouided, were difgrace,
'Twere fit they had fome warning; Now, doe you

Fetch but a warrant, from the Iuſtice Sir;
You vnderſtand mee.
   Old Lio. Yes, I doe.
   Reig. To attach
Him of ſuſpected murder, Ile fee't feru'd;
Did he deny't? And in the intrim, I
Will giue them notice, you are now ariu'd,
And long to fee your purchaſe.
   Old Lio. Councell'd well;
And meet ſome halfe houre hence.
   Reig. This plunge well paſt,
All things fall euen, to Crowne my Braine at laſt.
Exeunt.

Enter Dalauill *and a* Gentleman.

   Gent. Where ſhall we dine to day?
   Dal. At th' Ordinarie.
I ſee Sir, you are but a ſtranger heere;
This Barnet, is a place of great reſort;
And commonly vpon the Market dayes,
Heere all the Countrey Gentlemen Appoint.
A friendly meeting; Some about affaires
Of Conſequence and Profit; Bargaine, Sale,
And to conferre with Chap-men, ſome for pleaſure,
To match their Horſes; Wager in their Dogs,
Or trie their Hawkes; Some to no other end,
But onely meet good Company, diſcourſe,
Dine, drinke, and ſpend their Money.

Enter Old Geraldine *and* Yong Geraldine.

   Gent. That's the Market, Wee haue to make this day.
   Dal. 'Tis a Commoditie, that will be eaſily vented:
What my worthy Friend,
You are happily encounter'd; Oh, y'are growne ſtrange,
To one that much reſpects you; Troath the Houſe

Hath all this time feem'd naked without you;
The good Old Man doth neuer fit to meat,
But next his giuing Thankes, hee fpeakes of you;
There's fcarce a bit, that he at Table taftes,
That can digeft without a Geraldine,
You are in his mouth fo frequent: Hee and Shee
Both wondering, what diftafte from one, or either,
So fuddenly, fhould alianate a Gueft,
To them, fo decrely welcome.
   Old Ger. Mafter Dalauill,
Thus much let me for him Apoligie;
Diuers defignes haue throng'd vpon vs late,
My weakeneffe was not able to fupport
Without his helpe; He hath bin much abroad,
At London, or elfe where; Befides 'tis Terme;
And Lawyers muft be followed, feldome at home,
And fcarcely then at leafure.
   Dal. I am fatisfied,
And I would they were fo too, but I hope Sir,
In this reftraint, you haue not vs'd my name?
   Old Ger. Not, as I liue.
   Dal. Y'are Noble——Who had thought
To haue met with fuch good Company; Y'are it feeme
But new alighted; Father and Sonne, ere part,
I vow weele drinke a cup of Sacke together;
Phificians fay, It doth prepare the appetite
And ftomacke againft dinner.
   Old Ger. Wee old men,
Are apt to take thefe courtefies.
   Dal. What fay you Friend?
   Y. Ger. Ile but enquire for one, at the next Inne,
And inftantly returne.
   Dal. 'Tis enough.   *Exit.*

   Enter Beffe *meeting* Y. Geraldine.

   Y. Ger. Beffe: How do'ft thou Girle?

Bess. Faith we may doe how we lift for you, you are growne so
Great a stranger: We are more beholding
To Master Dalauill, Hee's a constant Guest:
And howsoere to some, that shall bee namelesse,
His presence may be gracefull; Yet to others——
I could say somewhat.
  Y. Ger. Hee's a noble fellow,
And my choice friend.
  Bess. Come come, he is, what he is; and that the end will prooue.
  Y. Ger. And how's all at home?
Nay, weele not part without a glasse of wine,
And meet so seldome: Boy.

Enter Drawer.

Drawer. Anon, anon Sir.
  Y. Ger. A Pint of Clarret, quickly. *Exit* Drawer.
Nay, sit downe: The newes, the newes, I pray thee;
I am sure, I haue beene much enquir'd of
Thy old Master, and thy young Mistris too.
  Bess. Euer your name is in my Masters mouth, and sometimes too
In hers, when she hath nothing else to thinke of:
Well well, I could say somewhat.

Enter Drawer.

Drawer. Heere's your wine Sir.   *Exit.*
  Y. Ger. Fill Boy: Here Besse, this glasse to both their healths;
Why do'st weepe my wench?
  Bess. Nay, nothing Sir.
  Y. Ger. Come, I must know.
  Bess. Introath I loue you Sir,
And euer wisht you well; You are a Gentleman,
Whom alwayes I respected; Know the passages
And priuate whisperings, of the secret loue

Betwixt you and my Miſtris; I dare ſweare,
On your part well intended: But——
   Y. Ger. But what?
   Beſſ. You beare the name of Land-lord, but another
Inioyes the rent; You doate vpon the ſhadow,
But another he beares away the ſubſtance.
   Y. Ger. Bee more plaine.
   Beſſ. You hope to inioy a vertuous widdow-hood;
But Dalauill, whom you eſteeme your friend,
Hee keepes the wife in common.
   Y. Ger. Y'are too blame,
And Beſſe, you make me angry; Hee's my friend,
And ſhe my ſecond ſelfe; In all their meetings,
I neuer ſaw ſo much as caſt of eye
Once entertain'd betwixt them.
   Beſſ. That's their cunning.
   Y. Ger. For her; I haue beene with her at all houres,
Both late and early; In her bed-chamber,
And often ſingly vſher'd her abroad:
Now, would ſhe haue bin any mans aliue,
Shee had bin mine; You wrong a worthy Friend,
And a chaſte Miſtris, y'are not a good Girle;
Drinke that, ſpeake better of her, I could chide you,
But I'le forbeare; What you haue raſhly ſpoke,
Shall euer heere be buried.
   Beſſ. I am ſorry my freeneſſe ſhould offend you,
But yet know, I am her Chamber-maid.
   Y. Ger. Play now the Market-maid,
And prethee bout thy buſineſſe.
   Beſſ. Well, I ſhall——that man ſhould be ſo fool'd.
                                            Exit.
   Y. Ger. Shee a Proſtitute?
Nay, and to him my troath plight, and my Friend;
As poſsible it is, that Heauen and Earth
Should be in loue together, meet and kiſſe,
And ſo cut off all diſtance: What ſtrange frenſie
Came in this wenches braine, ſo to ſurmiſe?

Were she so base? his noblenesse is such,
He would not entertaine it for my sake:
Or he so bent? His hot and lust burnt appetite
Would be soone quencht, at the meere contemplation
Of her most Pious and Religious life.
The Girle was much too blame; Perhaps her Mistris
Hath stirr'd her anger, by some word or blow,
Which she would thus reuenge; Not apprehending
At what a high price Honour's to be rated;
Or else some one that enuies her rare vertue,
Might hire her thus to brand it; Or, who knowes
But the yong wench may fixe a thought on me;
And to diuert me from her Mistris loue,
May raise this false asperfion? howsoeuer,

Enter Clo. *with a letter*.

My thoughts on these two columnes fixed are,
She's good as fresh, and purely chaste as faire.

Clo. Oh Sir, you are the Needle, and if the whole County of Middlesex had bin turn'd to a meere Bottle of Hay, I had bin inioyn'd to haue found you out, or neuer more return'd backe to my old Master: There's a Letter Sir.

Y. Ger. I know the hand that superscrib'd it well; Stay but till I peruse it, and from me
Thou shalt returne an answere.

Clo. I shall Sir: This is Market-day, and heere acquaintance commonly meet; and whom haue I encounter'd? my gossip Pint-pot, and brim full; nay, I meane to drinke with you before I part, and how doth all your worshipfull kindred? your sister Quart, your pater-Pottle, (who was euer a Gentlemans fellow) and your old grandsier Gallon; they cannot chuse but be all in health, since so many healthes haue beene drunke out of them: I could wish them all heere, and in no worse state then I see you are in at this present; howsoeuer gossip, since I haue met you hand to hand, I'le make bould to drinke to you——Nay, either you must pledge me, or get one to doo't for you; Doe you open your mouth towards me? well, I know what you would fay; Heere Roger, to your Mafter and Miftris, and all our good friends at home; gramercy gofsip, if I fhould not pledge thee, I were worthy to be turn'd out to Graffe, and ftand no more at Liuery; And now in requitall of this courtefie I'le begin one health to you and all your fociety in the Celler, to Peter Pipe, Harry Hogfhead, Bartholomew Butt and little mafter Randall Rundlet, to Timothy Tafter, and all your other great and fmall friends.

Y. Ger. Hee writes mee heere,
That at my difcontinuance hee's much grieu'd;
Defiring me, as I haue euer tender'd
Or him or his, to giue him fatisfaction
Touching my difcontent; and that in perfon,
By any priuate meeting.

Clo. I Sir, 'tis very true; The Letter fpeakes no more
Then he wifht me to tell you by word of mouth.

Y. Ger. Thou art then of his councell?

Clo. His Priuy and pleafe you.

Y. Ger. Though neere fo ftrict hath bin my fathers charge,
A little I'le difpenfe with't, for his loue;
Commend me to thy Mafter, tell him from me,
On Munday night (then will my leafure ferue)
I will by Heauens afsiftance vifit him.

Clo. On Munday Sir:
That's as I remember, iuft the day before Tuefday.

Y. Ger. But 'twill be midnight firft, at which late houre,
Pleafe him to let the Garden doore ftand ope,
At that I'le enter; But conditionally,
That neither Wife, Friend, Seruant, no third foule
Saue him, and thee to whom he trufts this meffage,
Know of my comming in, or pafsing out:
When, tell him, I will fully fatisfie him
Concerning my forct abfence.

Clo. I am fomething obliuious; Your meffage

would bee the truelier deliuered if it were fet downe in blacke and white.

 Y. Ger. I'le call for Pen and Incke,
And inſtantly diſpatch it.   *Exeunt.*

Actus Quartus. Scena Prima.

Enter Reignald.

 Reig. Now impudence, but ſteele my face this once,
Although I neere bluſh after; Heere's the houſe,
Ho, whoſe within? What, no man to defend
           Enter Mr. Ricot.
Theſe innocent gates from knocking?
 Ric. Whoſe without there?
 Reig. One Sir that euer wiſht your worſhips health;
And thoſe few houres I can find time to pray in,
I ſtill remember it.
 Ric. Gramercy Reignald,
I loue all thoſe that wiſh it: You are the men
Leade merry liues, Feaſt, Reuell, and Carowſe;
You feele no tedious houres; Time playes with you,
This is your golden age.
 Reig. It was, but now Sir,
That Gould is turned to worſe then Alcamy,
It will not ſtand the teſt; Thoſe dayes are paſt,
And now our nights come on.
 Ric. Tell me Reignald, is he return'd from Sea?
 Reig. Yes, to our griefe already, but we feare
Hereafter, it may prooue to all our coſt's.
 Ric. Suſpects thy Maſter any thing?
 Reig. Not yet Sir;
Now my requeſt is, that your worſhip being
So neere a Neighbour, therefore moſt diſturb'd,
Would not be firſt to peach vs.
 Ric. Take my word;

With other Neighbours make what peace you can,
I'le not be your accufer.
  Reig. Worfhipfull Sir;
I fhall be ftill your Beads-man; Now the bufineffe
That I was fent about, the Old Man my Mafter
Claiming fome intereft in acquaintance paft,
Defires (might it be no way troublefome)
To take free view of all your Houfe within.
  Ric. View of my Houfe? Why 'tis not fet to Sale,
Nor bill vpon the doore; Looke well vpon't:
View of my Houfe?
  Reig. Nay, be not angry Sir,
Hee no way doth difable your eftate;
As farre to buy, as you are loath to fell;
Some alterations in his owne hee'd make,
And hearing yours by worke-men much commended,
Hee would make that his Prefident.
  Ric. What fancies
Should at this age poffeffe him; Knowing the coft,
That hee fhould dreame of Building.
  Reig. 'Tis fuppos'd,
He hath late found a Wife out for his Sonne;
Now Sir, to haue him neere him, and that neereneffe
Too, without trouble, though beneath one roofe,
Yet parted in two Families; Hee would build
And make what's pickt, a perfit quadrangle,
Proportioned iuft with yours, were you fo pleafed,
To make it his example.
  Rio. Willingly; I will but order fome few things
    within,
And then attend his comming.   *Exit*
  Reig. Moft kind cox-combe,
Great *Alexander*, and *Agathocles*,
Cæfar, and others, haue bin Fam'd, they fay,
And magnified for high Facinerous deeds;
Why claime not I, an equall place with them?
Or rather a prefedent: Thefe commanded
Their Subiects, and their feruants; I my Mafter,
And euery way his equalls, where I pleafe,

Lead by the nofe along; They plac'd their burdens
On Horfes, Mules, and Camels; I, old Men
Of ftrength and wit, loade with my knauerie,

Enter Old Lionell.

Till both their backs and braines ake; Yet poore animalls,
They neere complaine of waight; Oh are you come Sir?
   Old Lio. I made what hafte I could.
   Reig. And brought the warrant?
   Old Lio. See heere, I hau't.
   Reig. 'Tis well done, but fpeake, runs it
Both without Baile and Maineprize?
   Old Lio. Nay, it carries both forme and power.
   Reig. Then I fhall warrant him;
I haue bin yonder Sir.
   Old Lio. And what fayes hee?
   Reig. Like one that offers you
Free ingreffe, view and regreffe, at your pleafure;
As to his worthy Land-lord.
   Old Lio. Was that all?
   Reig. Hee fpake to me, that I would fpeake to you,
To fpeake vnto your Sonne; And then againe,
To fpeake to him, that he would fpeake to you;
You would releafe his Bargaine.
   Old Lio. By no meanes,
Men muft aduife before they part with Land,
Not after to repent it; 'Tis moft iuft,
That fuch as hazzard, and disburfe their Stockes,
Should take all gaines and profits that accrew,

Enter Mr. Ricot *againe walking before the gate.*

As well in Sale of Houfes, as in Barter,
And Traficke of all other Merchandize.
   Reig. See, in acknowledgement of a Tenants duty,
Hee attends you at the gate; Salute him Sir.

Old Lio. My worthy Friend.
Ric. Now as I liue, all my beſt thoughts and wiſhes
Impart with yours, in your ſo ſafe returne;
Your ſeruant tels me, you haue great deſire
To take ſuruiew of this my houſe within.
Old Lio. Bee't Sir, no trouble to you.
Ric. None, enter bouldly;
With as much freedome, as it were your owne.
Old Lio. As it were mine; Why Reignald, is it not?
Reig. Lord Sir, that in extremity of griefe,
You'le adde vnto vexation; See you not
How ſad hee's on the ſuddaine,
Old Lio. I obſerue it.
Reig. To part with that which he hath kept ſo long;
Eſpecially his Inheritance; Now as you loue
Goodneſſe, and Honeſty, torment him not
With the leaſt word of Purchaſe.
Old Lio. Councell'd well;
Thou teacheſt me Humanitie.
Ric. Will you enter?
Or ſhall I call a ſeruant, to conduct you
Through euery Roome and Chamber?
Old Lio. By no means;
I feare wee are too much troubleſome of our ſelues.
Reig. See what a goodly Gate?
Old Lio. It likes me well.
Reig. What braue caru'd poaſts; Who knowes but heere,
In time Sir, you may keepe your Shreualtie;
And I be one oth' Seriants.
Old Lio. They are well Caru'd.
Ric. And coſt me a good price Sir; Take your pleaſure,
I haue buſineſſe in the Towne.   *Exit.*
Reig. Poore man, I pittie him;
H'ath not the heart to ſtay and ſee you come,

As 'twere, to take Poſſeſsion; Looke that way Sir,
What goodly faire Baye windowes?   *Bayes.*
  Old Lio. Wondrous ſtately.
  Reig. And what a Gallerie, How coſtly Seeled;
What painting round about?
  Old Lio. Euery freſh object to good, adds better-
    neſſe.
  Reig. Tarraſt aboue, and how below ſupported;
    doe they pleaſe you?
  Old Lio. All things beyond opinion; Truſt me
    Reignald,
I'le not forgoe the Bargaine, for more gaine
Then halfe the price it coſt me.
  Reig. If you would? I ſhould not ſuffer you; Was
    not the
Money due to the Vſurer, tooke vpon good ground,
That prou'd well built vpon? Wee were no fooles
That knew not what wee did.
  Old Lio. It ſhall be ſatisfied.
  Reig. Pleaſe you to truſt me with 't, I'le ſee 't diſ-
    charged.
  Old Lio. Hee hath my promiſe, and I'le doo 't
    my ſelfe:
Neuer could Sonne haue better pleas'd a Father,
Then in this Purchaſe: Hie thee inſtantly
Vnto my houſe ith' Countrey, giue him notice
Of my arriue, and bid him with all ſpeede
Poaſte hither.
  Reig. Ere I ſee the warrant ſeru'd?
  Old Lio. It ſhall be thy firſt buſineſſe; For my
    Soule
Is not at peace, till face to face, I approoue
His Husbandrie, and much commend his Thrift;
Nay, without pauſe, be gone.
  Reig. But a ſhort iourney;
For hee's not farre, that I am ſent to ſeeke:
I haue got the ſtart, the beſt part of the Race
Is runne already, what remaines, is ſmall,
And tyre now, I ſhould but forfeit all.

Old Lio. Make haſte, I doe intreat thee. *Exeunt.*

Enter the Clowne.

Clo. This is the Garden gate; And heere am I ſet to ſtand Centinell, and to attend the comming of Young Maſter Geraldine: Maſter Dalauill's gone to his Chamber; My Miſtreſſe to hers; 'Tis now about Mid-night; A Banquet prepared, bottles of Wine in readineſſe, all the whole Houſhold at their reſt; And no creature by this, honeſtly ſtirring, ſauing I and my Old Maſter; Hee in a bye Chamber, prepared of purpoſe for their priuate Meeting: And I heere to play the Watchman, againſt my will; Chauelah,

Enter Young Geraldine.

Stand; Who goes there?
Y. Ger. A Friend.
Clo. The Word?
Y. Ger. Honeſt Roger.
Clo. That's the Word indeed; You haue leaue to paſſe freely
Without calling my Corporall.
Y. Ger. How goe the affaires within?
Clo. According to promiſe, the buſineſſe is com-poſed, and the feruants difpoſed, my young Miſtris re-poſed, my old Maſter according as you propoſed, attends you if you bee expoſed to giue him meeting; Nothing in the way being interpoſed, to tranſpoſe you to the leaſt danger: And this I dare be depoſed, if you will not take my word, as I am honeſt Roger.
Y. Ger. Thy word ſhall be my warrant, but ſecur'd Moſt in thy Maſters promiſe, on which building;
By this knowne way I enter.
Clo. Nay, by your leaue,
I that was late but a plaine Centinell will now be your Captaine conducter: Follow me. *Exeunt.*

Table and Stooles set out; Lights: a Banquet, Wine.

Enter Master Wincott.

Winc. I wonder whence this strangenesse should proceed,
Or wherein I, or any of my house,
Should be th' occasion of the least distaste;
Now, as I wish him well, it troubles me;

Enter Clow. *and* Y. Ger.

But now the time growes on, from his owne mouth
To be resolu'd; And I hope satisfied:
Sir, as I liue, of all my friends to me
Most wishedly, you are welcome: Take that Chaire,
I this: Nay, I intreat no complement;
Attend——Fill wine.

Clo. Till the mouthes of the bottles yawne directly vpon the floore, and the bottomes turne their tayles vp to the seeling; Whil'st there's any blood in their bellies, I'le not leaue them.

Winc. I first salute you thus.

Y. Ger. It could not come
From one whom I more honour; Sir, I thanke you.

Clo. Nay, since my Master begun it, I'le see 't goe round
To all three.

Winc. Now giue vs leaue.

Clo. Talke you by your selues, whilest I find something to say to this: I haue a tale to tell him shall make his stony heart relent.   *Exit.*

Y. Ger. Now, first Sir, your attention I intreat:
Next, your beliefe, that what I speake is iust,
Maugre all contradiction.

Winc. Both are granted.

Y. Ger. Then I proceed; With due acknowledgement

Of all your more then many curtefies:
Y'aue bin my fecond father, and your wife,
My noble and chafte Miftris; All your feruants
At my command; And this your bounteous Table,
As free and common as my Fathers houfe;
Neither 'gainft any, or the leaft of thefe,
Can I commence iuft quarrell.
  Winc. What might then be
The caufe of this conftraint, in thus abfenting
Your felfe from fuch as loue you?
  Y. Ger. Out of many,
I will propofe fome few: The care I haue
Of your (as yet vnblemifhed) renowne;
The vntoucht honour of your vertuous wife;
And (which I value leaft, yet dearely too)
My owne faire reputation.
  Winc. How can thefe,
In any way be queftioned?
  Y. Ger. Oh deare Sir,
Bad tongues haue bin too bufie with vs all;
Of which I neuer yet had time to thinke,
But with fad thoughts and griefes vnfpeakeable:
It hath bin whifper'd by fome wicked ones,
But loudly thunder'd in my fathers eares,
By fome that haue malign'd our happineffe;
(Heauen, if it can brooke flander, pardon them)
That this my cuftomary comming hither,
Hath bin to bafe and forded purpofes:
To wrong your bed; Iniure her chaftity;
And be mine owne vndoer: Which, how falfe?
  Wenc. As Heauen is true, I know 't.
  Y. Ger. Now this Calumny
Ariuing firft vnto my fathers eares,
His eafie nature was induc'd to thinke,
That thefe things might perhaps be pofsible:
I anfwer'd him, as I would doe to Heauen:
And cleer'd my felfe in his fufpitious thoughts,
As truely, as the high all-knowing Iudge
Shall of thefe ftaines acquit me; which are meerely

Afperfions and vntruthes: The good old man
Poffeft with my fincerity, and yet carefull
Of your renowne, her honour, and my fame;
To ftop the worft that fcandall could inflict;
And to preuent falfe rumours, charges me,
The caufe remoou'd, to take away the effect;
Which onely could be, to forbeare your houfe
And this vpon his blefsing: You heare all.

   Winc. And I of all acquit you: This your ab-
fence,
With which my loue moft cauell'd; Orators
In your behalfe. Had fuch things paft betwixt
you,
Not threats nor chidings could haue driuen you
hence:
It pleads in your behalfe, and fpeakes in hers;
And armes me with a double confidence,
Both of your friendfhip, and her loyalty:
I am happy in you both, and onely doubtfull
Which of you two doth moft impart my loue:
You fhall not hence to night.

   Y. Ger. Pray pardon Sir.
   Winc. You are in your lodging.
   Y. Ger. But my fathers charge.
   Winc. My coniuration fhall difpence with that;
You may be vp as early as you pleafe;
But hence to night you fhall not.

   Y. Ger. You are powerfull.
   Winc. This night, of purpofe, I haue parted
beds,
Faining my felfe not well, to giue you meeting;
Nor can be ought fufpected by my Wife,
I haue kept all fo priuate: Now 'tis late,
I'le fteale vp to my reft; But howfoeuer,
Let 's not be ftrange in our writing, that way
dayly
We may conferre without the leaft fufpect,
In fpight of all fuch bafe calumnious tongues

So, Now good-night sweet friend.   *Exit.*
  Y. Ger. May he that made you
So iuſt and good, ſtill guard you. Not to bed,
So I perhaps might ouer-ſleepe my ſelfe,
And then my tardy wakeing might betray me
To the more early houſhold ; Thus as I am,
I'le reſt me on this Pallat ; But in vaine,
I finde no ſleepe can faſten on mine eyes,
There are in this diſturbed braine of mine
So many mutinous fancies : This, to me,
Will be a tedious night ; How ſhall I ſpend it ?
No Booke that I can ſpie ? no company ?
A little let me recollect my ſelfe ;
Oh, what more wiſht company can I find,
Suiting the apt occaſion, time and place ;
Then the ſweet contemplation of her Beauty ;
And the fruition too, time may produce,
Of what is yet lent out ? 'Tis a ſweet Lady,
And euery way accompliſht : Hath meere accident
Brought me thus neere, and I not viſit her ?
Should it ariue her eare, perhaps might breed
Our laſting ſeparation ; For 'twixt Louers,
No quarrell's to vnkindneſſe, Sweet opportunity
Offers preuention, and inuites me too't :
The houſe is knowne to me, the ſtaires and roomes ;
The way vnto her chamber frequently
Trodden by me at mid-night, and all houres :
How ioyfull to her would a meeting be,
So ſtrange and vnexpected ; Shadowed too
Beneath the vaile of night ; I am reſolu'd
To giue her viſitation, in that place
Where we haue paſt deepe vowes, her bed-chamber :
My fiery loue this darkeneſſe makes ſeeme bright,
And this the path that leades to my delight.
    He goes in at one doore, and comes out at another.
And this the gate vntoo't ; I'le liſten firſt,
Before too rudely I diſturbe her reſt :
And gentle breathing ; Ha ? ſhee's ſure awake,

For in the bed two whifper, and their voyces
Appeare to me vnequall ;——One a womans——
And hers ;——Th' other fhould be no maids tongue,
It beares too big a tone ; And harke, they laugh ;
(Damnation) But lift further ; 'Tother founds——
Like——'Tis the fame falfe periur'd traitor, Dalauill,
To friend and goodneffe : Vnchaft impious woman,
Falfe to all faith, and true coniugall loue ;
There's met, a Serpent and a Crockadell ;
A Synon and a Circe : Oh, to what
May I compare you ?——But my Sword,
I'le act a noble execution,
On two vnmatcht for fordid villanie :——
I left it in my Chamber, And thankes Heauen
That I did fo ; It hath preuented me
From playing a bafe Hang-man ; Sinne fecurely,
Whilft I, although for many, yet leffe faults,
Striue hourely to repent me ; I once loved her,
And was to him intir'd ; Although I pardon,
Heauen will find time to punifh, I'le not ftretch
My iuft reuenge fo farre, as once by blabbing,
To make your brazen Impudence to blufh ;
Damne on, reuenge too great ; And to fuppreffe
Your Soules yet lower, without hope to rife,
Heape Offa vpon Pelion ; You haue made mee
To hate my very Countrey, becaufe heere bred :
Neere two fuch monfters ; Firft I'le leaue this Houfe,
And then my Fathers ; Next I'le take my leaue,
Both of this Clime and Nation, Trauell till
Age fnow vpon this Head : My pafsions now,
Are vnexpreffable, I'le end them thus ;
Ill man, bad Woman, your vnheard of trecherie,
This vniuft cenfure, on a Iuft man giue,
To feeke out place, where no two fuch can liue.
Exit.

Enter Dalauill *in a Night-gowne :* Wife *in a night-tyre, as comming from Bed.*

Dal. A happy Morning now betide you Lady,

To equall the content of a fweet Night.
 Wife. It hath bin to my wifh, and your defire;
And this your comming by pretended loue
Vnto my Sifter Pru. cuts off fufpition
Of any fuch conuerfe 'twixt you and mee.
 Dal. It hath bin wifely carried.
 Wife. One thing troubles me.
 Dal. What's that my Dearest?
 Wife. Why your Friend Geraldine,
Should on the fudden thus abfent himfelfe?
Has he had thinke you no intelligence,
Of thefe our priuate meetings.
 Dal. No, on my Soule,
For therein hath my braine exceeded yours;
I ftuddying to engroffe you to my felfe,
Of his continued abfence haue bin caufe;
Yet hee of your affection no way iealous,
Or of my Friendfhip——How the plot was caft,
You at our better leafure fhall partake;
The aire growes cold, haue care vnto your health,
Sufpitious eyes are ore vs, that yet fleepe,
But with the dawne, will open; Sweet retire you
To your warme Sheets; I now to fill my owne,
That haue this Night bin empty.
 Wife. You aduife well;
Oh might this Kiffe dwell euer on thy Lips,
In my remembrance.
 Dal. Doubt it not I pray,
Whileft Day frights Night, and Night purfues the day:
Good morrow.   *Exeunt.*

Enter Reignald, Y. Lionell, Blanda, Scapha, Rioter,
and two Gallants, Reig. *with a Key in his hand.*

 Reig. Now is the Goale deliuerie; Through this backe gate
Shift for your felues, I heere vnprifon all.
 Y. Lio. But tell me, how fhall we difpofe our felues?

Wee are as farre to feeke now, as at the firſt;
What is it to repreeue vs for few houres,
And now to ſuffer, better had it bin
At firſt, to haue ſtood the triall, ſo by this,
Wee might haue paſt our Pennance.
 Bla. Sweet Reignald.
 Y. Lio. Honeſt rogue.
 Rio. If now thou faileſt vs, then we are loſt for euer.
 Reig. This ſame ſweete Reignald, and this honeſt rogue,
Hath bin the Burgeſſe, vnder whoſe protection
You all this while haue liu'd, free from Arreſts,
But now, the Seſsions of my power's broake vp,
And you expos'd to Actions, Warrants, Writs;
For all the helliſh rabble are broke looſe,
Of Seriants, Sheriffes, and Baliffes.
 Omn. Guard vs Heauen.
 Reig. I tell you as it is; Nay, I my ſelfe
That haue bin your Protector, now as ſubiect
To euery varlots Peſtle, for you know
How I am engag'd with you——At whoſe ſuit ſir.
 Omn. Why didſt thou Start. *All Start.*
 Reig. I was afraid ſome Catchpole ſtood behind me,
To clap me on the Shoulder.
 Rio. No ſuch thing;
Yet I proteſt thy feare did fright vs all.
 Reig. I knew your guilty conſciences.
 Y. Lio. No Braine left?
 Bla. No crotchet for my ſake?
 Reig. One kiſſe then Sweete,
Thus ſhall my crotchets, and your kiſſes meete.
 R. Lio. Nay, tell vs what to truſt too.
 Reig. Lodge your ſelues
In the next Tauerne, ther's the Caſh that's left,
Goe, health it freely for my good ſucceſſe;
Nay, Drowne it all, let not a Teaſter ſcape
To be conſum'd in rot-gut; I haue begun,

And I will ſtand the period.
Y. Lio. Brauely ſpoke.
Reig. Or periſh in the conflict.
Rio. Worthy Reignald.
Reig. Well, if he now come off well, Fox you all;
Goe, call for Wine; For ſinglie of my ſelfe
I will oppoſe all danger; But I charge you,
When I ſhall faint or find my ſelfe diſtreſt;
If I like braue *Orlando*, winde my Horne,
Make haſte vnto my reſcew.
Y. Lio. And die in't.
Reig. Well haſt thou ſpoke my noble Charlemaine,
With theſe thy Peeres about thee.
Y. Lio. May good Speede
Attend thee ſtill.
Reig. The end ſtill crownes the deede. *Exeunt.*

Enter Old Lionell, *and the firſt Owner of the Houſe.*

Own. Sir ſir, your threats nor warrants, can fright me;
My honeſtie and innocency's knowne
Alwayes to haue bin vnblemiſht; Would you could
As well approue your owne Integrity,
As I ſhall doubtleſſe acquit my ſelfe
Of this ſurmiſed murder.
Old Lio. Rather Surrender
The price I paid, and take into thy hands
This haunted manſion, or I'le proſecute
My wrong, euen to the vtmoſt of the Law,
Which is no leſſe then death.
Own. I'le anſwere all
Old Lionell, both to thy ſhame and ſcorne;
This for thy Menaces.

Enter the Clowne.

Clo. This is the Houſe, but where's the noyſe that

was wont to be in't? I am sent hither, to deliuer a Noate, to two young Gentlemen that heere keepe Reuell-rout; I remember it, since the last Massacre of Meat that was made in't; But it seemes, that the great Storme that was raised then, is chast now; I haue other Noates to deliuer, one to Master Rycott——and ——I shall thinke on them all in order; My Old Master makes a great Feast, for the parting of young Master Geraldine, who is presently vpon his departure for Trauell, and the better to grace it, hath inuited many of his Neighbours and Friends; Where will be Old Master Geraldine——his Sonne, and I cannot tell how many; But this is strange, the Gates shut vp at this time a day, belike they are all Drunke and laid to sleepe, if they be, I'le wake them, with a Murraine.

Knockes.

Old Lio. What desperate fellowe's this, that ignorant
Of his owne danger, thunders at these Gates?

Clo. Ho, Reignald, Riotous Reignald, Reuelling Reignald.

Old Lio. What madnesse doth possesse thee, honest Friend,
To touch that Hammers handle?

Clo. What madnesse doth possesse thee, honest Friend,
To aske me such a question?

Old Lio. Nay, stirre not you?

Own. Not I; The game begins.

Old Lio. How doest thou, art thou well?

Clo. Yes very well, I thanke you, how doe you Sir?

Old Lio. No alteration; What change about thee?

Clo. Not so much change about me at this time, As to change you a Shilling into two Teasters.

Old Lio. Yet I aduise thee Fellow, for thy good, Stand further from the Gate.

Clo. And I aduise thee Friend, for thine owne good, stand not betwixt mee and the Gate, but giue me leaue to deliuer my errant; Hoe, Reignald, you mad Rafcall.

Old Lio. In vaine thou thunder'ſt at theſe ſilent Doores,
Where no man dwels to anſwere, ſauing Ghoſts,
Furies, and Sprights.

Clo. Ghoſts; Indeed there has bin much walking, in and about the Houſe after Mid-night.

Old Lio. Strange noyſe oft heard.

Clo. Yes, terrible noiſe, that none of the neighbours could take any reſt for it, I haue heard it my ſelfe.

Old Lio. You heare this; Heere's more witneſſe.

Own. Very well Sir.

Old Lio. Which you ſhall dearely anſwere—— whooping.

Clo. And hollowing.

Old Lio. And ſhouting.

Clo. And crying out, till the whole houſe rung againe.

Old Lio. Which thou haſt heard?

Clo. Oftner then I haue toes and fingers.

Old Lio. Thou wilt be depos'd of this?

Clo. I'le be ſworne too't, and that's as good.

Old Lio. Very good ſtill; Yet you are innocent:
Shall I intreat thee friend, to auouch as much
Heere by to the next Iuſtice.

Clo. I'le take my fouldiers oath on't.

Old Lio. A fouldiers oath, What's that?

Clo. My corporall oath; And you know Sir, a Corporall is an office belonging to a fouldier.

Old Lio. Yet you are cleere?
Murder will come to light.

Enter Robin, *the old ſeruing-man.*

Own. So will your gullery too.

Rob. They ſay my old Maſter's come home; I'le

see if hee will turne me out of doores, as the young man has done: I haue laid rods in piſſe for ſomebody, ſcape Reignald as hee can, and with more freedome then I durſt late, I bouldly now dare knocke.

Robin knocks.

Old Lio. More mad-men yet; I thinke ſince my laſt voyage,
Halfe of the world's turn'd franticke: What do'ſt meane,
Or long'ſt thou to be blaſted?

Rob. Oh Sir, you are welcome home; 'Twas time to come
Ere all was gone to hauocke.

Old Lio. My old ſeruant? before I ſhall demand of further buſines,
Reſolue me why thou thunder'ſt at theſe doores,
Where thou know'ſt none inhabits?

Rob. Are they gone Sir?
'Twas well they haue left the houſe behind;
For all the furniture, to a bare bench,
I am ſure is ſpent and waſted.

Old Lio. Where's my ſonne,
That Reignald poaſting for him with ſuch ſpeed,
Brings him not from the Countrey?

Rob. Countrey Sir?
'Tis a thing they know not; Heere they Feaſt,
Dice, Drinke, and Drab; The company they keepe,
Cheaters and Roaring-Ladds, and theſe attended
By Bawdes and Queanes: Your ſonne hath got a Strumpet,
On whom he ſpends all that your ſparing left,
And heere they keepe court; To whoſe damn'd abuſes,
Reignald giues all encouragement.

Old Lio. But ſtay ſtay;
No liuing ſoule hath for theſe ſixe moneths ſpace
Heere enter'd, but the houſe ſtood deſolate.

Rob. Laſt weeke I am ſure, ſo late, and th' other day,

Such Reuells were here kept.
  Old Lio. And by my sonne?
  Rob. Yes, and his servant Reignald.
  Old Lio. And this house at all not haunted?
  Rob. Saue Sir with such Sprights.

      Enter Master Ricott.

  Own. This Murder will come out.
  Old Lio. But see, in happy time heere comes my
    Neighbour
Of whom he bought this mansion; He, I am sure
More amply can resolue me: I pray Sir,
What summes of moneys haue you late receiued
Of my young sonne?
  Ric. Of him? None I assure you.
  Old Lio. What of my seruant Reignald?
  Ric. But deuise
What to call lesse then nothing, and that summe
I will confesse receiu'd.
  Old Lio. Pray Sir, be serious;
I doe confesse my selfe indebted to you,
A hundred pound.
  Ric. You may doe well to pay't then, for heere's
    witnesse
Sufficient of your words.
  Old Lio. I speake no more
Then what I purpose; Iust so much I owe you,
And ere I sleepe will tender.
  Ric. I shall be
As ready to receiue it, and as willing,
As you can bee to pay't.
  Old Lio. But prouided,
You will confesse seuen hundred pounds receiued
Before hand of my sonne?
  Ric. But by your fauour;
Why should I yeeld seuen hundred [pounds] receiu'd
Of them I neuer dealt with? Why? For what?

What reafon? What condition? Where or when
Should fuch a fumme be paid mee?
    Old Lio. Why? For this bargaine: And for what?
        This houfe:
Reafon? Becaufe you fold it: The conditions?
    Such
As were agreed betweene you: Where and When?
That onely hath efcapt me.
    Ric. Madneffe all.
    Old Lio. Was I not brought to take free view
        thereof,
As of mine owne poffefsion?
    Ric. I confeffe;
Your feruant told me you had found out a wife
Fit for your fonne, and that you meant to build;
Defir'd to take a friendly view of mine,
To make it your example: But for felling,
I tell you Sir, my wants be not fo great,
To change my houfe to Coyne.
    Old Lio. Spare Sir your anger,
And turne it into pity; Neighbours and friends,
I am quite loft, was neuer man fo fool'd,
And by a wicked feruant; Shame and blufhing
Will not permit to tell the manner how,
Left I be made ridiculous to all:
My feares are to inherit what's yet left;
He hath made my fonne away.
    Rob. That's my feare too.
    Old Lio. Friends, as you would commiferate a
        man
Depriu'd at once, both of his wealth and fonne;
And in his age, by one I euer tender'd
More like a fonne then feruant: By imagining
My cafe were yours, haue feeling of my griefes
And helpe to apprehend him; Furnifh me
With Cords and Fetters, I will lay him fafe
In Prifon within Prifon.
    Ric. Weel afsift you.

Rob. And I.

Clo. And all;
But not to doe the leaſt hurt to my old friend Reignald.

Old Lio. His Leggs will be as nimble as his Braine,
And 'twill be difficult to ſeaze the ſlaue,

> *Enter* Reignald *with a Horne in his pocket*: *they withdraw behind the Arras.*

Yet your endeauours, pray peace, heere hee comes.

Reig. My heart miſ-giues, for 'tis not poſsible
But that in all theſe windings and indents
I ſhall be found at laſt : I'le take that courſe
That men both troubled and affrighted doe,
Heape doubt on doubt, and as combuſtions riſe,
Try if from many I can make my peace,
And worke mine owne atonement.

Old Lio. Stand you cloſe,
Be not yet ſeene, but at your beſt aduantage
Hand him, and bind him faſt : Whil'ſt I diſſemble
As if I yet knew nothing.

Reig. I ſuſpect
And find there's trouble in my Maſters lookes ;
Therefore I muſt not truſt my ſelfe too farre
Within his fingers.

Old Lio. Reignald ?

Reig. Worſhipfull Sir.

Old Lio. What ſayes my ſonne ith' Countrey ?

Reig. That to morrow,
Early ith' morning, heele attend your pleaſure,
And doe as all ſuch dutious children ought ;
Demand your bleſsing Sir.

Old Lio. Well, 'tis well.

Reig. I doe not like his countenance.

Old Lio. But Reignald ? I ſuſpect the honeſty
And the good meaning of my neighbour heere,
Old maſter Ricott ; Meeting him but now,
And hauing ſome diſcourſe about the houſe,
He makes all ſtrange, and tells me in plaine
 termes,

Hee knowes of no fuch matter.

Reig. Tell mee that Sir?

Old Lio. I tell thee as it is: Nor that fuch moneys,
Tooke vp at vfe, were euer tender'd him
On any fuch conditions.

Reig. I cannot blame your worfhip to bee pleafant,
Knowing at what an vnder-rate we bought it, but you euer
Were a moft merry Gentleman.

R. Lio. (Impudent flaue)
But Reignald, hee not onely doth denie it,
But offers to depofe Himfelfe and Seruants,
No fuch thing euer was.

Reig. Now Heauen, to fee to what this world's growne too.
I will make him——

Old Lio. Nay more, this man will not confeffe the Murder.

Reig. Which both fhall deerely anfwere; You haue warrant
For him already; But for the other Sir,
If hee denie it, he had better——

Old Lio. Appeare Gentlemen,   *Softly.*
'Tis a fit time to take him.

Reig. I difcouer the Ambufh that's laid for me.

Old Lio. Come neerer Reignald.

Reig. Firft fir refolue me one thing, amongft other Merchandize
Bought in your abfence by your Sonne and me,
Wee ingroft a great comoditie of Combes,
And how many forts thinke you?

Old Lio. You might buy
Some of the bones of Fifhes, fome of Beafts,
Box-combes, and Iuory-combes.

Reig. But befides thefe, we haue for Horfes Sir,
Mayne-combes, and Curry-combes; Now Sir for men,
Wee haue Head-combes, Beard-combes, I and Cox-combes too;

Take view of them at your pleafure, whil'ſt for my part,
I thus beſtow my ſelfe.

They all appeare with Cords and Shackels,
Whileſt hee gets vp.

Clo. Well ſaid Reignald, nobly put off Reignald,
Looke to thy ſelfe Reignald.
  Old Lio. Why doſt thou climbe thus?
  Reig. Onely to practice
The nimbleneſſe of my Armes and Legges,
Ere they prooue your Cords and Fetters.
  Old Lio. Why to that place?
  Reig. Why? becauſe Sir 'tis your owne Houſe; It hath bin my Harbour long, and now it muſt bee my Sanctuary; Diſpute now, and I'le anſwere.
  Own. Villaine, what deuiliſh meaning had'ſt thou in't,
To challenge me of Murder?
  Reig. Oh ſir, the man you kil'd is aliue at this preſent to iuſtifie it:
I am, quoth he, a Tranſ-marine by birth——
  Ric. Why, challenge me receipt of Moneys, and to giue abroad,
That I had ſold my Houſe?
  Reig. Why? becauſe ſir,
Could I haue purchaſt Houſes at that rate,
I had meant to haue bought all London.
  Clo. Yes, and Middleſex too, and I would haue bin thy halfe Reignald.
  Old Lio. Yours are great,
My wrongs inſufferable; As firſt, to fright mee
From mine owne dwelling, till they had confumed
The whole remainder of the little left;
Beſides, out of my late ſtocke got at Sea,
Diſcharge the clamorous Vſurer; Make me accuſe
This man of Murder; Be at charge of warrants;
And challenging this my worthy Neighbour of

Forſwearing Summes hee neuer yet receiued;
Foole mee, to thinke my Sonne that had ſpent all,
Had by his thrift bought Land; I and him too,
To open all the ſecrets of his Houſe
To mee, a Stranger; Oh thou inſolent villaine,
What to all theſe canſt anſwere?

   Reig. Guiltie, guiltie.
   Old Lio. But to my Sonnes death, what thou ſlaue?
   Reig. Not Guiltie.
   Old Lio. Produce him then; Ith' meane time, and——
Honeſt Friends, get Ladders.
   Reig. Yes, and come downe in your owne Ropes.
   Own. I'le fetch a Peece and ſhoote him.
   Reig. So the warrant in my Maſters pocket, will ſerue for my Murder; And euer after ſhall my Ghoſt haunt this Houſe.
   Clo. And I will ſay like Reignald,
This Ghoſt and I am Friends.
   Old Lio. Bring faggots, I'le ſet fire vpon the Houſe,
Rather then this indure.
   Reig. To burne Houſes is Fellony, and I'le not out
Till I be fir'd out; But ſince I am Beſieged thus,
I'le ſummon ſupplies vnto my Reſcue.

Hee windes a Horne. **Enter** Young Lionell, Rioter, *two* Gallants Blanda, &c.

   Y. Lio. Before you chide, firſt heere mee, next your Bleſsing,
That on my knees I begge; I haue but done
Like miſ-ſpent youth, which after wit deere bought,
Turnes his Eyes inward, ſorrie and aſhamed;
Theſe things in which I haue offended moſt,
Had I not prooued, I ſhould haue thought them ſtill

Essential things, delights perdureable;
Which now I find meere Shaddowes, Toyes and
   Dreames,
Now hated more then earst I doated on;
Best Natures, are soonest wrought on; Such was
   mine;
As I the offences, So the offendors throw
Heere at your feete, to punish as you please;
You haue but paid so much as I haue wasted,
To purchase to your selfe a thrifty Sonne;
Which I from henceforth, Vow.

Old Lio. See what Fathers are,
That can three yeeres offences, fowle ones too,
Thus in a Minute pardon; And thy faults
Vpon my selfe chastise, in these my Teares;
Ere this Submission, I had cast thee off;
Rife in my new Adoption: But for these——

Clo. The one you haue nothing to doe withall,
here's his Ticket for his discharge; Another for you
Sir, to Summon you to my Masters Feast, For you,
and you, where I charge you all to appeare, vpon his
displeasure, and your owne apperils.

Y. Lio. This is my Friend, the other one I
   loued,
Onely becaufe they haue bin deere to him
That now will striue to be more deere to you;
Vouchsafe their pardon.

Old Lio. All deere, to me indeed, for I haue payd
   for't soundly,
Yet for thy sake, I am atton'd with all; Onely that
   wanton,
Her, and her Company, abandon quite;
So doing, wee are friends.

Y. Lio. A iust Condition, and willingly sub-
   scrib'd to.

Old Lio. But for that Villaine; I am now de-
   uising
What shame, what punishment remarkable,

G 2

To inflict on him.
　Reig. Why Mafter? Haue I laboured,
Plotted, Contriued, and all this while for you,
And will you leaue me to the Whip and Stockes;
Not mediate my peace.
　Old Lio. Sirra, come downe.
　Reig. Not till my Pardon's fealed, I'le rather ftand heere
Like a Statue, in, in the Fore-front of your houfe
For euer; Like the picture of Dame Fortune
Before the Fortune Play-houfe.
　Y. Lio. If I haue heere
But any Friend amongft you, ioyne with mee
In this petition.
　Clo. Good Sir, for my fake, I refolued you truly
Concerning Whooping, the Noyfe, the Walking, and the Sprights,
And for a need, can fhew you a Ticket for him too.
　Own. I impute my wrongs rather to knauifh Cunning,
Then leaft pretended Malice.
　Ric. What he did,
Was but for his Young Mafter, I allow it
Rather as fports of Wit, then iniuries;
No other pray efteeme them.
　Old Lio. Euen as freely,
As you forget my quarells made with you;
Rais'd from the Errours firft begot by him;
I heere remit all free; I now am Calme,
But had I feaz'd vpon him in my Spleene——
　Reig. I knew that, therefore this was my Inuention,
For Pollicie's the art ftill of Preuention.
　Clo. Come downe then Reignald, firft on your hands and feete, and then on your knees to your Mafter; Now Gentlemen, what doe you fay to your inuiting to my Mafters Feaft.
　Ric. Wee will attend him.

Old Lio. Nor doe I loue to breake good company;
For Mafter Wincott is my worthy Friend,

Enter Reignald.

And old acquaintance ; Oh thou crafty Wag-ftring,
And could'ft thou thus delude me ? But we are Friends ;
Nor Gentlemen, let not what's heere to paft,
In your leaft thoughts difable my Eftate ;
This my laft Voyage hath made all things good,
With furplus too ; Be that your comfort Sonne :
Well Reignald——But no more.
   Reig. I was the Fox,
But I from henceforth, will no more the Cox——
Combe, put vpon your pate.
   Old Lio. Let's walke Gentlemen.
               Exeunt Omnes.

Actus Quintus.   Scena Prima.

Enter Old Geraldine, *and* Young Geraldine.

Old Ger. Sonne, let me tell you, you are ill aduifed ;
And doubly to be blam'd, by vndertaking
Vnneceffary trauell ; Grounding no reafon
For fuch a rafh and giddy enterprife :
What profit aime you at, you haue not reapt ;
What Nouelty affoords the Chriftian world,
Of which your view hath not participated
In a full meafure ; Can you either better
Your language or experience ? Your felfe-will
Hath onely purpofe to depriue a father

Of a loued fonne, and many noble friends,
Of your much wifht acquaintance.

Y. Ger. Oh, deare Sir,
Doe not, I doe intreat you, now repent you
Of your free grant; Which with fuch care and ftuddy,
I haue fo long, fo often laboured for.

Old Ger. Say that may be difpens'd with, fhew me reafon
Why you defire to fteale out of your Countrey,
Like fome Malefactor that had forfeited
His life and freedome; Heere's a worthy Gentleman
Hath for your fake inuited many guefts,
To his great charge, onely to take of you
A parting leaue: You fend him word you cannot,
After, you may not come: Had not my vrgence,
Almoft compulfion, driuen you to his houfe,
Th' vnkindneffe might haue forfeited your loue,
And raced you from his will; In which he hath giuen you
A faire and large eftate; Yet you of all this ftrangeneffe,
Show no fufficient ground.

Y. Ger. Then vnderftand;
The ground thereof tooke his firft birth from you;
'Twas you firft charg'd me to forbeare the houfe,
And that vpon your bleffing: Let it not then
Offend you Sir, if I fo great a charge
Haue ftriu'd to keepe fo ftrictly.

Old Ger. Mee perhaps,
You may appeafe, and with fmall difficulty,
Becaufe a Father; But how fatisfie
Their deare, and on your part, vnmerited loue?
But this your laft obedience may falue all:
Wee now grow neere the houfe.

Y. Ger. Whofe doores, to mee,
Appeare as horrid as the gates of Hell:
Where fhall I borrow patience, or from whence?

Enter Wincott, Wife, Ricott, *the two* Lionells, Owner, Dalauill, Prudentilla, Reignald, Rioter.

To giue a meeting to this viperous brood,
Of Friend and Miſtris.
  Winc. Y'aue entertain'd me with a ſtrange diſ-
    courſe
Of your mans knauiſh wit, but I reioyce,
That in your ſafe returne, all ends ſo well:
Moſt welcome you, and you, and indeed all;
To whom I am bound, that at ſo ſhort a warning,
This friendly, you will deigne to viſit me.
  Old Lio. It ſeemes my abſence hath begot ſome
    ſport,
Thanke my kinde feruant heere.
  Reig. Not ſo much worth Sir.
  Old Lio. But though their riots tript at my eſtate,
They haue not quite ore-throwne it.
  Winc. But ſee Gentlemen,
Theſe whom we moſt expected, come at length;
This I proclaime the maſter of the Feaſt,
In which to expreſſe the bounty of my loue,
I'le ſhew my ſelfe no niggard.
  Y. Ger. Your choiſe fauours
I ſtill taſte in abundance.
  Wife. Methinks it would not miſ-become me Sir,
To chide your abſence; That haue made your ſelfe,
To vs, ſo long a ſtranger.

Hee turnes away ſad, as not being minded.

  Y. Ger. Pardon mee Sir,
That haue not yet, ſince your returne from Sea,
Voted the leaſt fit opportunity,
To entertaine you with a kind ſalute.
  Old Lio. Moſt kindly Sir I thanke you.
  Dal. Methinks friend,

You fhould expect greene rufhes to be ftrow'd,
After fuch difcontinuance.

Y. Ger. Miftris Pru,
I haue not feene you long, but greet you thus,
May you be Lady of a better husband
Then I expect a wife.

Winc. I like that greeting:
Nay, enter Gentlemen; Dinner perhaps
Is not yet ready, but the time we ftay,
Weele find fome frefh difcourfe to fpend away.

Exeunt.

Manet Dalauill.

Dal. Not fpeake to me? nor once vouchfafe an
  anfwere,
But fleight me with a poore and bafe neglect?
No, nor fo much as caft an eye on her,
Or leaft regard, though in a feeming fhew
Shee courted a reply? 'twixt him and her,
Nay him and mee, this was not wont to be;
If fhe haue braine to apprehend as much

Enter Young Geraldine *and* Wife.

As I haue done, fheele quickly find it out:
Now as I liue, as our affections meete,
So our conceits, and fhee hath fingled him
To fome fuch purpofe: I'le retire my felfe,
Not interrupt their conference. *Exit.*

Wife. You are fad Sir.
Y. Ger. I know no caufe.
Wife. Then can I fhew you fome;
Who could be otherwayes, to leaue a Father
So carefull, and each way fo prouident?
To leaue fo many, and fuch worthy Friends?
To abandon your owne countrey? Thefe are fome,
Nor doe I thinke you can be much the merrier
For my fake?

Y. Ger. Now your tongue fpeakes Oracles;
For all the reft are nothing, 'tis for you,
Onely for you I cannot.
  Wife. So I thought;
Why then haue you bin all this while fo ftrange?
Why will you trauell? fuing a diuorce
Betwixt vs, of a loue infeperable;
For heere fhall I be left as defolate
Vnto a frozen, almoft widdowed bed;
Warm'd onely in that future, ftor'd in you;
For who can in your abfence comfort me?
  Y. Ger. Shall my oppreffed fufferance yet breake
      foorth
Into impatience, or endure her more?
  Wife. But fince by no perfwafion, no intreats,
Your fetled obftinacy can be fwai'd,
Though you feeme defperate of your owne deare
      life,
Haue care of mine, for it exifts in you.
Oh Sir, fhould you mifcarry I were loft,
Loft and forfaken; Then by our paft vowes,
And by this hand once giuen mee, by thefe teares,
Which are but fprings begetting greater floods,
I doe befeech thee, my deere Geraldine,
Looke to thy fafety, and preferue thy health;
Haue care into what company you fall;
Trauell not late, and croffe no dangerous Seas;
For till Heauens bleffe me in thy fafe returne,
How will this poore heart fuffer?
  Y. Ger. I had thought
Long fince the Syrens had bin all deftroy'd;
But one of them I find furuiues in her;
Shee almoft makes me queftion what I know,
An Hereticke vnto my owne beliefe:
Oh thou mankinds feducer.
  Wife. What? no anfwere?
  Y. Ger. Yes, thou haft fpoke to me in Showres,
I will reply in Thunder; Thou Adultreffe,
That haft more poyfon in thee then the Serpent,

Who was the firft that did corrupt thy fex,
The Deuill.
 Wife. To whom fpeakes the man?
 Y. Ger. To thee,
Falfeft of all that euer man term'd faire;
Hath Impudence fo fteel'd thy fmooth foft skin,
It cannot blufh? Or finne fo obdur'd thy heart,
It doth not quake and tremble? Search thy con-
 fcience,
There thou fhalt find a thoufand clamorous tongues
To fpeake as loud as mine doth.
 Wife. Saue from yours,
I heare no noife at all.
 Y. Ger. I'le play the Doctor
To open thy deafe eares; Munday the Ninth
Of the laft Moneth; Canft thou remember that?
That Night more blacke in thy abhorred finne,
Then in the gloomie darkneffe; That the time.
 Wife. Munday?
 Y. Ger. Wouldeft thou the place know? Thy pol-
 luted Chamber,
So often witneffe of my fin-leffe vowes;
Wouldeft thou the Perfon? One not worthy Name,
Yet to torment thy guilty Soule the more,
I'le tell him thee, That Monfter Dalauill;
Wouldeft thou your Bawd know? Mid-night, that the
 houre:
The very words thou fpake; Now what would Geral-
 dine
Say, if he faw vs heere? To which was anfwered,
Tufh hee's a Cox-combe, fit to be fo fool'd:
No blufh? What, no faint Feauer on thee yet?
How hath thy blacke fins chang'd thee? Thou
 Medufa,
Thofe Haires that late appeared like golden Wyers,
Now crawle with Snakes and Adders; Thou art
 vgly.
 Wife. And yet my glaffe, till now, neere told me
 fo;

Who gaue you this intelligence?
  Y. Ger. Onely hee,
That pittying fuch an Innocencie as mine,
Should by two fuch delinquents bee betray'd,
Hee brought me to that place by mirracle;
And made me an eare witneffe of all this.
  Wife. I am vndone.
  Y. Ger. But thinke what thou haft loft
To forfeit mee; I not withftanding thefe,
(So fixt was my loue and vnutterable)
I kept this from thy Husband, nay all eares,
With thy tranfgrefsions fmothering mine owne wrongs,
In hope of thy Repentance.
  Wife. Which begins
Thus low vpon my knees.
  Y. Ger. Tufh, bow to Heauen,
Which thou haft moft offended; I alas,
Saue in fuch (Scarce vnheard of) Treacherie,
Moft finfull like thy felfe; Wherein, Oh wherein,
Hath my vnfpotted and vnbounded Loue
Deferu'd the leaft of thefe? Sworne to be made a
    ftale
For terme of life; And all this for my goodneffe;
Die, and die foone, acquit me of my Oath,
But prethee die repentant; Farewell euer,
'Tis thou, and onely thou haft Banifht mee,
Both from my Friends and Countrey.
  Wife. Oh, I am loft.   *Sinkes downe.*

Enter Dalauill *meeting* Young Geraldine *going out.*

  Dal. Why how now, what's the bufineffe?
  Y. Ger. Goe take her Vp, whom thou haft oft throwne Downe,
Villaine.
  Dal. That was no language from a Friend,
It had too harfh an accent; But how's this?
My Miftreffe thus low caft vpon the earth
Grauelling and breathleffe, Miftreffe, Lady, Sweet——

Wife. Oh tell me if thy name be Geraldine,
Thy very lookes will kill mee?
　Dal. View me well,
I am no fuch man; See, I am Dalauill.
　Wife. Th'art then a Deuill, that prefents before mee
My horrid fins; perfwades me to difpaire;
When hee like a good Angel fent from Heauen,
Befought me of repentance; Swell ficke Heart,
Euen till thou burft the ribs that bound thee in;
So, there's one ftring crackt, flow, and flow high,
Euen till thy blood diftill out of mine eyes,
To witneffe my great forrow.
　Dal. Faint againe,
Some helpe within there, no attendant neere?
Thus to expire, in this I am more wretched,
Then all the fweet fruition of her loue
Before could make me happy.

Enter Wincott, Old Geraldine, Young Geraldine, *the two* Lionells, Ricott, Owner, Prudentilla, Reignald, Clowne.

　Winc. What was hee
Clamor'd fo lowd, to mingle with our mirth
This terrour and affright?
　Dal. See Sir, your Wife in thefe my armes expiring.
　Winc. How?
　Prud. My fifter?
　Winc. Support her, and by all meanes pofsible
Prouide for her deere fafety.
　Old Ger. See, fhee recouers.
　Winc. Woman, looke vp.
　Wife. Oh Sir, your pardon;
Conuey me to my Chamber, I am ficke,
Sicke euen to death, away thou Sycophant,
Out of my fight, I haue befides thy felfe,

Too many finnes about mee.
Clo.   My fweet Miftreffe.
Dal.   The ftorme's comming, I muft prouide for harbour.   *Exit.*
Old Lio.   What ftrange and fudden alteration's this,
How quickly is this cleere day ouercaft;
But fuch and fo vncertaine are all things,
That dwell beneath the Moone.
Y. Lio.   A Womans qualme,
Frailties that are inherent to her fex,
Soone ficke, and foone recouer'd.
Winc.   If fhee misfare,
I am a man more wretched in her loffe,
Then had I forfeited life and eftate;
Shee was fo good a creature.
Old Ger.   I the like
Suffer'd, when I my Wife brought vnto her graue;
So you, when you were firft a widower;
Come arme your felfe with patience.
Ric.   Thefe are cafualties
That are not new, but common.
Reig.   Burying of Wiues,
As ftale as fhifting fhirts, or for fome feruants,
To flout and gull their Mafters.
Own.   Beft to fend
And fee how her fit holds her.

Enter Prudentilla *and* Clowne.

Prud.   Sir, my Sifter
In thefe few Lines commends her laft to you,
For fhe is now no more; What's therein writ,
Saue Heauen and you, none knowes; This fhe defir'd
You would take view of; and with thefe words expired.
Winc.   Dead?

Y. Ger.   She hath made me then a free releafe,
Of all the debts I owed her.
  Winc.   My feare is beyond pardon, Dalauill
Hath plaid the villaine, but for Geraldine,
Hee hath bin each way Noble——Loue him ftill,
My peace already I haue made with Heauen;
Oh be not you at warre with me; My Honour
Is in your hands to punifh, or preferue;
I am now Confeft, and only Geraldine
Hath wrought on mee this vnexpected good;
The Inke I write with, I wifh had bin my blood,
To witneffe my Repentance——Dalauill?
Where's hee? Goe feeke him out.
  Clo.   I fhall, I fhall Sir.   *Exit.*
  Winc.   The Wills of Dead folke fhould be ftill
    obeyed;
How euer falfe to mee, I'le not reueale't;
Where Heauen forgiues, I pardon Gentlemen,
I know you all commiferate my loffe;
I little thought this Feaft fhould haue bin turn'd

Enter Clowne.

Into a Funerall; What's the newes of him?
  Clo.   Hee went prefently to the Stable, put the
Sadle vpon his Horfe, put his Foote into the Stirrup,
clapt his Spurres into his fides, and away hee's Gallopt,
as if hee were to ride a Race for a Wager.
  Winc.   All our ill lucks goe with him, farewell hee;
But all my beft of wifhes wait on you,
As my chiefe Friend; This meeting that was made
Onely to take of you a parting leaue,
Shall now be made a Marriage of our Loue,
Which none faue onely Death fhall feparate.
  Y. Ger.   It calles me from all Trauell, and from
    henceforth,
With my Countrey I am Friends.
  Winc.   The Lands that I haue left,

You lend mee for the fhort fpace of my life;
As foone as Heauen calles mee, they call you Lord;
Firſt feaſt, and after Mourne; Wee'le like fome Gallants
That Bury thrifty Fathers, think't no finne,
To weare Blacks without, but other Thoughts within.

Exeunt omnes.

FINIS.

A Pleasant Comedy, called

A

MAYDEN-HEAD WELL LOST.

As it hath beene publickly Acted at the *Cocke-pit in Drury-lane, with much Applause*: By her Maiesties Seruants.

Written by THOMAS HEYVVOOD.

Aut prodesse solent, aut delectare.

LONDON,
Printed by *Nicholas Okes* for *Iohn Iackson* and *Francis Church*, and are to be sold at the *Kings Armes* in *Cheape-side*. 1634.

To the Reader.

Ourteous Reader, (of what sexe soever) let not the Title of this Play any way deterre thee from the perusall thereof: For there is nothing herein contained, which doth deuiate either from Modesty, *or good* Manners. *For though the Argument be drawne from a* Mayden-head *lost, yet to be well lost, cleares it from all aspersion. Neither can this be drawne within the Criticall censure of that most horrible* Histriomastix, *whose vncharitable doome having damned all such to the flames of Hell, hath it selfe already suffered a most remarkeable fire here vpon Earth. This hath beene frequently, and publickly Acted without exception, and I presume may be freely read without distaste; and of all in generall: excepting such, whose prepared palats, disgusting all* Poems *of this nature, are poysoned with the bitter iuice of that* Coloquintida *and* Hemlocke, *which can neither relish the peace of the* Church *nor* Common-weale. *Nothing remaineth further to be said, but read charitably, and then censure without preiudice.*

By him who hath beene euer studious of thy fauour,

Thomas Heywood.

Dramatis Perſonæ.

The Duke of *Florence.*
The Prince of *Florence.*
Mounſieur, the Tutor to the Prince.
The Widdow of the Generall.
Sforſa.
Their Daughter *Lauretta.*
The Clowne their Seruant.
A Huntſman.
A Lord of *Florence.*

The Duke of *Millaine.*
The Prince of *Parma.*
Julia Daughter to *Millain.*
Stroza Secretary to the Duke.
A Souldier of *Sforza'es.*
Three maimed Souldiers.
A Lord of *Millaine.*
Attendants.
Other Lords, &c.

The Prologue.

PRologues to Playes *in vse, and common are,*
  As Vshers to Great Ladies : *Both walke bare,*
And comely both ; conducting Beauty they
And wee appeare, to vsher in our Play.
Yet, be their faces foule, or featur'd well,
Be they hard-fauoured, or in lookes excell,
Yet being Vsher, he owes no lesse duty
Vnto the most deformed, then the choise Beautie.
It is our case ; we vsher Acts *and* Scenes,
Some honest, and yet some may proue like Queanes.
(Loose and base stuffe) yet that is not our fault,
We walke before, but not like Panders hault
Before such cripled ware : Th' *Acts we present*
We hope are Virgins, drawne for your content
Vnto this Stage : Maides *gratefull are to Men,*
Our Scenes *being such, (like such) accept them then.*

A
MAYDEN-HEAD
WELL LOST.

Actus primus, Scena prima.

Enter Iulia and Stroza.

Iulia.

Hat shee should doo't?
   Stroza. Shee?
   Iul. May we build vpon't?
   St. As on a base of Marble; I haue seene
Strange passages of loue, loose enterchanges
Of hands and eyes betwixt her and the Prince,
Madame looke too't.
   Iul. What hope hath he in one
So meanly bred? or shee t'obtaine a Prince
Of such discent and linnage?
   Str. What but this
That you must vndergoe the name of wife,
And shee to intercept the sweetes of loue
Due to your bed.
   Iul. To be his strumpet *Stroza*?
   Str. Madame a woman may guesse vnhappily.

Iul. Thou shouldst be honest *Stroza.*

Str. Yes, many should
Be what they are not: but I alwayes was,
And euer will be one, (that's still my selfe.)

Iul. The Generall *Sforsaes* daughter? is't not she?

Str. Is that yet questioned? as if the chaste Court
Had saue her selfe one so degenerate,
So dissolutely wanton, so profuse
In prostitution too, so impudent
And blushlesse in her proud ambitious aime,
As if no man could her intemperance pleafe,
Saue him whom Heaven hath destin'd to your bed.

Iul. I never saw them yet familiar.

Str. Ha, ha, as if they'd send for you to see't,
To witnesse what they most striue to conceale,
Be guld? be branded: 'las to me, all's nothing,
I shall ne're smart for't, what is't to me?
If being a Bride, you haue a widdowed fortune;
If being married, you must throw your selfe
Vpon a desolate bed, and in your armes,
Claspe nought but Ayre, whilst his armes full of pleasure
Borrow'd from a stolne beauty, shall this grieue
Or trouble me? breake my sleepes? make me starte
At midnight vp, and fill the house with clamours?
Shall this bring strange brats to be bred and brought
Vp at my fire, and call me Dad? No: this
Concernes not me more then my loue to you
To your high Soueraignty.

Iul. I now repent
Too late, since I too lauishly haue giuen him
The vtmost he could aske, and stretcht my honour
Beyond all lawfull bounds of modesty.
Hee's couetous of others, and neglects

A Mayden-head well loſt.

His owne ; but I will part thoſe their ſtolne
   pleaſures,
And croſſe thoſe luſtfull ſports they haue in chaſe,
Not be the pillow to my owne diſgrace.   *Exit.*
  Str. The game's on foote, and there's an eaſie
   path
To my reuenge ; this beauteous *Millanois*
Vnto th' Duke ſole heire, ſtill courted, crau'd,
And by the *Parma* Prince ſollicited,
Which I ſtill ſtudy how to breake, and caſt
Aſperſions betwixt both of ſtrange diſlike ;
But wherein hath the other innocent Mayde
So iniur'd me, that I ſhould ſcandall her ?
Her Father is the Generall to the Duke :
For when I ſtuddied to be rais'd by Armes,
And purchaſe me high eminence in Campe,
He croſt my fortunes, and return'd me home
A Caſhierd Captaine ; for which iniury
I ſcandall all his meanes vnto the Duke,
And to the Princeſſe all his daughters vertues
I labour to inuert, and bring them both
Into diſgracefull hatred.

Enter Prince Parma.

  Par. Storza ?
  Str. My Lord ?
  Par. Saw you the Princeſſe ?
  Str. Iulia ?
  Par. She ?
  Str. I haue my Lord of late no eare of hers,
Nor ſhe a tongue of mine ; the time hath bin
Till ſoothing Sycophants and Court Paraſites
Supplanted me.
  Par. I haue the power with her
To bring thee into grace.
  Str. Haue you the power
To keepe your ſelfe in ? doe you ſmile my Lord ?

Par. I tell thee *Stroza*, I haue that intereſt
In *Iulias* boſome, that the proudeſt Prince
In *Italy* cannot ſupplant me thence.
   Str. Sir,
I no way queſtion it: but haue I not knowne
A Prince hath bin repulſt, and meaneſt perſons
Boſom'd? the Prince would once have lookt vpon me,
When ſmall intreaty would haue gain'd an eye,
An eare, a tongue, to ſpeake yea, and a heart,
To thinke I could be ſecret.
   Par. What meanes *Stroza*?
   Str. But 'tis the fate of all mortality:
Man cannot long be happy; but my paſſion
Will make me turne blab, I ſhall out with all.
   Par. Whence comes this? 'tis ſuſpicious, and I muſt be
Inquiſitiue to know't.
   Str. A Ieſt my Lord,
I'le tell you a good Ieſt.
   Par. Prithee let's heare it.
   Str. What will you ſay, if at your meeting next
With this faire Princeſſe? ſhee begins to raue,
To raile vpon you, to exclaime on your
Inconſtancy, and call the innocent name
Of ſome chaſte Maide in queſtion, whom perhaps
You neuer ey'd my Lord.
   Par. What of all this?
   Str. What but to excuſe her owne: (I'le not ſay what)
Put off the purpos'd Contract: and my Lord
Come, come, I know you haue a pregnant wit.
   Par. We parted laſt with all the kindeſt greeting
Louers could adde fare-well with: but ſhould this change
Suite thy report, I ſhould be forc't to thinke
That, which euen Oracles themſelues could neuer
Force me to that ſhe is.

Str. All women are not
Sincerely conſtant, but obſerue my Lord.

Enter Iulia, *the Generals Wife, and* Lauretta
her Daughter.

Iul. Minion is'ſt you ? there's for you, know your owne.
     Iulia meets her and ſtrikes her, then ſpeakes.
Str. Obſeru'd you that my Lord ?
Lau. Why did you ſtrike me Madame ?
Iul. Strumpet, why ?
Dare you conteſt with vs ?
Lau. Who dare with Princeſſe ? ſubjects muſt forbeare
Each ſtep I treade I'le water with a teare.
     Exeunt Mother and Lauretta *weeping.*
Str. I ſpy a ſtorme a comming, Ile to ſhelter.
        Exit Stro.
Par. Your meaning Madame ?
Iul. Did it Sir with yours
But correſpond, it would be bad indeede.
Par. Why did you ſtrike that Lady ?
Iul. Cauſe you ſhould pitty her.
Par. Small cauſe for blowes.
Iul. I ſtrucke her publickly.
You give her blowes in priuate.
Par. Stroza ſtill ?
Iul. Go periurd and diſpoſe thy falſe allurements
'Mongſt them that will beleeue thee, thou haſt loſt
Thy credit here for euer.
Par. I ſhall finde
Faith elſe-where then.
Iul. Eye ſpread thy ſnares
To catch poore innocent Maides : and hauing tane them
In the like pit-fall, with their ſhipwrackt honours,
Make ſeaſure of their liues.

Par. Iniurious Lady,
All thou canſt touch my Honour with, I caſt
On thee, and henceforth I will flye thee as
A Baſaliſke. I haue found the change of luſt,
Your looſe inconſtancy, which is as plaine
To me, as were it writ vpon thy brow,
You ſhall not caſt me off: I hate thy ſight,
And from this houre I will abiure thee quite.
Exit Parma.

Iul. Ile call him backe : if *Stroza* be no villaine,
He is not worth my clamour. What was that
Startled within me ? Oh I am diſhonoured
Perpetually ; for he hath left behinde
That pledge of his acquaintance, that will for euer
Cleaue to my blood in ſcandall, I muſt now
Sue, fend, and craue, and what before I ſcorn'd
By prayers to grant, ſubmiſſiuely implore. *Exit* Iulia.

A flouriſh. *Enter the* Duke *of* Millenie, *the Generals
wife, and deliuers a petition with* Stroza, Lauretta,
and attendants.

Duke. Lady your ſuite ?
Wife. So pleaſe your Grace peruſe it,
It is included there.
Duk. Our generals Wife ?
We know you Lady, and your beauteous Daughter,
Nay you ſhall ſpare your knee.
Str. More plot for mee ;
My brain's in labour, and muſt be deliuered
Of ſome new miſcheife ?
Duk. You petition heere
For Men and Money ! making a free relation
Of all your Husbands fortunes, how ſupplyes
Haue beene delay'd, and what extremities
He hath indurd at *Naples* dreadfull Seige ;
Wee know them all, and withall doe acknowledge
All plentious bleſſings by the power of Heauen,
By him wee doe obtaine, and by his valour

Lady we greue he hath beene fo neglected.
  Wife.   O Roiall Sir, you ftill were Gratious,
But twixt your Vertues and his Merits there
Hath beene fome interception, that hath ftopt
The current of your fauours.
  Duk.   All which fhal bee remou'd, and hee appeare
Henceforth a bright ftarre in our courtly fpheare.
  Str.   But no fuch Comet here fhall daze my fight,
Whilft I a Cloud am to Eclips that light. *Exit Stroza.*
  Duk.   We fent out our Commiflions two Monthes fince
For Men and Money, nor was't our intent
It fhould bee thus delayd: though we are Prince,
We onely can command, to execute
Tis not in vs but in our Officers,
We vnderftand that by their negligence
He has beene put to much extremity
Of Dearth and Famine, many a ftormy night
Beene forc'd to roofe himfelfe i'th open field,
Nay more then this, much of his owne reuenue
He hath expended, all to pay his Souldiers:
Yet Reuerend Madame, but forget what's paft,
Though late, weele quit his merit at the laft.

Enter Iulia and Stroza whifpering.

  Wife.   Your Highneffe is moft Royall?
  Stro.   Her Father fhall be in the Campe releiu'd,
She grac'd in Court, how will fhe braue you then?
If fuffer this take all? why the meaneft Lady
Would neuer brooke an equall? you a Princeffe?
And can you brooke a bafe competitor?
  Iulia.   It fhall not, we are fixt and ftand immou'd,
And will be fwaid by no hand.
  Duk.   Iulia?
  Iulia.   A Sutor to that Lady Royall Father,
Before fhe be a widdow that you are
So priuate in difcourfe?

Duk. O you mistake,
For shee the sutor is, and hath obtain'd.
 Iulia. I am glad I haue found you in the giuing vaine,
Will you grant me one boone to?
 Duk. Question not,
To hast your Marriage with the former Prince,
Or at the least the contract, is't not that?
 Iulia. Say twere my Lord?
 Duk. It could not be denide.
But speake? thy suite?
 Iulia. To haue this modest Gentlewoman
Banisht the Court.
 Wife. My Daughter Royall princesse,
Show vs some cause I beg it?
 Iulia. Lady though
You be i'th begging vaine, I am not now
In the giuing, will you leaue vs?
 Lauretta. Wherein O Heauen
Haue I deseru'd your wrath, that you should thus
Persue me? I haue searcht, indeed beyond
My vnderstanding, but yet cannot finde?
Wherein I haue offended by my chastity.
 Iulia. How chastity?
A thing long sought 'mongst Captains wiues and daughters,
Yet hardly can bee found.
 Duk. Faire Lady yeild
Vnto my daughters spleen her rage blowne 'ore,
Feare not, Ile make your peace, as for your suite
Touching your husband, that will I secure.
 Iul. Haste *Stroza*, vnto the Prince his chamber,
Giue him this letter, it concernes my honor,
My state, my life, all that I can call good
Depends vpon the safe deliuery
Of these few broken Letters.
 Str. Maddam, tis done———   *Exit.*
 Iul. What stayes she to out-face me?
 Lau. Madam, I yeeld

Way to your spleene, not knowing whence it growes,
Bearing your words more heauy then your blowes.
  Wife. Small hope there is to see the Father righted
When the child is thus wrong'd.

Enter a Souldier and Stroza.

  Soul. Must speake with the Duke.
  Str. Must fellow? stay your howre, and dance attendance
Vntill the Duke's at leisure.
  Soul. Ile doe neither,
I come in haste with newes.
  Str. Why then keepe out sir.
  Soul. Ha Milksop? know percullist gates
Though kept with Pikes & Muskets, could nere kepe me out
And dost thou thinke to shut me out with Wainscot?
  Duk. What's he?
  Soul. A Souldier.
  Duk. Whence?
  Soul. The Campe.
  Duk. The newes?
  Soul. A mighty losse; a glorious victory.
  Duke. But which the greater?
  Soul. Tis vncertaine sir:
But will you heare the best or bad newes first?
  Duke. Cheere me with conquest first, that being arm'd
With thy best newes, we better may endure
What sounds more fatall.
  Soul. Heare me then my Lord,
We sack't the Citty after nine Moneths siege,
Furnisht with store of all warres furniture,
Our (neuer to be prais'd enough) braue Generall
Fought in the Cannons face, their number still
Increast, but ours diminisht; their souldiers pay
Doubled, and ours kept backe: but we (braue spirits)

The leffe we had of Coyne, the more we tooke
Vnto our felues of Courage, but when all
Our furniture was fpent euen to one day,
And that to morrow we muft be inforc't
To raife a fhameful fiege, then ftood our General
(Our valiant General) vp, and breath'd vpon vs
His owne vndaunted fpirit, which fpred through
The Campe, return'd it doubly arm'd againe :
For he did meane to lay vpon one fhott
His ftate and fortune, and then inftantly
He bad vs arme and follow : On then he went,
We after him ; oh ! 'twas a glorious fight,
Fit for a Theater of Gods to fee,
How we made vp and mauger all oppofure,
Made way through raging ftormes of fhowring bullets ;
At laft we came to hooke our ladders, and
By them to skale. The firft that mounted, was
Our bold couragious Generall : after him
Ten thoufand, fo we inftantly were made
Lords of the Citty, purchas'd in two houres
After a nine Moneths fiege : all by the valour
Of our approued Generall.

Duke. I neuer heard a brauer victory,
But what's our loffe ?
Soul. Oh that, which ten fuch Conquefts
Cannot make good, your worthy Generall.
Wife. My Lord and husband ? fpare me paffion,
I muft with-draw to death. *Exit.*
Duke. How perifh't he ?
What dy'de he by the fword ?
Soul. Sword ? No alas,
No fword durft byte vpon his noble flefh,
Nor bullet raze his skinne : he whom War feared,
The Cannon fpar'd, no fteele durft venture on.
No Duke, 'twas thy vnkinde ingratitude
Hath flaine braue *Sforza*.
Duke. Speake the caufe ?
Soul. I fhall :
This Citty feaz'd, his purpofe was the fpoyle

To give his Souldiers; but when his feal'd Commiffion
He had vnript, and faw expreffe command,
To deale no farther then to victory,
And that his great Authority was curb'd,
And giuen to others, that refpect their profit
More then the worth of fouldiers: euen for griefe,
That he could neither furnifh vs with pay
Which was kept back, nor guerdon vs with fpoile,
What was about him he diftributed,
Euen to the beft deferuers, as his garments,
His Armes, and Tent, then fome few words fpake,
And fo oppreft with griefe, his great heart brake.

   Str. There's one gone then.
   Duke. Attend for thy reward,
So leaue vs.
   Soul. Pray on whom fhall I attend?
Who is't muft pay me?
   Str. I fir.
   Soul. You fir? tell me,
Will it not coft me more the waiting for,
Then the fumme comes to when it is receiu'd?
I doe but aske the queftion.
   Str. You are a bold
And faucy fouldier.
   Soul. You are a cunning flaue,
And cowardly Courtier.
   Duke. See all things be difpatcht
Touching conditions of attoned peace
'Twixt vs and *Naples*: fee that fouldier to
Haue his reward.
   Soul. Come will you pay me fir?   *Exit Soul.*
   Str. Sir, will you walke: as for your faucineffe
I'le teach you a Court-tricke: you fhal be taught
How to attend.
   Duke. But that our General's loft:
   Str. Is't not now peace, what fhould a Generall doe?
Had he return'd, he would haue lookt for honours,
This fuite and that for fuch a follower:

Now Royall fir, that debt is quite difcharg'd.
  Duke. But for his wife, we muft be mindefull of her,
And fee we doe fo.   *Exit Duke.*
  Iul. Speake, will he come?
  Str. Madam, I found him ready to depart
The Court with expedition: but at my vrgence
He promis't you a parley.
  Iul. It is well:
If prayers or teares can moue him, Ile make way
To faue my owne fhame, and enforce his ftay.
                                      Exeunt.

Enter three fouldiers: one without an arme.

  1 *Soul.* Come fellow fouldiers, doe you know the reafon
That we are fummon'd thus vnto the houfe
Of our dead Generall?
  2 *Soul.* Sure 'tis about
Our pay.
  3 *Soul.* But ftand afide, here comes the Lady.

Enter the Mother, Lauretta, *and Clowne.*

  Wife. Are all thefe Gentlemen fummond together,
That were my Husbands followers, and whofe fortunes
Expir'd in him?
  Clo. They are if pleafe your Ladifhip: though I
was neuer Tawny-coate, I haue playd the fummoners
part, and the reft are already paide, onely thefe three
attend your Ladifhips remuneration.
  Wife. Welcome Gentlemen,
My Husband led you on to many dangers
Two yeares, and laft to pouerty: His reuenewes
Before hand he fold to maintaine his Army,
When the Dukes pay ftill fail'd, you know you were
Stor'd euer from his Coffers.

2 Soul. He was a right
And worthy Generall.
　2. Soul. He was no leſſe.
　Clo. He was no leſſe; and all you know hee was
no more, well, had he liu'd, I had beene plac't in ſome
houſe of office or other ere this time.
　Wife. It was his will, which to my vtmoſt power
I will make good, to ſatisfie his ſouldiers
To the vtmoſt farthing. All his Gold and Iewels
I haue already added, yet are we ſtill
To ſcore to ſouldiery? what is your ſumme?
　1 Soul. Pay for three Moneths.
　Wife. There's double that in Gold.
　1. Soul. I thanke your Ladiſhip.
　Wife. What yours?
　2. Soul. Why Madam,
For foure Moneths pay.
　Wife. This Iewell ſurmounts that.
　2. Soul. I am treble ſatisfied.
　Wife. You are behinde hand too.
　Clo. Ey but Madam, I thinke he be no true
ſouldier.
　Wife. No true Souldier? your reaſon?
　Clo. Marry becauſe he walkes without his Armes.
　Wife. The Dukes Treaſure
Cannot make good that loſſe, yet are we rich
In one thing:
Nothing we haue that were of nothing made,
Nothing we owe, my Husbands debts are payd.
Morrow Gentlemen.
　All. Madam, Hearts, Swords and hands, reſt ſtill
At your command.
　Wife. Gentlemen I'me ſorry that I cannot pay you
　　better,
Vnto my wiſhes and your owne deſert,
'Tis plainely ſeene great Perſons oft times fall,
And the moſt Rich cannot giue more then all.
Good morrow Gentlemen.

All. May you be euer happy.
Exeunt Souldiers.

Clo. I but Madam, this is a hard cafe being truly confidered, to giue away all, why your Shoe-maker, though he hath many other Tooles to worke with, he will not giue away his All.

Wife. All ours was his alone, it came by him,
And for his Honour it was paid againe.

Clo. Why, fay I had a peece of Meate I had a mind to, I might perhaps giue away a Modicum, a Morcell, a Fragment or fo, but to giue away and bee a hungry my felfe, I durft not doo't for my Guts, or fay I fhould meete with a friend that had but one Penny in his Purfe, that fhould giue mee a Pot of Ale, that fhould drinke to me, and drinke vp all, I'le ftand too't there's no Confcience in't.

Lau. What hath beene done was for my Fathers Honor.

Clo. Shee might haue giuen away a little, and a little, but when all is gone, what's left for me?

Wife. Wee will leaue *Millaine* and to *Florence*
  ftraight,
Though wee are poore, yet where we liue vn-
  knowne
'Tis the leffe griefe, firrah, will you confort
With vs, and beare a part in our misfortunes?

Clo. Troth Madam, I could find in my heart to goe with you but for one thing.

Wife. What's that?

Clow. Becaufe you are too liberall a Miftreffe: and that's a fault feldome found among Ladies: For looke, you vfe to giue away all, and I am all that is left; and I am affraide when you come into a ftrange Countrey, you'le give away me too, fo that I fhall neuer liue to be my owne man.

Wife. Tufh, feare it not.

Clo. Why then I'le goe with you in fpite of your teeth.

Wife. Leaue *Milleine* then, to *Florence* be our guide,
Heauen when man failes, muſt for our helpe prouide.
Exeunt.

Actus Secundus, Scena prima.

Enter Parma *reading a Letter: after him* Julia.

Par. This Letter came from you, 'tis your Character.
Iul. That hand in Contract you ſo long haue had,
Should not ſeeme ſtrange to you now.
Par. You are with-childe,
So doth your Letter ſay: what change your face?
Iu. My bluſhes muſt ſpeake for me.
Par. And this Childe
You would beſtow on me: y'are very liberall Lady,
You giue me more then I did meane to aske.
Iu. And yet but what's your owne Sir, I am ſerious,
And it will ill become your Oathes and Vowes
To ieſt at my vndoeing.
Par. You would ſay
Rather your doing.
Iu. In doing thus, you ſhould vndoe me quite.
Par. What doe you weepe, that late did rayle in clamor?
Your thunders turnd to ſhowres? It is moſt ſtrange.
Iu. You haue diſhonoured me, and by your flattery
Haue rob'd me of my chaſte Virginity:
Yet ere I yeelded, we were man and wife,
Sauing the Churches outward Ceremony.
Par. But Lady, you that would be wonne by me

To such an act of lust, would soone consent
Vnto another.
 Iu. Can this be found in man?
 Par. This *Strozas* language moues me, and I
  intend
To try what patience, constancy, and loue
There can be found in woman: why do you weepe?
You are not hungry, for your bellie's full;
Lady, be rul'd by me: take the aduice
A Doctor gaue a Gentleman of late,
That sent to him to know, whether Tobacco
Were good for him or no: My friend quoth he,
If thou didst neuer loue it, neuer take it;
If thou didst euer loue it, neuer leaue it;
So I to thee; if thou wert as thou hast
Beene alwayes honest, I could wish thee still
So to continue; but being a broken Lady,
Your onely way's to make vse of your Talent,
Farewell, I'le to my Countrey.   *Exit Parma.*
 Iu. Oh miserable,
Let me but reckon vp ten thousand ills
My loosenesse hath committed, the asperson
And scandalous reputation of my Childe,
My Father too, 'tmust come vnto his eare,
Oh——

    Enter Milleine.

 Duke. Iulia.
 Iu. Away.
 Duke. Come hither, but one word.
 Iu. That all those blacke occurrents should con-
  spire,
And end in my disgrace.
 Duke. Ha! what's the businesse?
 Iu. If all men were such,
I should be sorry that a man begot me,
Although he were my father.
 Duke. Iulia, how's that?

Iul. Oh Sir, you come to know whether Tobacco be good for you or no; Ile tell you, if you neuer tooke it, neuer take it then, or if you euer vs'd it, take it ſtill; Nay, I'me an excellent Phiſitian growne of late I tell you.

Duke. What meane theſe ſtrange Anagrams? I am thy Father and I loue thee ſweete.

Iul. Loue me thou doſt not.

Duke. Why thou doeſt know I doe.

Iul. I ſay thou doeſt not: lay no wager with me, For if thou doſt, there will be two to one On my ſide againſt thee.

Duke. Ha! I am thy Father, Why *Iulia*?

Iu. How my Father! then doe one thing For me your Daughter.

Duke. One thing? any thing, Ey all things.

Iu. Inſtantly then draw your ſword, And pierce me to the heart.

Duke. I loue thee not ſo ill, To be the Author of thy death.

Iu. Nor I my ſelfe ſo well, as to deſire A longer life: if you be then my Father, Puniſh a ſinne that hath diſgrac't your Daughter, Scandald your blood, and poyſon'd it with mud.

Duke. Be plaine with vs.

Iu. See, I am ſtrumpeted, A baſtard iſſue growes within my wombe.

Duke. Whoſe fact?

Iu. Prince *Parmaes*.

Duke. *Stroza*.

Str. My Lord.

Duke. Search out Prince *Parma*, bring the Traytour backe againe Dead or aliue.

Str. My Lord, he is a Prince.

Duke. No matter; for his head ſhall be the ranſome

Of this foule Treafon. When I fay begon.
But as for thee bafe and degenerate——

Iul. Doe fhew your felfe a Prince: let her no longer
Liue, that hath thus difgrac't your Royall blood.

Duk. Nature preuailes 'boue honour: her offence
Merits my vengeance, but the name of Childe
Abates my Swords keene edge: yet Royalty
Take th' vpper hand of pitty: kill the ftrumpet,
And be renown'd for Iuftice.

Iul. Strike, I'le ftand.

Duke. How eafie could I period all my care,
Could I her kill, and yet her Infant fpare:
A double Murder I muft needes commit,
To ruine that which neuer offended yet.
Oh Heauen! in this I your affiftance craue,
Punifh the faulter, and the innocent faue.

Iul. You are not true to your owne honour Father,
To let me longer liue.

Duke. Oh *Iulia, Iulia,*
Thou haft ouerwhelm'd vpon my aged head
Mountaines of griefe, t'oppreffe me to my graue.
Is *Parma* found?

Str. My Lord, hee's priuately
Fled from the Court.

Duke. Then flye thou after villaine.

Str. Sir, are you madde?

Duke. What's to be done? Alacke,
I cannot change a father and a Prince
Into a cruell Hang-man: tell me *Iulia,*
Is thy guilt yet but priuate to thy felfe?

Iul. It is my Lord.

Duke. Conceale it then: wee'le ftudy
To falue thy honour, and to keepe thy loofeneffe
From all the world conceal'd, compreffe thy griefe,
And I will ftudy how to fhadow mine.
Wipe from thy cheekes thefe teares: oh curfed Age,

When Children 'gainſt their Parents all things dare,
Yet Fathers ſtill proue Fathers in their care. *Exeunt.*

Enter Mother, Lauretta, *and* Clowne.

Moth. Oh miſery beyond compariſon!
When ſaue the Heauens we haue no roofe at all
To ſhelter vs.

Clow. That word all ſtickes more in my ſtomacke
then my victuals can : For indeede wee can get none
to eate now : I told you, you were ſo prodigall we
ſhould pinch for't.

Wife. What place may wee call this? what Clime?
what Prouince?

Clow. Why this is the Duke-dome of *Florence*, and
this is the Forreſt where the hard-hearted Duke hunts
many a Hart : and there's no Deere ſo deare to him,
but hee'le kill it : as goodly a large place to ſtarue
in, as your Ladiſhip can deſire to ſee in a Summers
day.

Wife. Yet here, ſince no man knowes vs, no
man can
Deride our miſery : better dye ſtaru'd,
Then baſely begge.

Clow. How better ſtarue then begge; all the
Ladies of *Florence* ſhal neuer make me of that beleefe.
I had rather beg a thouſand times, then ſtarue once,
doe you ſcorne begging? Your betters doe not, no
Madam; get me a Snap-ſacke, I'le to *Florence* : I'le
make all the high-wayes ring of me with for the Lords
ſake. I haue ſtudied a Prayer for him that giues, and
a Poxe take him that giues nothing : I haue one for
the Horſe-way, another for the Foote-way, and a third
for the turning-ſtile. No Madam, begging is growne
a gentleman-like Calling here in our Countrey.

Wife. I haue yet one poore piece of Gold reſeru'd,
Step to the Village by and fetch ſome Wine.

Clow. You had better keepe your Gold, and truſt

to my begging Oratory, yet this is the worſt they can ſay to mee, that I am my Ladies Bottle-man.

Exit Clowne.

 Wife. Here's a ſtrange change: we muſt be patient,
Yet can I not but weepe thinking on thee.
 Lau. Madam on me? there is no change of Fortune
Can puffe me or deieƈt me; I am all one
In rich abundance and penurious want:
So little doe my miſeries vexe me,
Or the faire Princeſſe wrong,
That I will end my paſſions in a Song.

A Song.

Sound Hornes within.

 Wife. It ſeemes the Duke is Hunting in the Forreſt,
Here let vs reſt our ſelues, and liſten to
Their Tones, for nothing but miſhap here lies;
Sing thou faire Childe, I'le keepe tune with my eyes.

Winde hornes. And enter the Prince of Florence *& Mounſieur.*

 Prince. This way the voyce was, let vs leaue the Chace.
 Moun. Behold my Lord two ſad deieƈted Creatures
Throwne on the humble verdure.
 Prince. Here's beauty mixt with teares, that pouerty
Was neuer bred in Cottage: I'le farther queſtion
Their ſtate and fortune.
 Wife. Wee're diſcouered,
Daughter ariſe.
 Prince. What are you gentle Creatures?

A Mayden-head well loft.

Nay anfwere not in teares.
If you by cafuall loffe, or by the hand
Of Fortune haue beene crufht beneath thefe forrowes,
He demands your griefe
That hath as much will as ability
To fuccour you, and for your owne faire fake ;
Nay beautious Damfell, you neede not queftion that.
   Lau. If by the front we may beleeue the heart,
Or by the out-fide iudge the inward vertue:
You faire Sir, haue euen in your felfe alone
All that this world can promife ; for I ne're
Beheld one fo compleate ; and were I fure
Although you would not pitty, yet at leaft
You would not mocke our mifery : I would relate
A Tale fhould make you weepe.
   Prince. Sweete if the Prologue
To thy fad paffion mooue thus : what will the Sceane
And tragicke act it felfe doe ?   Is that Gentlewoman
Your Mother fweete ?
   Lau. My wretched Mother Sir.
   Prince. Pray of what Prouince ?
   Lau. Milleine.
   Prince. What fortune there ?
   Lau. My Father was a Noble Gentleman,
Rank't with the beft in Birth, and which did adde
To all his other vertues, a bold Souldier ;
But when he dy'de——
   Prince. Nay, proceede beauteous Lady,
How was your Father ftil'd ?
   Lau. To tell you that,
Were to exclaime vpon my Prince, my Countrey,
And their Ingratitude : For he being dead,
With him our fortunes and our hopes both fail'd ;
My Mother loath to liue ignobly bafe,
Where once fhe flourifht, hauing fpent her meanes
Not loofely nor in riot, but in the honour
Of her dead Husband : left th' ingratefull Land,
Rather to fpend her yeares in pouerty,
Mongft thofe that neuer knew her height of Fortune,

Then with her thankeleſſe Friends and Countrey-men,
Fled here to periſh.
  Prince. More then her charming beauty
Her paſſion moues me: where inhabit you?
  Lau. Here, euery where.
  Prince. Beneath theſe Trees?
  Lau. We haue
No other roofe then what kinde Heauen lends.
  Prince. Gentle Creature,
Had you not told me that your Birth was Noble,
I ſhould haue found it in your face and geſture.
Mounſieur.
  Mounſieur. My Lord.
  Prince. Goe winde thy Horne abroad, and call to vs
Some of our traine: we pitty theſe two Ladies,
And we will raiſe their hope: Cheere you old Madam,
You ſhall receiue ſome bounty from a Prince.

  Enter a Huntſ-man.

Who keepes the Lodge below?
  Huntſ. Your Highneſſe Huntſ-man.
  Prince. Command him to remoue, and inſtantly
We giue it to theſe Ladies: beſides, adde
Vnto our Gueſt three thouſand pounds a yeare:
We'le ſee it furniſht too with Plate and Hangings.
'Las pretty Maide, your Father's dead you ſay,
We'le take you now to our owne Patronage,
And truſt me Lady, while wee're Prince of *Florence*,
You ſhall not want nor foode, nor harborage.
  Wife. Pardon Great Sir, this our neglect of duty
Vnto a Prince ſo gracious and compleate
In vertuous indowments.
  Lau. To excuſe
Our former negligence, behold I caſt
Me at your foote.

Prince. Arife fweete, pray your name?
Lau. Lauretta.
Prince. Faire *Lauretta*, you fhall be henceforth
  ours,
Oh Mounfieur! I ne're faw where I could loue
Till now.
Moun. How now my Lord, remember pray,
What you are to this poore deiected Maide.
Prince. Well Mounfieur, well; when e're I match,
  pray Heauen,
We loue fo well: but loue and toyle hath made vs
Euen fomewhat thirfty, would we had fome Wine.

Enter Clowne.

Clow. Nay, now I thinke I haue fitted you with a
Cup of Mipfilato.
Movn. How now firrah, what are you?
Clow. What am I? Nay what art thou?
I thinke you'le proue little better then a fmell-
  fmocke,
That can finde out a pretty wench in fuch a Corner.
Wife. Peace firrah, 'tis the Prince.
Clow. What if he be? he may loue a Wench as
well as another man.
Prince. What haft thou there?
Clow. A bottle of Wine and a Manchel that my
Lady fent me for.
Prince. Thou ne're couldft come to vs in better
  time,
Reach it vs Mounfieur.
Moun. Your bottle quickly firrah, come I fay.
Clow. Yes, when? can you tell? doe you thinke
I am fuch an Affe, to part fo lightly with my liquor?
Know thou my friend, before I could get this bottle
fill'd, I was glad to change a piece of gold, and call
for the reft againe: And doe you thinke I'le loofe my
liquor, and haue no Gold nor reft againe? Not fo
my Friend, not fo.

Moun. There's Gold fir.

Clow. Madam, will you giue me a Licence to fell Wine? I could get no Plate in the Forreft but a woodden Difh.

Wife. Fill to the Prince *Lauretta*.

Lau. Will it pleafe
Your Highneffe drinke out of a woodden Mazer?

Prince. Yes fweete with thee in any thing: you know
Wee are a Prince, and you fhall be our tafter.

Lau. Why fhould I loue this Prince? his bounteous gifts
Exalt me not, but make me much more poore,
I'me more deiected then I was before.

Wife. Sir.

Moun. Lady, thankes: I feare me he is caught,
But if he be, my Counfell muft diuert him.

Clow. The bottome of the bottle is at your feruice Sir,
Shall you and I part ftakes?

Moun. There's more Gold for you.

Clow. I had rather you had broke my pate then my draught, but harke you Sir, are you as a man fhould fay, a belonger to?

Hunt. A belonger to? what's that fir?

Clow. Oh ignorant! are you a follower?

Hunt. I feldome goe before when my betters are in place.

Clow. A Seruing-man I take it.

Hunt. Right fir.

Clow. I defire you the more complement: I haue the courtefie of the Forreft for you.

Hunt. And I haue the courtefie of the Court for you fir.

Clow. That's to bring me to Buttery hatch, and neuer make me drinke.

Prince. Sirrah, conduct thofe Ladies to the Lodge,
And tell the keeper we haue ftor'd for him,
A better fortune: you fhall heare further from vs,

A Mayden-head well loſt.

You vſher them.

Hunt. Come Ladies will you walke?

Clow. How now ſawce-boxe, know your manners: was not I Gentleman vſher before you came? Am not I hee that did the bottle bring? Come Ladies follow me. *Exit Clowne with Ladies, with Huntſman.*

Moun. Your purpoſe Sir, is to loue this Lady,
And hazard all your hopes.

Prince. Oh gentle Friend,
Why was I borne high? but to raiſe their hopes
That are deiected—ſo much for my bounty.

Moun. But for your loue.

Prince. It is with no intent
To make the Maide my wife, becauſe I know
Her fortunes cannot equall mine.

Moun. Then 'twere more diſhonorable
To ſtrumpet her.

Prince. Still thou miſtak'ſt, mine
Is honourable loue, and built on vertue;
Nor would I for the Emperours Diademe
Corrupt her whom I loue.

Moun. Braue Prince I'me glad
That ere I kept thy company.

Prince. Come Mounſieur, night ſteales on, not many yeares
Shall paſſe me, but I purpoſe to reuiſite
This my new Miſtreſſe, my auſpicious fate
To thee my happy loue I conſecrate. *Exeunt.*

A Dumbe ſhow. Enter the Duke *of Milleine, a Midwife with a young Childe, and after them* Stroza: *the Duke ſhewes the Childe to* Stroza, *hee takes it: then the Duke ſweares them both to ſecrecy vpon his Sword, and exit with the Midwife: then* Stroza *goes to hide it, and* Parma *dogs him: when hee hath laid the Childe in a Corner, he departs in haſte, and* Parma *takes vp the Childe and ſpeakes.*

Par. Thou ſhouldſt be mine: and durſt I for my Head

Euen in the open Court I'de challenge thee,
But I haue so incenſt th' offended Duke,
And layd ſuch heauy ſpots vpon her head,
I cannot doo't with ſafety: methinks this Child
Doth looke me in the face, as if 'twould call
Me Father, and but this ſuſpected *Stroza*
Stuft my too credulous eares with iealouſies.
For thee ſweete Babe I'le ſweare, that if not all,
Part of my blood runnes in thy tender veynes,
For thoſe few drops I will not ſee thee periſh;
Be it for her ſake whom once I lov'd,
And ſhall doe euer: Oh iniurious *Stroza!*
I now begin to feare; for this ſweete Babe
Hath in his face no baſtardy, but ſhewes
A Princely ſemblance: but *Stroza* and the Duke,
This will I keepe as charie as her honour,
The which I prize aboue the Vniuerſe.
Though ſhe were forc't to be vnnaturall,
I'le take to me this Infants pupillage;
Nor yet reſolu'd, till I a way haue found
To make that perfect which is yet vnfound.   *Exit.*

Explicit Actus Secundus.

Actus Tertius.

Enter Milleine *with Lords and* Iulia.

Milleine. Forbeare my Lords for a few priuate
  words:
Faire Daughter, wee'le not chide you farther now,
Nor adde vnto your bluſhes by our rude reproofes:
Your faults are couered with theſe your ſighes,
Since all your fire of luſt is quencht in aſhes.

Iul. Durſt I preſume my Lord, to know
Whither you haue ſent my ſonne?
　Mil. I'le not haue it queſtion'd.
I ſtriue to ſalue thy honour, and thou ſeek'ſt
To publiſh thy diſgrace: my ſtudy is
Where I may picke thee out a noble Husband,
To ſhadow theſe diſhonours, and keepe thee
From the like ſcandall.
　Iul. Whom but *Parmaes* Prince.
　Mil. Oh name him not thou ſtrumpet.
　Iul. I haue done.
　Mil. There's a Prince of noble hopes and for-
　　tunes,
The Prince of *Florence*: what if I ſent to him
About a ſpeedy Marriage? for I feare,
Delay may breed ſtrange doubts.
　Iul. Since I haue loſt the name of Child,
I am a ſeruant now and muſt obey.

　　　　Enter Stroza *and Lords*.

　Mil. *Stroza*.
　Str. Your eare my Lord, 'tis done.
　Mil. Laid out?
　Str. To ſafety as I hope.
　Mil. What, and ſuſpectleſſe?
　Str. Vnleſſe the ſilent Groue of Trees ſhould
　　blabe,
There is no feare of ſcandall, mantled cloſe,
I left the fucking Babe where the next paſſenger
Muſt finde it needes, and ſo it hapned for
Some two yeares after,
Paſſing that way to know where 'twas become,
'Twas gone, and by ſome courteous hand I hope
Remou'd to gentle foſterage.
　Mil. My excellent friend,
For this wee'le boſome thee: your counſel *Stroza*,
Our Daughter's growne to yeares, and we intend
To picke her out a Husband, in whoſe iſſue

Her name may flourish, and her honours liue.
All Lords. Most carefully deuis'd.
Mil. But where my Lords
May we prouide a match to equall her?
  1. *Lord.* *Ferrara* hath a faire and hopefull Heire.
  2. *Lord.* And so hath *Mantua*.
  3. *Lord.* How do you prize the Noble *Florentine*?
  1. *Lord.* In fame no whit inferior.
  2. *Lord.* But in state
Many degrees excelling: aime no further Sir,
If that may be accepted.
  Duke. To *Florence* then wee'le streight dispatch Embassadours,
Stroza, bee't your care to mannage this high businesse.
Oh to see
How Parents loue descends: and howsoe're
The Children proue vngratefull and vnkinde,
Though they deride, we weepe our poore eyes blinde.
                              Exeunt.

Enter Clowne *gallant, and the* Huntsman.

Clow. Nay, nay, the case is alter'd with mee since you saw me last: I was neuer in any hope to purchase any other suite then that I wore yesterday; but now I can say *Ecce signum*, the case is alter'd. Now euery begger comes vpon me with *good Gentleman, good Gentleman*: when yesterday Gentlemen would haue shun'd the way for feare I should haue begg'd of them. Then comes another vpon mee with *good your Worship, good your Worship*, then doe I double my fyles, and cast him a single two pence.
  Hunt. Sirrah, thou mayst thanke the Prince for this.
  Clow. Thou say'st true; for he hath chang'd our woodden Dishes to Siluer Goblets: goodly large Arras that neuer yet deseru'd hanging, he hath caus'd to be hang'd round about the Chamber: My Lady and Mistresse, now my Lady and Mistresse lyes ouer head

and eares in Downe and Feathers: well, if they be rul'd by me, I would haue them to keepe their beds.

Hunt. Why wouldſt thou haue them lye a bed all day?

Clow. Oh dull ignorant! I meane knowing how hard they haue bin lodg'd in the Forreſt; I would not haue them ſell away their beds, and lie vpon the boords.

Hunt. Oh now I vnderſtand you ſir.

Clow. Ey, ey; thou may'ſt get much vnderſtanding by keeping my company: But Sir, does not the new Gowne the Prince ſent my Miſtreſſe, become her moſt incomparably?

Hunt. 'Tis true: 'tis ſtrange to ſee how Apparrell makes or marres.

Clow. Right: for yeſterday thou wouldſt haue taken me for a very Clowne, a very Clowne; and now to ſee, to ſee.—

Enter Mother and the young Lady gallant.

Wife. Sirrah.
Clow. Madam.
Lau. Why doſt view me thus?
Clow. To ſee if the Tayler that made your Gowne, hath put ne're an M. vnder your Girdle, there belongs more to beaten Sattin then ſirrah.
Lau. What thinke you Mother of the Prince his bounty,
His vertue, and perfection?
Wife. He's a mirrour, and deſerues a name
Amongſt the famous Worthies.
Lau. Heighoe.
Wife. Why ſigh you?
Lau. Pray tell me one thing Mother: when you were
Of my yeares, and firſt lou'd, how did you feele
Your ſelfe?

Wife. Loue Daughter?

Clow. Shee talkes now, as if she should be enamored of my comely shape; for I haue (as they say) such a foolish yong and relenting heart, I should neuer say her nay, I should neuer weare off this.

Lau. Stand farther off sir.

Clow. No, I'le assure your Ladiship 'tis beaten Sattin.

Lau. Then take your Sattin farther.

Clow. Your Ladiship hath coniur'd me, and I will auoide Satan.

Lau. Had you not sometimes musings, sometimes extasies,
When some delicate man 'boue other
Was present?

Wife. I aduise you curbe your sence in time,
Or you will bring your selfe into the way
Of much dishonour.

Lau. And speake you by experience Mother? then
I doe begin to feare lest that his shape
Should tempt me, or his bounty worke aboue
My strength and patience; pray Mother leaue vs neuer,
Lest that without your Company, my loue
Contending with my weakenesse, should in time
Get of 't the vpper hand.

Wife. For this I loue thee.

Enter Clowne *running.*

Clow. So hoe Mistris Madam, yonder is the Prince, and two or three Gentlemen come riding vpon the goodliest Horses that euer I set my eyes vpon: and the Princes Horse did no sooner see me, but he weeighed and wagg'd his tayle: now I thinking he had done it to take acquaintance of me, said againe to him, Gramercy Horse; so I left them, and came to tell your Ladiship.

Lau.   Goe fee them ſtabled, my foule leapt within me
To heare the Prince but named.

Enter Prince *and* Mounſieur.

Prince.   Now my faire Friend.
Lau.   Your hand-mayd mighty Prince.
Prince.   Looke Mounſieur,
Can ſhe be leſſe then Noble? nay deſerues ſhe
Thus habited, to be tearm'd leſſe then Royall,
What thinkſt thou Mounſieur?
Moun.   Faith my Lord,
I neuer loue a woman for her habite,
When Sir I loue, I'le ſee my loue ſtarke naked.
Prince.   Right courteous Lady,
Our bounty is too ſparing for your worth,
Yet ſuch as 'tis accept it.
Wife.   Royall ſir,
'Tis beyond hope or merit.
Prince.   I prithee Mounſieur,
A little complement with that old Lady,
Whilſt I conferre with her.
Moun.   I thanke you Sir:
See, you would make me a ſir Panderus,
Yet farre as I can ſee you, I will truſt you.
                    Hee talkes with the old Lady.
Sweete Lady, how long is't—nay keepe that hand,
Since thoſe fierce warres 'twixt *Florence* and great
    Millaine?
Nay that hand ſtill.
Prince.   And haue you ne're a loue then?
Lau.   Yes my Lord:
I ſhould belye my owne thoughts to deny,
And ſay I had none.
Prince.   Pray acquaint me with him,
And for thy ſake I'le giue him ſtate and Honours,
And make him great in *Florence.*   Is he of birth?
Lau.   A mighty Duke-domes Heire.

Prince. How now my *Lauretta*?
I prithee fweete where liues he?
  Lau. In his Countrey.
  Prince. Honour me fo much
As let me know him.
  Lau. In that your Grace muft pardon me.
  Prince. Muft? then I will. Is he of prefence fweete?
  Lau. As like your Grace as one Prince to another.
  Prince. Honour me fo much then, as let me know him.
  Lau. In that excufe me Sir.
  Prince. Thee, loue I will
In all things: wherefore ftudy you?
  Lau. Why my Lord?
I was euen wifhing you a mighty harme;
But pardon me 'twas out euen vnawares.
  Prince. Harme? there's none can come from thee *Lauretta,*
Thou art all goodneffe, nay confeffe it fweete.
  Lau. I was wifhing with my felfe that you were poore:
Oh pardon me my Lord, a poore, a poore man.
  Prince. Why my *Lauretta*?
  Lau. Sir, becaufe that little
I haue, Might doe you good: I would you had
No money, nay, no meanes: but I fpeake idly,
Pray pardon me my Lord.
  Prince. By all my hopes,
I haue in *Florence,* would thou wert a Dutcheffe,
That I might court thee vpon equall tearmes;
Or that I were of low deiected fortunes,
To ranke with thee in Birth: for to enioy
Thy beauty, were a greater Dowre then *Florence*
Great Duke-dome.

        Enter Clowne.
  Clow. Oh my Lord, my Lord,

Are you clofe at it ? and you too crabbed Age,
And you—there's Rods in piffe for fome of you.
　Prince. Now fir, the newes?
　Clow. Oh my Lord, there's a Nobleman come
from the Court to fpeake with you.
　Prince. Mounfieur,
Vpon my life 'tis fome Embaffadour.
　Moun. Good Sir make hafte, left I be challeng'd
for you.
　Prince. No worthy Friend, for me thou fhalt not
　　fuffer,
At our beft leafur'd houres we meane to vifite you;
Now giue me leaue to take a fhort fare-well.
　　　　　　　　　　Exeunt Prince *and* Mounfieur.
　Lau. Your pleafure is your owne,
To part from him I am rent quite afunder.
　Clow. And you can but keepe your leggs clofe,
Let him rend any thing elfe and fpare not.　*Exeunt.*

Enter Florence *and* Lords *with* Stroza Embaffadour.

　Flo. Speake the true Tenor of your Embaffie.
　Str. If *Florence* prize the Duke of *Millaines*
　　loue,
His indear'd Amity : If he haue minde
To mixe with him in confanguinity,
To ftrengthen both your Realmes : he makes this pro-
　　iect
To your faire Treaty, that your hopefull Heire
Shall with the Princeffe *Iulia* his faire Daughter,
Be ioyn'd in Marriage ; her large Dowre fhall be
A fpacious Duke-dome after his deceafe.
But which my Lord counts moft, is a faire League
'Twixt your diuided Duke-domes.
　Florence. We doe conceite you :
But for the Dowre you craue?
　Str. Ten thoufand Crownes
By th'yeare.

Flo. 'Tis granted : onely our Sonnes confent
Is wanting : but fee here, he wifht for comes.

Enter Prince and Mounfieur.

Prince. Mounfieur, what are thofe ?
Moun. Embaffadours my Lord.
Prince. Whence are thefe Lords ?
Dake. From *Millaine*.
Prince. Their bufineffe Royall Sir ?
Flo. About a match,
Which if you't pleafe, we highly fhall applaud.
They offer you a faire and vertuous Princeffe
Vnto your bed.
Prince. Vnto my bed my Lord ?
I am not fo affraide of fpirits Sir,
But I can lye alone without a bed-fellow.
Flo. 'Tis the faire Princeffe *Iulia* you muft marry.
Prince. Marry my Lord ?
Flo. I marry muft you Sir,
Or you diuorce your felfe from our deare loue.
Prince. But is fhe faire ?
Stro. As euer *Hellen* was.
Prince. What, and as Chafte ?
Stroza. It were not Princely in you, Royall Sir,
To queftion fuch a Princeffe Chaftity :
I could haue inftanc'd *Lucrece*.
Prince. Would you had,
For both were rauifht.
Moun. How's this my Lord ?
They offer loue and beauty, which being both
So freely offer'd, doe deferue acceptance.
Stroza. Your anfwere Sir ?
Prince. That I am yours : the States ;
And if you pleafe fo to difpofe me, hers,
What ere fhe be : come friend, I muft impart
My Loue this newes, or it will rend my heart.

Exit Prince.

Stroza. I shall returne this answere.
Flo. Faithfully
As we intend it : But you first shall taste
The bounty of our Court, with royall Presents
Both to the Duke your master, and the Princesse;
It done, prepare we for this great solemnity,
Of Hymeneall Iubilies. Fixt is the day,
Wherein rich *Florens* shall her pompe display.
                                                                Exeunt.

    Enter Parma *and a Lord of* Millaine.

Parm. Onely to you, of all the *Millaine* Peeres,
I dare expose my safety.
Lord. In these armes
My Lord, you are Sanctuared.
Parm. I doe not doubt it :
But I pray you tell me, since I left the Court,
How is my absence taken ?
Lord. Of the Duke,
With much distaste.
Parm. But of the Princesse *Iulia ?*
Lord. Full two Moneths
Shee kept her Chamber, grieuously distracted,
They say, meere griefe for your departure hence.
Parm. Brauely manag'd,
The Duke I see was more kind to her fame,
Then to his prettie grand-childe; well Ile salt it all,
But what thinke you if after all I should
Send Letters to her, or Ambassadors ?
I should not win her, for I know
They haue her heart in bondage.
Lord. Why worthy Prince,
Haue you not heard the newes : Shee hath beene offered
Vnto the Florentine, the match accepted,
And the Nuptiall day the tenth of the next Moneth.
Parm. No more : Pray leaue mee Sir.
Lord. I will : Pray Sir

Regard your safety. Exit *Lord*.

Parm. To bee married, *Ruimus in vestitum semper*,
I did neglect her, but being deni'd,
I doate upon her beautie : Methinkes 'tis fit,
If I begot the Child ? I wed the Mother :
The Prince, I pitie hee should bee so wrong'd,
And I the Instrument : Now helpe mee braine,
That neare was wont to fayle mee : 'Tis decreed
Something to Plot, although I fayle to speede.

Exit *Parma*.

Enter Clowne, Mother, *and* Lauretta.

Clowne. I wonder you should bee so sad and melanchollie, Ile lay a yeeres wages before hand Ile tell your disease, as well as any Doctor in *Florence*, and let me but feele your pulse.

Lauret. Away, you are a foole, and trouble vs.

Clowne. That's no matter whether I bee a foole or a phisitian, if I loose, Ile pay, that's certain.

Wife. Try the fooles counsell daughter, but bee sure
To forfit, and to pay.

Lauret. Now sir, your skill.

Clowne. Nay I must feele your pulse first, for if a Womans pulse bee neere a place, I know there's few heere of my yeeres but would bee glad to turne Doctors.

Lauret. Now sir, you see I doe not smile.

Clawne. Nay, if it bee nothing else, Ile fetch that will cure you presently. Exit *Clowne*.

Wife. Child I must chide you, you giue too much way
Vnto this humour : It alters much your beautie.

Enter the Clowne.

Clowne. Oh young Mistris, where are you, the Prince,

A Mayden-head well loſt.   139

The Prince.
  Lauret. Oh Mother, doe you heare the newes, the
    Prince,
The Prince is comming : Where is hee. oh where ?
  Clowne. Where is hee ? Why at the Court ; where
ſhould hee bee ? I did but doo't to make you ſmile :
Nay, Ile tickle you for a Doctor : Madam I haue a
yeeres wages before hand.
  Lauret. Is hee not come then ?
  Clowne. No marrie is hee not.
  Lauret. My foule did leape within, to heare the
    Prince
But nam'd : It ſtarted every ioynt.
  Clowne. Nay Madam, the Prince is come.
  Wife. Away, your foolerie's vnſeaſonable,
Weele not beleeve you.

        Enter the Prince *and* Mounſieur.

  Clowne. If you will not belieue mee, will you
    beleeue theſe ?
  Lauret. Welcome my Lord : And wherefore doe
    you ſigh ?
  Prince. I ſigh *Lauretta*, cauſe I cannot chuſe.
  Lauret. Nor could I chuſe, ſhould you but ſigh
    againe.
  Prince. Ile tell thee Loue, ſtrange newes : I muſt
    be married.
  Lauret. Married my Lord !
  Prince. Why doe you weepe ? You blam'd mee now
    for ſighing :
Why doe you melt in teares ? Sweet what's the
    cauſe ?
  Lauret. Nay, nothing.
  Prince. And as I told thee Sweete ; I muſt bee
    married,
My Father and the State will haue it ſo ;
And I came inſtantly to tell the newes

To thee *Lauretta* ; As to one, from whom
I nothing can conceale.
    Lauret. Why fhould you grieue
For that? For I, my Lord, muft haue a Husband
too.
    Prince. Muft you? But when's the day?
    Lauret. When's yours my Lord?
    Prince. The tenth of the next moneth.
    Lauret. The felfe fame day,
And felfe fame houre that you inioy your loue,
My Princely Husband I muft then inioy.
    Prince. But doe you loue him?
    Lauret. Not my felfe more deere.
    Prince. How happie are you aboue mee faire
friend,
That muft inioy where you affect? When I
Am tide to others fancies : It was your promife
That I fhould know him further.
    Lauret. You fhall fee him
That day, as richly habited as the great
Heire of *Florence:* But royall Sir, what's fhee
That you muft bed then?
    Prince. 'Tis *Iulia*,
The Duke of *Millaines* daughter : Why change your
    Face?   *Lauretta fpeakes to her felfe.*
    Lauret. That fhee that hates mee moft fhould liue
to inioy
Him I affect beft : O my ominous fate,
I thought to haue hid mee from thee in thefe
defarts,
But thou doft dogg mee euery where.
                                         Shee Swounes.
    Prince. Looke to her fafety, not for the Crowne
Of *Florence* I would haue her perifh.
    Wife. Helpe to fupport her.
                              Exit with Mother and Clowne.
    Prince. Oh Friend, that I fhould change my
Royaltie

To weakneffe now: I doe thinke this lodge
A Pallace, and this Beautious Mayden-head
Of greater worth then *Iulia*.
 Moun. Come my Lord,
Lay by thefe idle thoughts, and make you ready
To entertaine your Bride.

Enter Parma *difguifed*.

 Parm. The Prince, the Prince,
I come to feeke the Prince, and was directed
Vnto this place.
 Prince. Thy newes.
 Parm. A Letter.
 Prince. Whence?
 Parm. Reade, the Contents will fhew you; their
eyes are from mee, and I muft hence.   Exit *Parma*.

The Prince *reades*.

 Prince. The *Millaine* Princeffe is betroathed; de-
 flowred,
Not worthy of your loue, beleeue this true
Vpon a Prince his word; when you fhall bed
 her,
And find her flawd in her Virginitie,
You fhall haue caufe to thinke vpon his loue
From whom you had this caution;
But doe it with that Princely management,
Her honour bee not flandered: Hee that loues,
Admires, and honours you:
Where's hee that brought this Letter?
 Moun. Fled my Lord.
 Prince. Poaft after; bring him backe,
Could hee not fet his hand to't——
How now, the newes?
 Moun. Hee's fled vpon a milke white Gennet
 Sir,
Seeming t' outftrip the winde, and I—loft him.

Prince. Thou haſt loſt mee quite.
Moun. What meanes this paſsion Sir?
Prince. Mounſieur reade there,
What will confound thee: Oh if ſhee bee vnchaſt!
Could they find none but mee to worke vpon.
Moun. It confounds mee my Lord.
Prince. If ſhee bee Chaſt,
How ſhall I wrong her, to queſtion her faire Vertues?
Moun. Right.
Prince. But if ſhee bee not right? I wrong my Honor,
Which after marriage, how ſhall I recall?
Moun. 'Tis certaine.
Prince. Yes: Oh how am I perplext!
Come, Ile to Court,
Ile not bee ſway'd: Were ſhee a Potent Queene,
Where Counſell fayles mee, Ile once truſt to ſpleene.
Exeunt.

Enter the Clowne *with his Table-bookes.*

Clowne. Let me ſee, the *Prince* is to bee married to morrow, and my young Miſtris meanes to keepe a Feaſt in the Forreſt, in honour of his wedding at the Court: Now am I ſent as Caterer into the City to prouide them with victualls, which they charg'd me to buy; no ordinary fare, no more it ſhall, and therefore I haue caſt it thus; Firſt and foremoſt, wee will haue—(yes downe it ſhall) we will haue a Gammon of Bacon roaſted, and ſtufft with Oyſters; And fixe Black-Puddings to bee ſerued vp in Sorrell-ſops; A pickell'd ſhoulder of Mutton, and a ſurloyne of Beefe in White-broth, ſo much for the firſt courſe. Now for the ſecond, we will haue a Cherry-Tart cut into Raſhers and broyled; A Cuſtard Carbonado'd on the coales; A liue Eele ſwimming in clowted Creame; And fixe Sheepes-heads baked, with the hornes peering out of the paſty-cruſt. The morrall is, becauſe it is a wedding-dinner.

Enter Stroza *with another Lord.*

Stro. The ioyfull day's to morrow. Paſſe this plunge
And we are made for euer.

Clowne. What, my old Polititian? hee that vndermin'd my old Lady and my yong Miſtris? now that I could find but one ſtratagem to blow him vp; I would toſſe him, I would blanket him i' th Ayre, and make him cut an Italian caper in the Clouds: Theſe Politicians can doe more execution with a pen, in their ſtudies, then a good Souldier with his ſword in the field, but he hath ſpi'd mee.

Stro. Thee friend I ſhould haue knowne?

Clowne. And you too, I ſhould haue knowne, but whether for a friend, or no, ther's the queſtion?

Stro. Thou ſeru'ſt the Generall *Sforza.*

Clow. I confeſſe it; but whether you haue ſeru'd him well, or no, there hangs a Tale.

Stro. How doth thy noble Lady, faire *Lauretta*? They have left *Millaine* long, reſide they here
Neere to the City *Florence*?

Clow. Some three miles off, here in the Forreſt, not halfe an houres riding.

Stro. I pray thee recommend me to them both,
And ſay, It ſhall goe hard with mine affaires
But Ile find ſeaſon'd houres to viſit them.

Clow. You ſhall not want directions to find the place, come when you will, you ſhall be moſt heartily ——poyſon'd.

Stro. Tell them, The newes that they are well
Is wondrous pleaſing to me, and that power
I haue in *Millaine* is reſeru'd for them,
To worke them into grace: I can but ſmile,
To ſee how cloſe I haue plotted their exile.
Now buſineſſe calls me hence: farewell. *Exit.*

Clow. And be hang'd, Mounſieur *Stroza*, whoſe deſcription my *Muſe* hath included in theſe few lines;

Stroza, *Thy Head is of a comely Block,*
And would shew well, crown'd with the combe of Cock:
His Face an Inne, his Brow a sluttish Roome,
His Nose the Chamberlaine, his Beard the Broome,
Or like New-market Heath, that makes theeues rich,
In which his Mouth stands iust like Deuills-ditch.
And so farewell to your worship, graue Mounsieur
Stroza, for I must about my market. *Exeunt.*

Actus Quartus.

A Dumbe shew. *Enter at one doore, the Duke of* Millaine, Iulia, Stroza, *and a* Bishop: *At the other doore, the Duke of* Florens, *the* Prince *and* Mounsieur, *with attendants:* Then *the* Bishop *takes their hands and makes signes to marry them, and then the* Prince *speakes.*

Prince. Stay till we be resolu'd.
Florens. What meanes our sonne ?
Princ. Not to be gull'd by the best Prince in Europe;
Much lesse by *Millaine.*
Millaine. Sir, be plaine with vs.
Prin. I much suspect that Ladies Chastity.
Millaine. Hers.
Prin. I haue said.
Stroza. Ther's Worme-wood.
Millaine. I came in termes of Honour,
Brought with me, all my comforts here on earth,
My daughter ; to bestow her on thy son :
Poore Lady, innocently comming, forsaking all,
Father and Countrey, to betake her selfe

Vnto his bofome; and is fhe for all this,
Branded with fhame?

 Stro. Who can accufe her, fpeake? what probabilities?
What ground? the place? the meanes? the feafon how
Shee did become corrupt?

 Prince. Sir, fo we haue heard.

 Stro. Produce the witneffe; and behould, I ftand
The Champion for her honour, and will auerre
Her Chafte, aboue degree; infinitely honeft:
Oh Prince! what, can you ground fuch iniury
Vpon vaine heare-fay? Speake for your felfe, take
 fpirit.

 Iulia. Came we thus farre, to be thus wrong'd?
           Apart to herfelfe.

 Stro. Was the flaue neuer Chriften'd, hath hee no
 name?

 Iulia. Haue you fent for me, to accufe me heere
In this ftrange Clime? It is not Princely done.

 Prince. O Heauen, how am I perplext!

 Floren. Sonne, Sonne, you wrong
Your felfe and me too, to accufe a Lady
Of fuch high birth and fame; vnleffe you confeffe
You felfe to haue err'd, you needs muft forfeit vs.

 Moun. My Lord, yeeld to your father, left you draw
His wrath vpon you.

 Prince. Well, fince I muft, I will:
Your pardon, Royall Father: Yours faire Princeffe:
And yours great Duke;
If I fhall find my felfe truely to haue err'd,
I fhall confeffe your chaftity much iniur'd.

 Iulia. Submiffion is to me full recompence.

 Milla. My daughters honour?

 Stro. Doe not ftand off my Lord,
If fhe be wrong'd, fhee's not much behind-hand.

 Milla. Oh let me alone *Stroza*.

 Flor. Nay, good Brother
Accept him as your Sonne.

 Milla. My hearts no clofet for reuenge; 'tis done

Prin. Now heare my proteftations: I receiue
This Ladies hand on thefe Conditions;
If you, my Lord, her father, or her felfe,
Know her felfe faulty, Oh confeffe it here,
Before the Ceremonies faften on me: for if hereafter
I find you once corrupted? by this right hand,
My future hopes, my Fathers royalty,
And all the honours due vnto our houfe,
Ile haue as many liues and heads for it,
As he hath Manners, Caftles, Liues and Towres;
It fhall be worthy to be lockt in Chronicles
Of all ftrange tongues: And therefore beautious Lady,
As you efteeme a Prince his name or honour,
That youd be a *Mecenas* vnto vertue;
If in the leaft of thefe you guilty be,
Pull backe your hand.

Stro. What if you find her chafte?

Prin. If chafte, fhe fhall be dearer farre to me
Then my owne foule: I will refpect her honour,
Equall with that of my great Anceftours;
All this I vow, as I am Prince and vertuous.

Stro. Then ioyne their hands.

Prin. Shee's mine: Set forwards then.

Exeunt all but Stroza.

Stro. All goes not well, This iugling will be found,
Then where am I? would I were fafe in *Millaine.*
Here Matchiuell thou waft hatcht: Could not the fame
Planet infpire this pate of mine with fome
Rare ftratagem, worthy a lafting Character:
No, 'twill not be; my braine is at a non-plus,
For I am dull.

Enter Millaine.

Milla. Stroza.

Stro. My Lord.

Milla. Oh now, or neuer *Stroza*!
Stro. I am turn'd Foole, Affe, Iddeot; Are they
   married?
Milla. Yes, and the Prince after the Ceremonie,
Imbrac'd her louingly.
Stro. But the hell is
That they muſt lie together, ther's the Deuill.
Milla. And then——
Stro. And then we are difgrac'd and fham'd.
Milla. Canſt thou not help't man?
Stro. Why you would make
A man—midwife, woo'd you? I haue no skill.
Milla. Stroza, awake, th'art drowfie.
Stro. Peace, interrupt me not,
I ha'te : fo to reuenge mee vpon her
Whom moſt I hate. To Strumpet her 'twere braue.
Milla. Counfell aduife me.
Stro. Youle make me mad my Lord :
And in this fweet reuenge, I am not onely
Pleas'd (with iuſt fatisfaction for all wrongs)
But the great Prince moſt palpably deceiu'd.
Milla. The time runs on, thinke on my honor
   Stroza.
Stro. If youle eate grapes vnripe, edge your owne
   teeth,
Ile ſtay the mellow'd feafon, doo't your felfe,
Vnleffe you giue me time for't.
Milla. But thinke with mine, on thine owne fafety
   Stroza.
Stro. Peace, giue me way my Lord, fo fhall the
   Prince
Bee palpably deceiu'd, Faire *Iulia's* honor
Moſt profperoufly preferu'd, The Duke my maſter,
Freed from all blame, Warre hindred, Peace con-
   firm'd,
And I fecur'd ; Oh I am fortunate
Beyond imagination !
Milla. O deare *Stroza*,
Helpe now, or neuer !

Stro.   Hee was a meere Affe
That rais'd Troy's Horfe : 'twas a pritty ftructure.
  Milla.   Oh mee !
  Stro.   Synon, a foole, I can doe more
With precious Gold, then hee with whining Teares.
  Milla.   Oh my tormented foule !
  Stro.   Pray my Lord, giue mee
Fiue hundred crownes.
  Milla.   What to doe with them man ?
  Stro.   See how you ftand on trifles ; when our liues,
Your honour ; all our fortunes lie a bleeding ;
What fhall I haue the Gold ?
  Milla.   Thy purpofe preethee ?
  Stro.   I know a defolate Lady, whom with Gold
I can corrupt.
  Milla.   There are fiue hundred Crownes,
Stroza bethinke thee what thou vndertak'ft,
Such an Act, would make huge *Atlas* bend his head
Vnto his heele.
  Stro.   But fay I cannot win her,
They bide the brunt of all, heere let them ftay,
With thefe fiue hundred Crownes Ile poaft away.

Exit Stroza, *and* Duke.

Enter Mother, Daughter, *and* Clowne.

  Clow.   Maddam, yonder's a Gentleman comes to fpeake with you in all haft.
  Lauret.   Admit him in.

Enter Stroza.

  Stro.   Lady bee happy, and from this bleft houre
Euer reioyce faire Virgin, for I bring you
Gold, and Inlargement ; with a recouerie
Of all your former loffe, and dignitie,
But for a two houres labour : Nay, that no labour
Nor toyle, but a meere pleafure.

Lau. Your words like mufick, pleafe me with delight,
Beyond imagination : Offered to vs?
Being exil'd our Countrey, and our friends,
Therefore good fir, delay not with long complement ;
But tell thefe hopes more plaine.
  Stro. Haue wee not heere
Too many eares?
  Lauret. Wee would bee priuate firra,
And therefore leaue vs.   Exit *Clowne.*
  Stro. You haue feene the Prince of *Florence* ?
  Lauret. Yes I haue.
  Stro. Is he not for his Feature, Beauty, Goodneffe,
The moft Compleate? So abfolute in all things.
  Lauret. All this is granted.
  Stro. How happy doe you thinke that Lady then
That fhall Inioy him? Nay, that fhall bee the firft
To prooue him, and exchange Virginitie,
Were't not bright Lady a great happineffe?
  Lauret. I wifh that happineffe were mine alone,
Oh my faint heart: Paffion ouer-fwayes me quite,
But hide thy griefe *Lauretta* : Sir, you'le make
Me fall in loue with him : Were I his equall,
I then fhould iudge him worthy of no leffe.
  Stro. Loue him : What's fhe doth not, if fhee haue eyes?
Were I my felfe a Woman : I would lay
My felfe a proftitute vnto the Prince :
Shee is not wife that would refufe him Lady.
  Lauret. Good Sir bee briefe :
To what pray tends thefe fpeeches?
  Stro. To thee fweete Lady : I offer all thefe pleafures,
Oh happie fate that hath felected mee
To be your raifer : Lady take this gold,
But that's not all : For there are greater honours

Prepared for you ; the Duke of *Millaine* doth
Commend him to you : *Iulia* his daughter
Hath in her honour late mifcarried,
Now't lies in you to falue and make all good.
 Wife. Who ? Lies this in my daughter.
 Stro. Yes, in her,
Shee hath the power to make the Duke her friend,
Iulia her fifter, and all *Millaine* bound
To offer vp for her their Orrifons.
 Lauret. Good Sir bee plaine.
 Stro. This night lie with the Prince
In *Iulia's* ftead : There's way made for you,
Who would not woo, for what you are wooed too ?
 Lauret. Doe you not blufh, when you deliuer this
Pray tell the Duke, all Women are not *Iulia*,
And though wee bee deiected, thus much tell him,
Wee hold our honour at too high a price,
For Gold to buy.
 Stro. Nay Lady, heare mee out ;
You fhall preferue her honour, gaine the Duke,
Redeeme your fortunes : Strengthen you in friends,
You fhall haue many Townes and Turrets ftanding,
Which future Warre may ruine : Thinke on that.
 Wife. *Lauretta*, oh behold thy mothers teares !
Thinke on thy Father, and his honour wonne,
And call to mind our exile : All the wrongs
Wee haue indured by her, to whom wee gaue
No caufe, and now are plundg'd in a deepe ftreame,
Which not refifted, will for euer blemifh
The name of *Sforfa* thy great Anceftors,
Thou'lt waken thy dead Father from his graue,
And caufe his honour'd wounds which hee receiu'd
From that vnthankfull Duke, to bleede afrefh,
Powring out new blood from his grifly wounds,
If thou confenteft to this abhorred fact,
Thy Mothers curfe will feaze on thee for euer :
Oh child, behold me on my knees : Ile follow thee ;

Oh doe not leaue me thus, and pull on thee
An euerlasting staine, to scandall all
Thy former Vertues, for the momentarie
Short pleasures of one night.

    Stro. She doth not councell well ; 'tis foolish rash-
nes,
Womanish Indiscretion.

    Lauret. Sir bee answered,
If *Iulia* bee disloyall : Let her bee found
So by the Prince she wedds : Let her be branded
With the vile name of strumpet : Shee disgrac'd
Mee, that nere thought her harme ; publikely strucke
    mee,
Nay in the Court : And after that, procur'd
My banishment : These Injuries I reap't
By her alone, then let it light on her.

    Stro. Now see your errour,
What better, safer, or more sweete reuenge,
Then with the Husband ? what more could woman
    aske ?

    Lauret. My blood rebells against my reason, and
I no way can withstand it : 'Tis not the Gold
Mooues mee, but that deere loue I beare the Prince,
Makes me neglect the credit and the honour
Of my deare Fathers house : Sir, what the Duke desires
I am resolued to doe his vtmost will.

    Wife. Oh my deare daughter.

    Lauret. Good Mother speake not, for my word is
    past,
And cannot bee recall'd, Sir will you away ?
I am resolute.

    Stro. Shee yeeldes vnto her shame ; which makes
    me blest,
Let Millions fall, so I bee crown'd with rest.

    Wife. Oh mee, vnhappie, that nere knew griefe
till now.   *Exeunt.*

    Musicke. A Dumbe Show. *Enter* Millaine, *to
    him* Stroza, *and brings in* Lauretta *masked,*

> *the* Duke *takes her and puts her into the Bed, and* Exit.

> *Enter both the* Duke *and* Iulia, *they make signes to her and* Exit: Stroza *hides* Iulia *in a corner, and stands before her.*

> *Enter againe with the* Prince *to bring him to bed. They cheere him on, and others snatch his Pointes, and so* Exit. *The* Dukes *Imbrace, and* Exeunt.

Actus Quintus.

Enter Millaine *to* Stroza.

Milla. Thou art our trusty Counsellor; if this passe currant
We're past all feare: What is shee preethee? What?
  Stro. What's that to you, bee shee what ere she can,
All's one to vs, so she be found a Virgin;
I haue hyred her, and shee's pleas'd.
  Milla. But gaue you charge
Assoone as ere the Prince was fast asleepe,
That shee should rise and giue place to our daughter?
  Stro. Doubt you not that; what, iealous already?
  Milla. How long she stayes, I faine would be a bed;
Pray heauen shee doe not fall
By him asleepe, and so forget her selfe.
  Stro. Heer's in my heart, a violent Feauer still;

Nor fhall I find my felfe in my true temper,
Vntill this brunt bee paft.
Milla. What, not yet?
Had fhe with *Parma* beene a bed fo long,
It would haue more perplext mee.

Enter Lauretta.

Stro. See, here fhee is;
The newes?
Lauret. The Prince is faft, all done.
Milla. Step in her place;
Nay when? and counterfeit fleepe prefently.
Stro, Away to bed my Lord: You to the Forreft,
I'le to my Coach, all's well.
Exeunt Stroza *and the* Duke.
Lauret. And for my part, it was not much amifle,
Becaufe my Lord the Prince had fuch content
Which caus'd him giue his Charter to my hand,
The full affurance of faire *Iulia's* dowre:
Day gins to breake, and I muft to the Lodge.
Oh what a griefe it was to leaue the Prince!
But leaue thofe thoughts: Thefe Gifts to me affign'd,
Are nothing worth the Iem I left behind. *Exit.*

Enter Prince *and* Mounfieur *with a Torch.*

Moun. What doe you not like your bed-fellow, my Lord,
That you are vp fo foone?
Prin. Oh friend, was neuer man bleft with a Bride
So chaft! I'me fcarce my felfe, till this be knowne
To my faire Forreft friend: Lett's mount away,
The nights quite fpent: and now begins the day.

Enter Mother *and* Clowne.

Wife. And what was it you faid firra?

Clow. Marry, I would intreat your Lady-ſhip to turne away my fellow *Ierom*, for I thinke hee's no true man.

Wife. No true man, Why?

Clo. Marry, we were both in the Tauerne together tother day——

Wife. And hee ſtole ſome Plate?

Clo. No Madam, but there ſtood at our elbow a pottle Pot——

Wife. And hee ſtole the Pot?

Clo. No Madam, but he ſtole the wine in the Pot, and drunke it off, And made himſelfe ſo drunke hee be-piſt himſelfe: Your Ladyſhip could not be better be-piſt in a Summers-day.

Enter Prince *and* Mounſieur.

Prin. Good morrow Lady: Wher's your daughter pray?

Wife. She tooke ſo little reſt laſt night, my Lord, I thinke ſhee is ſcarce well.

Prin. Pray may wee ſee her?

Wife. My Lord, you may.

Shee's drawne out vpon a Bed.

Song.

Hence with *Paſsion, Sighes and Teares,*
  Deſaſters, Sorrowes, Cares and Feares.
See, *my Loue (my Loue) appeares,*
  That thought himſelfe exil'd.
Whence might all theſe loud Ioyes grow?
Whence might Myrth, and Banquet's flow?
But that hee's come (hee's come) I know.
  Faire Fortune thou haſt ſmil'd.

2.

Giue to theſe blind windowes, Eyes;
Daze the Stars, and mocke the Skies,

And let vs two (vs two) deuife,
  To lauifh our beft Treafures
Crowne our Wifhes with Content,
Meete our Soules in fweet confent,
And let this night (this night) bee fpent
  In all aboundant pleafures.

  Prince. Oh good morrow Lady,
I come to tell you newes!
  Lauret. They are wellcome to me my Lord.
  Prin. You know the Princeffe *Iulia* was fuppos'd
To bee adulterate———
  Lauret. So we haue heard it rumor'd.
  Prin. Oh but faire friend, fhe was indeed bely'd!
And I this morning rofe from her chaft bed:
But wherefore fweet caft you that blufhing fmile?
But you haue broak promife with me: For you told me
That the fame day and houre I tooke my Bride,
You fhould Inioy a Princely Husband.
  Lauret. Trew
My Lord, I did.
  Prin. And are you married then?
  Lauret. And lay with him laft night.
  Prin. Is hee off fortunes?
  Lauret. That you may foone coniecture by this gift.
  Prin. What haue you then, fome tokens that were his?
  Lauret. Some few my Lord, amongft the reft, this diamond
Hee put vpon my finger.
  Prin. You amaze mee!
Yet Rings may bee alike: If then your husband
Bee of fuch ftate and fortunes, What dowre are you allotted.
  Lauret. Sir, ten thoufand crownes by th' yeere.
  Prin. I gaue no more vnto my *Iulia.*
But where is the fecurity you haue

For the performance of it?
 Lauret. See here, My Lord,
Sir, Is not that fufficient for a dowry?
 Prin. This is the Indenture that I gaue to *Iulia*;
Preethee *Lauretta*, but refolue me true,
How came you by this Charter?
 Lauret. Pardon great Prince; for all that loue you
  fpake
To *Iulia*, you whifper'd in my eare:
Shee is vnchaft; which, left you fhould haue found,
Her father fent mee here, fiue hundred crownes
By *Stroza*; but neither his gold, nor all
His fly temptations, could one whit mooue mee;
Onely the loue I euer bare your honour,
Made me not prife my owne. No luftfull appetite
Made me attempt fuch an ambitious practife,
As to afpire vnto your bed my Lord.
 Prin. Rife, doe not weepe, Oh I am ftrangely
  rapt
Into deepe ftrange confufion?
 Moun. *Millaine* fhould know, were it my cafe my
  Lord,
A better Prince then hee fhould not wrong me.
 Prin. I haue bethought already how to beare
  mee;
This Charter and this Ring, faire Loue, keepe you;
And when I fend for you, you fhall repaire
Vnto the Court: This all I fhall inioyne you.
 Lauret. Great Sir, I fhall.
 Prin. Come *Mounfieur*, now 'tis caft,
Reuenge neere rules, fo it be found at laft.
         Exeunt omnes.

  Enter the two Dukes with Iulia, Stroza *and*
     attendants.

 Milla. Who faw the Prince laft? Is't a cuftome
  with him
To rife thus early?

Floren. Sir, hee neuer ſleepes
Longer then th' day, nor keepes his bed by Sunne:
'Tis not the loue of the faireſt Lady liues,
Can make him leaue his morning exerciſe.
　Iulia. He neuer exercis'd with me, I'm ſure;
I might haue layne as ſafe, free, and vntoucht,
By any Lady liuing.

Enter the Prince *and* Mounſi.

　Prince. Pardon Lords,
I haue ſtay'd you long, your bleſsing royall Father.
My cuſtome is, euer to riſe before
A womans houre: Now heare me ſpeake my Lords,
I'm married to a Lady, whoſe chaſte honour,
Reports and falſe Suggeſtions, did inforce me
To call in publike queſtion; but that we leaue
Vnto our laſt nights reſt.
　Stro. True my good Lord;
But did you find me faulty?
　Prin. I doe proteſt, my Lords, I boſom'd with
As true and chaſte a Virgin, as ere lodg'd
Within a Princes armes; All this I vow
As I am Royall.
　Stro. All's well my Lord?
　Milla. All's excellent *Stroza.*
　Princ. Now for amends and publike ſatisfaction,
For the foule wrong I did her, queſtioning
Her Vertue, Ile confirme her dowre, and that
Before I eate: Sweet Lady, reach the Charter
I gaue you laſt night, 'fore you were full mine?
　Iulia. I receiu'd none Sir.
　Prin. Sweet, will you tell mee that?
With which you did receiue a Ring the Duke
My father gaue me.
　Iulia. When?
　Prince. Laſt night.
　Iulia. Where?
　Prince. In your Bed.

Iulir. 'Twas in my dreame then.
Prince. Being broad awake.
Stro. I like not this: I smell a Rat.
Milla. *Stroza*, I feare too.
Stro. Brazen fore-head, Wilt
Thou leaue me now: 'Tis true my Lord. You did
Receiue them both, Haue you forgot sweet Lady,
This very morning, that you gaue them both
To me? The Princesse iested, to see how
You woo'd but take it.
Moun. Excellent Villaine!
Prince. 'Twas well put off:
'Tis strange shee's so forgetfull: I prethee *Stroza*
Where are they?
Stroza. Where are they? they are——
Prince. Where?
Why studdy you?
Stro. They are there——
Prince. Where man?
Stro. I posted them
To *Millaine*, sent them safe, dare you not trust my
    word.
Prince. Not till I see my deeds.
Stro. By one oth' Princes Traine.
Prince. See which of the Traine is wanting.
Moun. I shall my Lord.
Stro. I would I were in *Turkey*.
Milla. Would I were on horse-backe.
Prin. Nay, looke not you deiected beautious
    Bride,
For this is done onely to honour you.

Enter a Seruing-man with a child in a couered Dish.

Gent. The Prince, my Master, hearing your so-
    lemnities,
Hath sent this dish, to adde a present to
Your royall Feasts, wishing himselfe therein
To be a wellcome guest.

Prince. Your Mafters name?
Gent. Prince *Parma.*
Prince. Giue this Gentleman
A 100. crownes: This will much grace our banquet.
   Flo. Ther's in that difh, fome Morrall.
   Milla. Comming from him,
Meethinks it fhould be feafon'd with fome ftrange
And dangerous poyfon: Touch't not, my Lord.
   Flo. There fhould be more in't, then a feafting difh;
What's here, a Child?
   Iulia. O my perplexed heart!
   Pri. Upon his breft ther's fomething writ, Ile read it.

   'Tis fit, if Iuftice bee not quite exil'd
   That he that wedds the mother, keepe the child.

This Child was fent to me.
   Stro. From whom? whom, *Parma?* breake the baftards necke,
As I would doe the Fathers, were hee here.
   Prin. Sure fpare't for the Mothers fake; t'was fent to vs: *Enter* Mounfieur.
Which of the trayne is wanting?
   Moun. None my Lord.
   Prin. Stroza, where is this Charter and the Ring?
   Stro. I know of none.
   Moun. Why, t'was confeft.
   Stro. Right, I confeft it; but your grace muft know,
'Twas but to pleafe your humour, which began
To grow into fome violence.
   Moun. I can forbeare no longer; Impudent *Stroza,*
Thou art a Villaine, periur'd, and forfworne:
That Duke difhonourable; and fhee vnchaft:
Befides, thou hyredft a Virgin in her roome;
(Slaue as thou art) to bofome with the Prince;

Gau'ſt her fiue hundred Crownes. That this is true,
I will maintaine by combat.

Stro. That I did this? Hee lies below his en-
trayles,
That dares to braue mee with ſuch a proud affront:
And in the honour of my Prince and Countrey
I will approoue thee recreant.

Prin. A ſtrife, that nought ſaue combat can defide,
The cauſe ſo full of doubts, and intricate.
See, they are both arm'd, and euenly, without odds,
Saue what the iuſtice of the cauſe can yeeld.

Exit Mounſieur *and* Stroza.

Enter Prince Parma.

Par. Bee't no intruſion held, if a ſtrange Prince
(Setting behind, all complementall leaue)
Amongſt ſtrange Princes enters: Let me know
Which is the Prince of *Florence?*

Prince. Wee are hee.

Parm. And *Parma?*

Iuli. *Parma?*

Prince. Excuſe mee Sir,
I know him not: But if I much miſtake not,
Wee are late indebted to you for a preſent.

Parm. It was a gift, I ſhould bee loath to part with,
But vpon good conditions. Am I then
To all a ſtranger: Doe you not know mee Lady?

Milla. Heare him not ſpeake, I charge thee by thine honor?

Prince. *Parma* ſpeake, and if thy ſpeech was bent to mee?

Parm. Ere I proceede, let mee behold this babe;
Nere a Nurſe heere? Pray hand it you ſweete Lady,
Till I find out a Mother.

Milla. Touch it not,
I charge thee on my bleſsing.

Iulia. Pardon Sir,
It well becomes my handling.
  Prince. *Parma* proceede.
  Parm. Then *Florence* know, thou haſt wrong'd me
    beyond thought;
Shipwrackt my Honour, and my Fame; nay ſtrumpeted
Her, whom I tearme my Bride.
  Prince. 'Tis falſe, I neuer ſaue with one imbrac'd,
And her, I found to be moſt truely chaſt.
  Parm. Then It maintaine: Haſt thou a Wife
    heere?
  Prince. Yes.
  Parm. Then Ile approue her to bee none of
    thine,
That thou haſt fetch't her from anothers armes.
Nay more, that ſhee's vnchaſt?
  Prin. Know *Parma*, thou haſt kindled ſuch a
    Flame,
That all the Oceans billowes ſcarce can quench:
Bee that our quarrells ground.
  Florence. Princes, forbeare:
Firſt ſee the Iſſue of the former Combat,
Before more blood you hazard.
  Prince. Wee are pleaſed.
  Parm. And wee content.

Enter Stroza *and the* Mounſieur, *they fight, and*
    Stroza *is ouercome.*

  Moun. Yeeld thy ſelfe recreant villaine, or thou
    dy'ſt.
  Stro. Saue mee, I will confeſſe; Is *Parma* heere?
  Parm. Yes, heere we are.
  Stro. I falſely ſtuft thy head with Iealouſies,
And for ſome priuate ends of my reuenge,
Diſgrac'd the Generall, and ſet odds betwixt
Lauretta and the Princeſſe: All theſe miſchiefes
Proceede from my ſuggeſtions.
  Milla. Damne him for it.

Stro. Is that your kindneſſe? giue me leaue to liue,
Bee't but to taynt his honour.
　Prince. Tell mee *Stroza*,
Was *Iulia* chaſte?
　Str. No.
　Prince. Did her Father know it?
　Str. Yes, and more too: I had the Gold from him,
To bribe the Generalls daughter.
　Florence. Iniuries,
Beyond the thought of man.
　Milla. Which wee'le no longer ſtriue with, ſince the heauens
Haue laid that ope moſt plaine and palpable,
Which moſt wee thought to conceale.
　Prince. Will *Parma* fight?
　Parm. Reſolue mee firſt? Was *Iulia* found chaſt?
　Priece. I heere proteſt, wee parted both, as cleere,
As at our firſt encounter.
　Parm. Then I accept her,
If you my Lord bee pleaſ'd ſo to part with her.
　Prince. Willingly.
　Iulia. Now haue I my deſires: Had I withall,
The Princely babe I boare.
　Parm. See *Iulia*,
Whom thy hard-hearted Father doom'd to death,
My care hath ſtill conſerued, Imbrace it Lady;
Nay, tis thy owne nere feare it.
　Prince. Then Prince *Parma*,
With your words Ile proceed.
'Tis fit all Iuſtice bee not quite exil'd,
That hee that wedds the Mother keepe the child.
　Florence. But Peeres, the Virgin that this *Stroza* hired
To Iuſtifie theſe wrongs?
　Prince. At hand my Lord:
Mounſieur conduct them hither?
　Moun. I ſhall Sir.

Milla. The Generalls Wife and Daughter.

Enter Lauretta, Wife, *and* Clowne.

Clow. Yes and their man too; all that's left of him.

Prince. This the Maide,
To whom I am so bound?

Lauret. Oh let me lie
As prostrate at your foot in Vassallage,
As I was at your pleasure.

Prince. Sweete arise.

Clow. Your Lordship hath bin vp already, when shee was downe: I hope if the thing you wott of goe no worse forward then it hath begun, and that you take charge of my young Lady, you neede not be altogether vnmindfull of her Gentleman-Vsher.

Florence. Of what birth is that Lady?

Milla. Euen the least
Enuy can speake, Shee is a Souldiers Daughter,
Descended from a noble parentage.

Wife. Who with her mother,
Thus kneeles to him, as to their Soueraigne,
Intreating grace and pittie.

Milla. You haue both:
Sure, sure, the heauens for our Ingratitude,
To noble *Sforza*, our braue generall,
Hath thus crost our proceedings; which to recom-
  pence,
Wee'le take you vnto our best patronage.

Wife. *Millaine* is honorable.

Prince. But by your fauour Sir,
This must bee our owne charge.

Florence. With which we are pleas'd.

Iulia. *Stroza* was cause of all, but his submission
Hath sau'd him from our hate, arise in grace.
Whil'st we thus greete *Lauretta.*

Lauret. Royall Princesse,
I still shall be your hand-maide.

Stroza. Who would ſtriue,
To bee a villaine, when the good thus thriue?
  Prince, You crowne me with your wiſhes, Royall
    father;
My Miſtris firſt, and next my bed-fellow,
And now my Bride moſt welcome. Excellent Sir,
Imbrace the *Millaine* Duke, whil'ſt I change hand
With Princely *Parma*; *Iulia*, once my Wife?
Backe to your husband I returne you chaſt:
Mounſieur, bee ſtill our friend: You our kind Mother:
And let ſucceeding Ages, thus much ſay:
Neuer was Maiden-head better giuen away.

Exeunt omnes.

F I N I S.

The Epilogue.

NEw Playes, are like new Fashions; If they
    take?
Followed and worne: And happy's hee can make
First into'th Garbe: But when they once haue past
Censure, and proue not well, they seldome last.
Our Play is new, but whether shaped well
In Act or Scane, Iudge you, you best can tell:
Wee hope the best, and 'tis our least of feare,
That any thing but comely should shew heere;
    However Gentlemen, 'tis in your powers,
    To make it last; or weare out, in two houres.

The late Lancashire VVITCHES.

A well received Comedy, lately Acted at the *Globe* on the *Banke-side*, by the Kings Majesties Actors.

WRITTEN,
By THOM. HEYVVOOD,
AND
RICHARD BROOME.

Aut prodesse solent, aut delectare.

LONDON,
Printed by *Thomas Harper* for *Benjamin Fisher*, and are to be sold at his Shop at the Signe of the *Talbot*, without *Aldersgate*.
1634.

THE PROLOGVE.

Orrantoes *failing, and no foot poſt late
Poſſeſſing us with Newes of forraine State,*
*No accidents abroad worthy Relation
Arriving here, we are forc'd from our owne Nation
To ground the Scene that's now in agitation.
The Project unto many here well knowne;
Thoſe Witches the fat Iaylor brought to Towne,
An Argument ſo thin, perſons ſo low
Can neither yeeld much matter, nor great ſhow.
Expect no more than can from ſuch be rais'd,
So may the Scene paſſe pardon'd, though not prais'd.*

ACTVS, I.   SCENA, I.

Enter Master Arthur, *Mr.* Shakstone, *Mr.* Bantam :
(*as from hunting.*)

Arthur.

As ever sport of expectation
Thus crost in th' height.
   Shak. Tush these are accidents all game
       is subject to.
  Arth. So you may call them
Chances, or crosses, or what else you please,
But for my part, Ile hold them prodigies,
As things transcending Nature.
  Bantam. O you speake this,
Because a Hare hath crost you.
  Arth. A Hare ? a Witch, or rather a Divell I
    think.
For tell me Gentlemen, was't possible
In such a faire course, and no covert neere,
We in pursuit, and she in constant view,
Our eyes not wandring but all bent that way,
The Dogs in chase, she ready to be ceas'd,
And at the instant, when I durst have layd
My life to gage, my Dog had pincht her, then
To vanish into nothing !
  Shak. Somewhat strange,
But not as you inforce it.
  Arth. Make it plaine
That I am in an error, sure I am

That I about me have no borrow'd eyes.
They are mine owne, and Matches.
   Bant. She might find
Some Muse as then not visible to us,
And escape that way.
   Shak. Perhaps some Foxe had earth'd there,
And though it be not common, for I seldome
Have knowne or heard the like, there squat her selfe,
And so her scape appeare but Naturall,
Which you proclaime a Wonder.
   Arth. Well well Gentlemen,
Be you of your own faith, but what I see
And is to me apparent, being in sence,
My wits about me, no way tost nor troubled,
To that will I give credit.
   Bant. Come, come, all men
Were never of one minde, nor I of yours.
   Shak. To leave this argument, are you resolv'd
Where we shall dine to day?
   Arth. Yes where we purpos'd.
   Bant. That was with Master *Generous*.
   Arth. True, the same.
And where a loving welcome is presum'd,
Whose liberall Table's never unprepar'd,
Nor he of guests unfurnisht, of his meanes,
There's none can beare it with a braver port,
And keepe his state unshaken, one who fels not
Nor covets he to purchase, holds his owne
Without oppressing others, alwayes prest
To indeere to him any knowne Gentleman
In whom he finds good parts.
   Bant. A Character not common in this age.
   Brth. I cannot wind him up
Vnto the least part of his noble worth.
Tis far above my strength.

Enter Whetstone.

   Shak. See who comes yonder,

A fourth, to make us a full Meſſe of gueſts
At Maſter *Generous* Table.

Arth. Tuſh let him paſſe,
He is not worth our luring, a meere Coxcombe,
It is a way to call our wits in queſtion,
To have him ſeene amongſt us.

Baut. He hath ſpy'd us,
There is no way to evade him.

Arth. That's my griefe ;
A moſt notorious lyar, out upon him,

Shak. Let's ſet the beſt face on't.

Whet. What Gentlemen? all mine old acquaintance?
A whole triplicity of friends together? nay then
'Tis three to one we ſhall not ſoone part Company.

Shak. Sweet Mr. *Whetſtone.*

Bant. Dainty Mr. *Whetſtone.*

Arth. Delicate Maſter *Whetſtone.*

Whet. You ſay right, Mr. *Whetſtone* I have bin, Mr. *Whetſtone* I am, and Mr. *Whetſtone* I ſhall be, and thoſe that know me, know withall that I have not my name for nothing, I am hee whom all the brave Blades of the Country uſe to whet their wits upon ; ſweet Mr. *Shakton*, dainty Mr. *Bantham*, and dainty Mr. *Arthur*, and how, and how, what all luſtick, all froligozone? I know, you are going to my Vncles to dinner, and ſo am I too, What ſhall we all make one randevous there, you need not doubt of your welcome.

Shak. No doubt at all kind Mr. *Whetſtone*; but we have not ſeene you of late, you are growne a great ſtranger amongſt us, I deſire ſometimes to give you a viſit ; I pray where do you lye?

Whet. Where doe I lye? why ſometimes in one place, and then againe in another, I love to ſhift lodgings ; but moſt conſtantly, wherefoere I dine or ſup, there doe I lye?

Arth. I never heard that word proceed from him I durſt call truth till now.

Whet. But where fo ever I lye 'tis no matter for that,
I pray you fay, and fay truth, are not you three now Going to dinner to my Vncles?

Bant. I thinke you are a Witch Mafter *Whetftone*.

Whet. How? A Witch Gentlemen? I hope you doe not meane to abufe me, though at this time (if report be true) there are too many of them here in our Country, but I am fure I look like no fuch ugly Creature.

Shak. It feemes then you are of opinion that there are Witches, for mine own part, I can hardly be induc'd to think there is any fuch kinde of people.

Whet. No fuch kinde of people! I pray you tell me Gentlemen, did never any one of you know my Mother?

Arth. Why was your Mother a Witch?

Whet. I doe not fay as Witches goe now a dayes, for they for the moft part are ugly old Beldams, but fhe was a lufty young Laffe, and by her owne report, by her beauty and faire lookes bewitcht my Father.

Bant. It feemes then your Mother was rather a yong wanton wench, than an old wither'd witch.

Whet. You fay right, and know withall I come of two ancient Families, for as I am a *Whetftone* by the Mother-fide, fo I am a *By-blow* by the Fathers.

Arth. It appeares then by your difcourfe, that you came in at the window.

Whet. I would have you thinke I fcorne like my Granams Cat to leape over the Hatch.

Shak. He hath confeft himfelfe to be a Baftard.

Arth. And I beleeve't as a notorious truth.

Whet. Howfoever I was begot, here you fee I am, And if my Parents went to it without feare or wit, What can I helpe it.

Arth. Very probable, for as he was got without feare,
So it is apparent he was borne without wit.

Whet. Gentlemen, it feemes you have fome private

bufineffe amongſt your felves, which I am not willing to interrupt, I know not how the day goes with you, but for mine owne part, my ſtomacke is now much upon 12. You know what houre my Vncle keepes, and I love ever to bee fet before the firſt grace, I am going before, fpeake, ſhall I acquaint him with your comming after?

Shak. We meane this day to fee what fare he keepes.

Whet. And you know it is his cuſtome to fare well, And in that refpect I think I may be his kinfman, And fo farewell Gentlemen, Ile be your fore-runner, To give him notice of your vifite.

Bant. And fo intyre us to you.

Shak. Sweet Mr. *Whetſtone*.

Arth. Kind Mr. *Byblow*.

Whet. I fee you are perfect both in my name & firname; I have bin ever bound unto you, for which I will at this time be your *Novcrint*, and give him notice that you *Vniverfi* will bee with him *per præfentes*, and that I take to be prefently. *Exit.*

Arth. Farewell *As in præfenti*.

Shak. It feemes hee's peece of a Scholler.

Arth. What becaufe he hath read a little Scriveners Latine, hee never proceeded farther in his Accidence than to *Mentiri non eſt meum;* and that was fuch a hard Leſſon to learne, that he ſtucke at *mentiri*; and cu'd never reach to *non eſt meum*: fince, a meere Ignaro, and not worth acknowledgement.

Bant. Are thefe then the beſt parts he can boaſt of?

Arth. As you fee him now, fo ſhall you finde him ever: all in one ſtrain, there is one only thing which I wonder he left out.

Shak. And what might that be.

Arth. Of the fame affinity with the reſt. At every fecond word, he is commonly boaſting either of his Aunt or his Vncle.

Enter Mr. Generous.

Bant. You name him in good time, see where he comes.

Gener. Gentlemen, Welcome, t'is a word I use,
From me expect no further complement:
Nor do I name it often at one meeting,
Once spoke (to those that understand me best,
And know I alwaies purpose as I speake)
Hath ever yet suffiz'd: so let it you;
Nor doe I love that common phrase of guests,
As we make bold, or we are troublesome,
Wee take you unprovided, and the like;
I know you understanding Gentlemen,
And knowing me, cannot persuade your selves
With me you shall be troublesome or bold,
But still provided for my worthy friends,
Amongst whom you are lifted.

Arth. Noble sir,
You generously instruct us, and to expresse
We can be your apt schollers: in a word
Wee come to dine with you.

Gener. And Gentlemen,
Such plainnesse doth best pleafe me, I had notice
Of so much by my kinsman, and to show
How lovingly I tooke it, instantly
Rose from my chayre to meet you at the gate,
And be my selfe your usher; nor shall you finde
Being set to meat, that i'le excuse your fare,[1]
Or say, I am sory it falls out so poore;
And had I knowne your comming wee'd have had
Such things and such, nor blame my Cooke, to say
This dish or that hath not bin sauc'st with care:
Words, fitting best a common Hostesse mouth,
When ther's perhaps some just cause of dislike,
But not the table of a Gentleman;
Nor is it my wives custome; in a word,
Take what you find, & so———

Arth. Sir without flattery
You may be call'd the fole furviving fonne
Of long fince banifht Hofpitality.
   Gener. In that you pleafe me not: But Gentlemen
I hope to be beholden unto you all,
Which if I proove, Ile be a gratefull debtor.
   Bant. Wherein good fir.
   Gener. I ever ftudied plaineneffe, and truth withall.
   Shak. I pray expreffe your felfe.
   Gener. In few I fhall. I know this youth to whom my wife is Aunt
Is (as you needs muft finde him) weake and fhallow:
Dull, as his name, and what for kindred fake
We note not, or at leaft, are loath to fee,
Is unto fuch well-knowing Gentlemen
Moft groffely vifible: If for my fake
You will but feeme to winke at thefe his wants,
At leaft at table before us his friends,
I fhall receive it as a courtefie
Not foone to be forgot.
   Arth. Prefume it fir.
   Gener. Now when you pleafe pray Enter Gentlemen.
   Arth. Would thefe my friends prepare the way before,
To be refolved of one thing before dinner
Would fomething adde unto mine appetite,
Shall I intreat you fo much.
   Bant. O fir you may command us.
   Gener. I'th meane time
Prepare your ftomackes with a bowle of Sacke.
                               Exit Bant. & Shak.
My Cellar can affoord it; now Mr. *Arthur*
Pray freely fpeake your thoughts.
   Arth. I come not fir
To preffe a promife from you, tak't not fo,
Rather to prompt your memory in a motion

Made to you not long fince.
　Gener. Waſt not about
A Mannor, the beſt part of your eſtate,
Morgag'd to one ſlips no advantages
Which you would have redeem'd.
　Arth. True ſir the ſame.
　Gener. And as I thinke, I promiſt at that time
To become bound with you, or if the uſurer
(A baſe, yet the beſt title I can give him)
Perhaps ſhould queſtion that ſecurity,
To have the money ready. Waſt not ſo?
　Arth. It was to that purpoſe wee diſcourſt.
　Gener. Provided, to have the Writings in my cuſtody.
Elſe how ſhould I ſecure mine owne eſtate.
　Arth. To denie that, I ſhould appeare to th' World
Stupid, and of no braine.
　Gener. Your monie's ready.
　Arth. And I remaine a man oblig'd to you.
Beyond all utterance.
　Gener. Make then your word good
By ſpeaking it no further, onely this,
It ſeemes your Vncle you truſted in ſo far
Hath failed your expectation.
　Arth. Sir he hath, not that he is unwilling or unable,
But at this time unfit to be ſolicited;
For to the Countries wonder, and my ſorrow,
Hee is much to be pitied.
　Gener. Why I intreat you.
　Arth. Becauſe hee's late become the ſole diſcourſe
Of all the countrey; for of a man reſpected
For his diſcretion and knowne gravitie,
As maſter of a govern'd Family,
The houſe (as if the ridge were fixt below,
And groundſils lifted up to make the roofe)
All now turn'd topſie turvy.

Gener. Strange, but how?

Arth. In fuch a retrograde & prepofterous way
As feldome hath bin heard of. I thinke never.

Gener. Can you difcourfe the manner?

Arth. The good man,
In all obedience kneeles vnto his fon,
Hee with an auftere brow commands his father.
The wife prefumes not in the daughters fight
Without a prepared courtefie. The girle, fhee
Expects it as a dutie; chides her mother
Who quakes and trembles at each word fhe fpeaks,
And what's as ftrange, the Maid fhe dominiers
O're her yong miftris, who is aw'd by her.
The fon to whom the Father creeps and bends,
Stands in as much feare of the groome his man.
All in fuch rare diforder, that in fome
As it breeds pitty, and in others wonder;
So in the moft part laughter.

Gener. How thinke you might this come.

Arth. T'is thought by Witchcraft.

Gener. They that thinke fo dreame,
For my beliefe is, no fuch thing can be,
A madneffe you may call it: Dinner ftayes,
That done, the beft part of the afternoone
Wee'le fpend about your bufineffe. *Exeunt.*

Enter old Seely and Doughty.

Seely. Nay but underftand me neighbor *Doughty.*

Doughty. Good mafter *Seely* I do underftand you, and over and over underftand you fo much, that I could e'ene blufh at your fondneffe; and had I a fonne to ferve mee fo, I would coniure a divell out of him.

See. Alas he is my childe.

Dough. No, you are his childe to live in feare of him, indeed they fay oldmen become children againe, but before I would become my childes childe, and make my foot my head, I would stand upon my head, and kick my heels at the skies.

Enter Gregory.

See. You do not know what an only son is, O see, he comes now if you can appease his anger toward me, you shall doe an act of timely charity.

Dou. It is an office that I am but weakly versd in
To plead to a sonne in the fathers behalfe,
Blesse me what lookes the devilish young Rascall
Frights the poore man withall!

Greg. I wonder at your confidence, and how you dare appeare before me.

Doug. A brave beginning.

See. O sonne be patient.

Greg. It is right reverend councell, I thanke you for it, I shall study patience shall I, while you practice waies to begger mee, shall I?

Dough. Very handsome.

See. If ever I transgresse in the like againe—

Greg. I have taken your word too often sir and neither can nor will forbeare you longer.

Dough. What not your Father Mr. *Gregory*?

Greg. Whats that to you sir?

Dough. Pray tell me then sir, how many yeares has hee to serve you.

Gre. What do you bring your spokesman now, your advocat,
What fee goes out of my estate now, for his Oratory?

Dou. Come I must tell you, you forget your selfe,
And in this foule unnaturall strife wherein
You trample on your father. You are falne
Below humanitie. Y'are so beneath
The title of a sonne, you cannot clayme

To be a man, and let me tell you were you mine
Thou shouldst not eat but on thy knees before me.
    Sec. O this is not the way.
This is to raise Impatience into fury.
I do not seek his quiet for my ease,
I can beare all his chidings and his threats,
And take them well, very exceeding well,
And finde they do me good on my owne part,
Indeed they do reclaim me from those errors
That might impeach his fortunes, but I feare
Th' unquiet strife within him hurts himselfe,
And wastes or weakens Nature by the breach
Of moderate sleepe and dyet ; and I can
No lesse than grieve to finde my weaknesses
To be the cause of his affliction,
And see the danger of his health and being.
    Dou. Alas poore man ? Can you stand open ey'd
Or dry ey'd either at this now in a Father ?
    Greg. Why, if it grieve you, you may look of ont,
I have seen more than this twice twenty times,
And have as often bin deceiv'd by his dissimulations
I can see nothing mended.
    Dou. He is a happy sire that has brought vp his son to this.
    Sec. All shall be mended son content your selfe,
But this time forget but this last fault.
    Greg. Yes, for a new one to morrow.
    Dou. Pray Mr. *Gregory* forget it, you see how
Submissive your poore penitent is, forget it,
Forget it, put it out o' your head, knocke it
Out of your braines. I protest, if my Father,
Nay if my fathers dogge should haue sayd
As much to me, I should have embrac't him.
What was the trespasse ? It c'ud not be so hainous.
    Greg. Wel Sir, you now shall be a Iudge for all your jeering.

Was it a fatherly part thinke you having a fonne
To offer to enter in bonds for his nephew, fo to indanger
My eftate to redeeme his morgage.

See. But I did it not fonne?

Gre. I know it very well, but your dotage had done it,
If my care had not prevented it.

Dou. Is that the bufineffe: why if he had done it, had hee not bin fufficiently fecur'd in having the morgage made over to himfelfe.

Greg. He does nothing but practice waies to undo himfelfe, and me: a very fpendthrift, a prodigall fire, hee was at the Ale club but tother day, and fpent a foure-penny.

See. 'Tis gone and paft fonne.

Greg. Can you hold your peace fir? And not long ago at the wine he fpent his teafter, and two pence to the piper, that was brave was it not?

Sec. Truely we were civily merry. But I have left it.

Greg. Your civility have you not? For no longer agoe than laft holiday evening he gam'd away eight double ring'd tokens on a rubbers at bowles with the Curate, and fome of his idle companions.

Dou. Fie Mr. *Gregory Seely* is this feemely in a fonne.
You'le have a rod for the childe your father fhortly I feare.
Alaffe did hee make it cry? Give me a ftroke and Ile beat him,
Bleffe me, they make me almoft as mad as themfelves.

Greg. 'Twere good you would meddle with your own matters fir.

See. Sonne, fonne.

Greg. Sir, Sir, as I am not beholden to you for houfe or Land, for it has ftood in the name of my anceſtry the *Seelyes* above two hundred yeares, ſo will I look you leave all as you found it.

Enter Lawrence.

Law. What is the matter con yeow tell?

Greg. O *Lawrence*, welcom, Thou wilt make al wel I am ſure.

Law. Yie whick way con yeow tell, but what the foule evill doone yee, heres ſick an a din.

Dou. Art thou his man fellow ha? that talkeſt thus to him.

Law. Yie ſir, and what ma' yoew o'that, he mainteynes me to rule him, and i'le deu't, or ma' the heart weary o'the weambe on him.

Dou. This is quite upſide downe, the ſonne controlls the father, and the man overcrowes his maſters coxſcombe, ſure they are all bewitch'd.

Greg. 'Twas but ſo, truely *Lawrence*; the peeviſh old man vex't me, for which I did my duty, in telling him his owne, and Mr. *Doughty* here maintaines him againſt me.

Law. I forbodden yeow to meddle with the old carle, and let me alone with him, yet yeow ſtill be at him, hee ſerv'd yeow but weell to baſt ye for't, ant he were ſtronk enough, but an I faw foule with yee an I ſwaddle yee not favorly may my girts braſt.

See. Prethee good *Lawrence* be gentle and do not fright thy Maſter ſo.

Law. Yie, at your command anon.

See. Enough good *Lawrence*, you have ſaid enough.

Law. How trow yeou that? A fine World when a man cannot be whyet at heame for buſie brain'd neighpors.

Dou. I know not what to ſay to any thing here, This cannot be but witchcraft.

Enter Ioane and Winny.

Win. I cannot indure it nor I will not indure it.

Dou. Hey day! the daughter upon the mother too.

Win. One of us two, chufe you which, muſt leave the houſe, wee are not to live together I fee that, but I will know, if there be Law in *Lancaſhire* for't, which is fit firſt to depart the houſe or the World, the mother or the daughter.

Ioane. Daughter I fay.

Win. Do you fay the daughter, for that word I fay the mother, unleſſe you can prove me the eldeſt, as my diſcretion almoſt warrant it, I fay the mother ſhall out of the houſe or take ſuch courſes in it as ſhall fort with ſuch a honſe and ſuch a daughter.

Joan. Daughter I fay, I wil take any courſe ſo thou wilt leave thy paſſion; indeed it hurts thee childe, I'le ſing and be merry, weare as fine clothes, and as delicate dreſſings as thou wilt have me, ſo thou wilt pacifie thy ſelfe, and be at peace with me.

Wiu. O will you ſo, in ſo doing I may chance to looke upon you, Is this a fit habite for a handfome young Gentlewomans mother, as I hope to be a Lady, you look like one o' the Scottiſh wayward ſiſters, O my hart has got the hickup, and all lookes greene about me, a merry ſong now mother, and thou ſhalt be my white girle.

Ioan. Ha, ha, ha! ſhe's overcome with joy at my converſion.

Dough. She is moſt evidently bewitcht.

Song.

Joane. *There was a deft Lad and a Laſſe fell in love,*
  with a fa la la, fa la la, Langtidowne dilly;

With kissing and toying this Maiden did prove,
  with a fa la la, fa la la, Langtidowne dilly;
So wide i' th wast, and her Belly so high,
That unto her mother the Maiden did cry,
  O Langtidowne dilly, O Langtidowne dilly,
  fa la la Langtidowne, Langtidowne dilly.

Enter Parnell.

Parn. Thus wodden yeou doone and I were dead, but while I live yoeu fadge not on it, is this aw the warke yeou con fine ?

Dough. Now comes the Mayd to set her Mistresses to work.

Win. Nay pri'thee sweet *Parnell*, I was but chiding the old wife for her unhandsomnesse, and would have been at my work presently, she tels me now she will weare fine things, and I shall dresse her head as I list.

Dough. Here's a house well govern'd ?

Parn. Dresse me no dressings, lessen I dresse yeou beth, and learne a new lesson with a wainon right now, han I bin a servant here this halfe dozen o' yeares, and con I see yeou idler then my selve !

Ioa. Win. Nay prithee sweet *Parnell* content, & hark thee—

Dough. I have knowne this, and till very lately, as well govern'd a Family as the Country yeilds, and now what a nest of severall humors it is growne, and all divellish ones, sure all the Witches in the Country, have their hands in this home-spun medley; and there be no few 'tis thought.

Parn. Yie, yie, ye shall ye shall, another time, but not naw I thonke yeou, yeou shall as soone pisse and paddle in't, as flap me in the mouth with an awd Petticoat, or a new paire o shoine, to be whyet, I cannot be whyet, nor I wonnot be whyet, to see sicky doings I.

Lawr. Hold thy prattle *Parnell*, aw's com'd about as weene a had it, wotst thou what *Parnell* ? wotst thou what ? o deare, wotst thou what ?

Parn. What's the fond wexen waild trow I.

Lawr. We han bin in love thefe three yeares, and ever wee had not enough, now is it com'd about that our love fhall be at an end for ever, and a day, for wee mun wed may hunny, we mun wed.

Parn. What the Deowl ayles the lymmer lowne, bin thy braines broke lowfe trow I.

Lawr. Sick a waddin was there never i' Loncofhire as ween couple at on Monday newft.

Par. Awa awaw, fayn yeou this fickerly, or done you but jaum me?

Lawr. I jaum thee not nor flam thee not, 'tis all as true as booke, here's both our Mafters have confented and concloyded, and our Miftreffes mun yeild toyt, to put aw houfe and lond and aw they have into our hands.

Parn. Awa, awaw.

Lawr. And we mun marry and be mafter and dame of aw.

Parn. Awa, awaw.

Lawr. And theyn be our Sijourners, becaufe they are weary of the world, to live in frendiblenefle, and fee what will come on't.

Par. Awa, awaw, agone.

Seel. & Greg. Nay 'tis true *Parnell*, here's both our hands on't, and give you joy.

Ioan & Win. And ours too, and 'twill be fine Ifackins.

Parn. Whaw, whaw, whaw, whaw!

Dou. Here's a mad bufineffe towards.

Seel. I will befpeake the Guefts.

Greg. And I the meat:

Ioan. I'le dreffe the dinner, though I drip my fweat.

Law. My care fhall fumptuous parrelments provide.

Win. And my beft art fhall trickly trim the Bride.

Parn. Whaw, whaw, whaw, whaw.

Greg. Ile get choyce mufick for the merriment.

Dough. And I will waite with wonder the event.
Parn. Whaw, whaw, whaw, whaw.

Actvs, II. Scæna, I.

Enter 4. Witches : (*feverally.*)

All. Oe! well met, well met.
   Meg. What new devife, what dainty ftraine
More for our myrth now then our gaine,
Shall we in practice put.
  Meg. Nay dame,
Before we play another game,
We muft a little laugh and thanke
Our feat familiars for the pranck
They playd us laft.
  Mawd. Or they will miffe
Vs in our next plot, if for this
They find not their reward.
  Meg. 'Tis right.
  Gil. Therefore fing *Mawd*, and call each fpright.
Come away, and take thy duggy.

Enter foure Spirits.

  Meg. Come my *Mamilion* like a Puggy.
  Mawd. And come my puckling take thy teat,
Your travels have deferv'd your meat.
  Meg. Now upon the Churles ground
On which we're met, lets dance a round ;
That Cocle, Darnell, Poppia wild,
May choake his graine, and fill the field.

Gil. Now spirits fly about the taske,
That we projected in our Maske. *Exit Spirlts.*
Meg. Now let us laugh to thinke upon
The feat which we have so lately done,
In the distraction we have set
In *Seelyes* house; which shall beget
Wonder and sorrow 'mongst our foes,
Whilst we make laughter of their woes.
All. Ha, ha ha!
Meg. I can but laugh now to foresee,
The fruits of their perplexity.
Gil. Of *Seely's* family?
Meg. I, I, I, the Father to the Sonne doth cry,
The Sonne rebukes the Father old;
The Daughter at the mother Scold,
The wife the husband check and chide,
But that's no wonder, through the wide
World 'tis common.
Gil. But to be short,
The wedding must bring on the sport
Betwixt the hare-brayn'd man and mayd,
Master and dame that over-sway'd.
All. Ha, ha, ha!
Meg. Enough, enough,
Our sides are charm'd, or else this stuffe
Would laughter-cracke them; let's away
About the Iig: we dance to day,
To spoyle the Hunters sport.
Gil. I that,
Be now the subject of our chat.
Meg. Then list yee well, the Hunters are
This day by vow to kill a Hare,
Or else the sport they will forsweare;
And hang their Dogs up.
Mawd. Stay, but where
Must the long threatned hare be found?
Gill. They'l search in yonder Meadow ground.
Meg. There will I be, and like a wily Wat,
Vntill they put me up; ile squat.
Gill. I and my puckling will a brace

Of Greyhounds be, fit for the race;
And linger where we may be tane
Vp for the courfe in the by-lane;
Then will we lead their Dogs a courfe,
And every man and every horfe;
Vntill they breake their necks, and fay—
   All. The Divell on Dun is rid this way. Ha, ha,
      ha, ha.
   Meg. All the doubt can be but this,
That if by chance of me they miffe,
And ftart another Hare.
   Gil. Then we'll not run
But finde fome way how to be gone.
I fhal know thee *Peg*, by thy griffel'd gut.
   Meg. And I you *Gilian* by your gaunt thin gut.
But where will *Mawd* beftow her felfe to day?
   Mawd. O' th' Steeple top; Ile fit and fee you
      play.   *Exeunt.*

*Enter Mr. Generous, Arthur, Bantam, Shakftone,
           and Whetftone.*

   Gener. At meeting, and at parting Gentlemen,
I onely make ufe of that generall word,
So frequent at all feafts, and that but once; y'are wel-
    come.
You are fo, all of you, and I intreat you
Take notice of that fpeciall bufineffe,
Betwixt this Gentleman my friend, and I.
About the Morgage, to which writings drawne,
Your hands are witneffe.
   Bant. & Shak. We acknowledge it.
   Whet. My hand is there too, for a man cannot fet
to his Marke, but it may be call'd his hand; I am a
Gentleman both wayes, and it hath been held that it
is the part of a Gentleman, to write a fcurvie hand.
   Bant. You write Sir like your felfe.
   Gener. Pray take no notice of his ignorance,
You know what I foretold you.

Arth. 'Tis confeft,
But for that word by you fo feldome fpoke
By us fo freely on your part perform'd,
We hold us much ingag'd.
Gener. I pray, no complement,
It is a thing I doe not ufe my felfe,
Nor doe I love't in others.
Arth. For my part,
Could I at once diffolve my felfe to words
And after turne them into matter; fuch
And of that ftrength, as to attract the attention
Of all the curious, and moft itching eares
Of this our Crittick age; it cou'd not make
A theame amounting to your noble worth:
You feeme to me to fuper-arrogate,
Supplying the defects of all your kindred
To innoble your own name: I now have done Sir.
Whet. Hey day, this Gentleman fpeakes like a
Country Parfon that had tooke his text out of *Ovids*
Metamorphofis.
Gener. Sir, you Hyperbolize;
And I coo'd chide you for't, but whil'ft you connive
At this my Kinfman, I fhall winke at you;
'Twil prove an equall match.
Gener. Your name proclaimes
To be fuch as it fpeakes, you, *Generous.*
Gener. Still in that ftraine!
Arth. Sir, fir, whilft you perfever to be good
I muft continue gratefull.
Gener. Gentlemen,
The greateft part of this day you fee is fpent
In reading deeds, conveyances, and bonds,
With fcaling and fubfcribing; will you now
Take part of a bad Supper.
Arth. We are like travellers
And where fuch bayt, they doe not ufe to Inne.
Our love and fervice to you.
Gener. The firft I accept,
The Laft I entertaine not, farewell Gentlemen.

Arth. We'l try if we can finde in our way home
When Hares come from their coverts, to reliffe,
A courfe or too.

Whet. Say you fo Gentlemen, nay then I am for your company ftill, 'tis fayd Hares are like ! Hermophrodites, one while Male, and another Female, and that which begets this yeare, brings young ones the next; which fome think to be the reafon that witches take their fhapes fo oft : Nay if I lye *Pliny* lyes too, but come, now I have light upon you, I cannot fo lightly leave you farewell Vnckle.

Gener. Cozen I wifh you would confort your felfe,
With fuch men ever, and make them your Prefident
For a more Gentile carriage.

Arth. Good Mafter *Generous*——
                    Exeunt, manet Generous.

Enter Robert.

Gen. *Robin.*
Rob. Sir.
Gen. Goe call your Miftreffe hither.
Rob. My Miftreffe Sir, I doe call her Miftreffe, as I doe call you Mafter, but if you would have me call my Miftreffe to my Mafter, I may call lowd enough before fhe can heare me.

Gener. Why fhe's not deafe I hope, I am fure fince Dinner
She had her hearing perfect.

Rob. And fo fhe may have at Supper too for ought I know, but I can affure you fhe is not now within my call.

Gener. Sirrah you trifle, give me the Key oth' Stable.
I will goe fee my Gelding ; i'th' meane time
Goe feeke her out, fay fhe fhall finde me there.

Rob. To tell you true fir, I fhall neither finde my Miftreffe here, nor you your Gelding there.

Gener. Ha! how comes that to paffe?

Rob. Whilft you were bufie about your writings, fhe came and commanded me to faddle your Beaft, and fayd fhe would ride abroad to take the ayre.

Gener. Which of your fellowes did fhe take along to wayte on her?

Rob. None fir.

Gener. None! hath fhe us'd it often?

Rob. Oftner I am fure then fhe goes to Church, and leave out Wednefdayes and Fridayes.

Gener. And ftill alone?

Rob. If you call that alone, when no body rides in her company.

Gen. But what times hath fhe forted for thefe journeyes?

Rob. Commonly when you are abroad, aud fometimes when you are full of bufineffe at home.

Gener. To ride out often and alone, what fayth fhe
When fhe takes horfe, and at her backe returne?

Rob. Onely conjures me that I fhall keepe it from you, then clappes me in the fift with fome fmall piece of filver, and then a Fifh cannot be more filent then I.

Gen. I know her a good woman and well bred,
Of an unqueftion'd carriage, well reputed
Amongft her neighbors, reckon'd with the beft
And ore me moft indulgent; though in many
Such things might breed a doubt and jealoufie,
Yet I hatch no fuch phrenfie. Yet to prevent
The fmalleft jarre that might betwixt us happen;
Give her no notice that I know thus much.
Befides I charge thee, when fhe craves him next
He be deny'd: if fhe be vext or mov'd
Doe not thou feare, Ile interpofe my felfe
Betwixt thee and her anger, as you tender
Your duty and my fervice, fee this done.

Rob. Now you have expreft your minde, I know what I have to doe; firft, not to tell her what I have

told you, & next to keep her side-faddle from comming upon your Gueldings backe; but howfoever it is
like to hinder me of many a round tefter.

Gener. As oft as thou deny'ft her, fo oft clayme
That teafter from me, 't fhall be roundly payd.

Rob. You fay well in that fir, I dare take your
word, you are an honeft Gentleman, and my Mafter;
and now take mine as I am your true fervant, before
fhe fhall backe your Guelding again in your abfence,
while I have the charge of his keeping; fhe fhall ride
me, or Ile ride her.

Gen. So much for that. Sirrah my Butler tels
me
My Seller is drunke dry, I meane thofe Bottles
Of Sack and Claret, are all empty growne
And I have guefts to morrow, my choyfe friends.
Take the gray Nag i'th' ftable, and thofe Bottles
Fill at *Lancafter*, there where you ufe to fetch it.

Rob. Good newes for me, I fhall fir.

Gen. O *Robin*, it comes fhort of that pure liquor
We drunke laft Terme in London at the *Myter*
In *Fleet-ftreet*, thou remembreft it; me thought
It was the very fpirit of the Grape,
Meere quinteffence of Wine.

Rob. Yes fir, I fo remember it, that moft certaine
it is I never fhal forget it, my mouth waters ever fince
when I but think on't, whilft you were at fupper
above, the drawer had me down into the Cellar below,
I know the way in againe if I fee't, but at that time to
finde the way out againe, I had the help of more eies
than mine owne: is the tafte of that *Ipfitate* ftil in
your pallat fir?

Gener. What then? But vaine are wifhes, take
thofe bottles
And fee them fil'd where I command you fir.

Rob. I fhall: never c'ud I have met with fuch a
faire opportunity: for iuft in the mid way lies my
fweet-heart, as lovely a laffe as any is in *Lancafhire*,

and kisses as sweetly: i'le see her going or comming, i'le have one smouch at thy lips, and bee with thee to bring *Mal Spencer*. *Exit.*

Gen. Go hasten your return, what he hath told me
Touching my wife is somewhat strange, no matter
Bee't as it will, it shall not trouble me.
Shee hath not lyen so long so neere my side,
That now I should be jealous.

Enter a souldier.

Sold. You seeme sir a Gentleman of quality, and no doubt but in your youth have beene acquainted with affaires military, in your very lookes there appeares bounty, and in your person humanity. Pleafe you to vouchsafe the tender of some small courtesie to help to beare a souldier into his countrey.

Gen. Though I could tax you friend, & justly too
For begging 'gainst the Statute in that name,
Yet I have ever bin of that compassion,
Where I see want, rather to pittie it
Than to use power. Where hast thou serv'd?

Sold. With the Russian against the Polack, a heavy war, and hath brought me to this hard fate. I was tooke prisoner by the Pole, & after some few weeks of durance, got both my freedom and passe. I have it about me to show, please you to vouchsafe the perusall.

Gener. It shall not need. What Countreyman.

Sold. Yorkeshire sir. Many a sharp battell by land, and many a sharpe storme at sea, many a long mile, and many a short meale, I have travel'd and suffer'd ere I c'ud reach thus far, I beseech you sir take my poore & wretched case into your worships noble consideration.

Gener. Perhaps thou lov'st this wandring life
To be an idle loitering begger, than
To eat of thine owne labour.

Sold. I fir! Loitering I defie fir, I hate lazineſſe as I do leproſie: It is the next way to breed the ſcurvie, put mee to hedge, ditch, plow, threſh, dig, delve, any thing: your worſhip ſhal find that I love nothing leſſe than loitering.

Gener. Friend thou ſpeakeſt well.

Enter Miller (his hands and face ſcratcht, and bloudy.

Miller. Your Mill quoth he, if ever you take me in your mill againe, i'le give you leave to caſt my fleſh to the dogges, and grinde my bones to pouder, betwixt the Milſtones. Cats do you call them, for their hugeneſſe they might bee cat a mountaines, and for their clawes, I thinke I have it here in red and white to ſhew, I pray looke here ſir, a murreine take them, ile be ſworne they have ſcratcht, where I am ſure it itcht not.

Gener. How cam'ſt thou in this pickle?

Mil. You ſee ſir, and what you ſee, I have felt, & am come to give you to underſtand i'le not indure ſuch another night if you would give mee your mill for nothing, they ſay we Millers are theeves: but I c'ud as ſoone bee hangd as ſteale one piece of a nap all the night long, good Landlord provide your ſelfe of a new tenant, the noiſe of ſuch catterwawling, & ſuch ſcratching and clawing, before I would indure againe, i'le bee tyed to the ſaile when the winde blowes ſharpeſt, and they flie ſwifteſt, till I be torne into as many fitters as I have toes and fingers.

Sold. I was a Miller my ſelfe before I was a ſouldier. What one of my own trade ſhould be ſo poorely ſpirited frighted with cats?
Sir truſt me with the Mill that he forſakes.
Here is a blade that hangs upon this belt
That ſpight of all theſe Rats, Cats, Wezells, Witches
Or Dogges, or Divels, ſhall ſo coniure them
I'le quiet my poſſeſſion.

Gener. Well fpoke Souldier.
I like thy refolution. Fellow, you then
Have given the Mill quite over.
  Mil. Over and over, here I utterly renounce it;
nor would I ftay in it longer, if you would give me
your whole eftate; nay if I fay it, you may take my
word Landlord.
  Sold. I pray fir dare you truft your mill with me.
  Gener. I dare, but I am loth, my reafons thefe.
For many moneths, fcarce any one hath lien there
But have bin ftrangely frighted in his fleepe,
Or from his warme bed drawne into the floore,
Or clawd and fcratcht, as thou feeft this poore man,
So much, that it ftood long untenanted,
Till he late undertooke it, now thine eies
Witneffe how he hath fped.
  Sold. Give me the keies, ile ftand it all danger.
  Gener. 'Tis a match: deliver them.
  Mil. Mary withall my heart, and I am glad, I am
fo rid of em.   *Exeunt.*

Enter Boy with a fwitch.

  Boy. Now I have gathered Bullies, and fild my
bellie pretty well, i'le goe fee fome fport. There are
gentlemen courfing in the medow hard by; and 'tis a
game that I love better than going to Schoole ten to
one.

*Enter an invifible fpirit. F. Adfon with a brace of
greyhounds.*

  What have we here a brace of Greyhounds broke
loofe from their mafters: it muft needs be fo, for they
have both their Collers and flippes about their neckes.
Now I looke better upon them, me thinks I fhould
know them, and fo I do: thefe are Mr. *Robinfons*
dogges, that dwels fome two miles off, i'le take them
up, & lead them home to their mafter; it may be

ſomthing in my way, for he is as liberall a gentleman, as any is in our countrie. Come *Hector*, come. Now if I c'ud but ſtart a Hare by the way, kill her, and carry her home to my ſupper, I ſhould thinke I had made a better afternoones worke of it than gathering of bullies. Come poore curres along with me.   *Exit.*

Enter Arthur, Bantam, Shakstone, and Whetſtone.

Arth. My Dog as yours.
Shak. For what?
Arth. A piece.
Shak. 'Tis done.
Bant. I ſay the pide dog ſhall outſtrip the browne.
Whe. And ile take the brown dogs part againſt the pide.
Bant. Yes when hee's at his lap youle take his part.
Arth. *Bantam* forbeare him prethee.
Bant. He talks ſo like an Aſſe I have not patience to indure his non ſence.
Whet. The browne dogge for two peeces.
Bant. Of what?
Whet. Of what you dare; name them from the laſt Farthings with the double rings, to the late Coy'ned peeces which they ſay are all counterfeit.
Bant. Well ſir, I take you: will you cover theſe, give them into the hands of either of theſe two gentlemen.
Whet. What needs that? doe you thinke my word and my money is not all one?
Bant. And weigh alike: both many graines too light.
Shak. Enough of that, I preſume Mr. *Whetſtone*, you are not ignorant what belongs to the ſport of hunting.
Whet. I thinke I have reaſon, for I have bin at the death of more Hares.

Bant. More then you shed the last fall of the leafe.

Whet. More then any man here I am sure. I should be loath at these yeares to be ignorant of hairing or whoring. I knew a hare close hunted, clime a tree.

Bant. To finde out birds nests.

Whet. Another leap into a river, nothing appearing above water, save onely the tip of her nose to take breath.

Shak. Nay that's verie likely, for no man can fish with an angle but his Line must be made of hare.

Whet. You say right, I knew another, who to escape the Dogges hath taken a house, and leapt in at a window.

Bant. It is thought you came into the World that way.

Whet. How meane you that?

Bant. Becaufe you are a bastard.

Whet. Bastard! O base.

Bant. And thou art base all over.

Arth. Needs must I now condemne your indiscretion.

To set your wit against his.

Whe. Bastard? that shall be tried; well Gentlemen concerning Hare-hunting you might have hard more, if he had had the grace to have said lesse, but for the word Bastard, if I do not tell my Vncle, I and my Aunt too, either when I would speake ought or goe of the skore for any thing, let me never be trusted, they are older than I, and what know I, but they might bee by when I was begot; but if thou *Bantam* do'st not heare of this with both thine eares, if thou hast them still, and not lost them by scribling, instead of *Whet-stone* call me *Grinde-stone*, and for *By-blow*, *Bulfinch*. Gentlemen, for two of you your companie is faire and honest; but for you *Bantam*, remember and take notice also, that I am a bastard, and so much i'le testifie to my Aunt and Vncle. *Exit.*

The Witches of Lancashire.

Arth. What have you done, 'twill grieve the good old Gentleman, to heare him baffled thus.

Bant. I was in a cold fweat ready to faint The time he ftaid amongft us.

Shak. But come, now the Hare is found and ftarted,
She fhall have Law, fo to our fport.   *Exit.*

Enter Boy with the Greyhounds.

A Hare, a Hare, halloe, halloe, the Divell take thefe curres, will they not ftir, halloe, halloe, there, there, there, what are they growne fo lither and fo lazie? Are Mr. *Robinfons* dogges turn'd tykes with a wanion? the Hare is yet in fight, halloe, halloe, mary hang you for a couple of mungrils (if you were worth hanging), & have you ferv'd me thus? nay then ile ferve you with the like fauce, you fhall to the next bufh, there will I tie you, and ufe you like a couple of curs as you are, & though not lafh you, yet lafh you whileft my fwitch will hold, nay fince you have left your fpeed, ile fee if I can put fpirit into you, and put you in remembrance what halloe, halloe meanes.

As he beats them, there appeares before him, Gooddy Dickifon, *and the Boy upon the dogs, going in.*

Now bleffe me heaven, one of the Greyhounds turn'd into a woman, the other into a boy! The lad I never faw before, but her I know well; it is my gammer *Dickifon.*

G. Dick. Sirah, you have ferv'd me well to fwindge me thus.
You yong rogue, you haue vs'd me like a dog.

Boy. When you had put your felf into a dogs skin, I pray how c'ud I help it; but gammer are not you a Witch? if you bee, I beg upon my knees you will not hurt me.

Dickif. Stand up my boie, for thou fhalt have no harme.

Be silent, speake of nothing thou hast seene.
And here's a shilling for thee.

Boy. Ile have none of your money gammer, becaufe you are a Witch : and now fhe is out of her foure leg'd fhape, ile fee if with my two legs I can out-run her.

Dickif. Nay, firra, though you be yong, and I old, you are not fo nimble, nor I fo lame, but I can overtake you.

Boy. But Gammer what do you meane to do with me
Now you have me ?

Dickif. To hugge thee, ftroke thee, and embrace thee thus,
And teach thee twentie thoufand prety things.
So thou tell no tales ; and boy this night
Thou muft along with me to a brave feaft.

Boy. Not I gammer indeedla, I dare not ftay out late,
My father is a fell man, and if I bee out long, vill both chide and beat me.

Dickif. Not firra, then perforce thou fhalt along,
This bridle helps me ftill at need,
And fhall provide us of a fteed.
Now firra, take your fhape and be
Prepar'd to hurrie him and me. *Exit.*
Now looke and tell mee wher's the lad become.

Boy. The boy is vanifht, and I can fee nothing in his ftead
But a white horfe readie fadled and bridled.

Dickif. And thats the horfe we muft beftride,
On which both thou and I muft ride,
Thou boy before and I behinde,
The earth we tread not, but the winde,
For we muft progreffe through the aire,
And I will bring thee to fuch fare
As thou ne're faw'ft, up and away,
For now no longer we can ftay.

She catches him up, & turning round. Exit.

Boy. Help, help.

Enter Robin and Mall.

Thanks my sweet Mall for thy courteous entertainment, thy creame, thy cheese-cakes, and every good thing, this, this, & this for all. *kisse.*

Mal. But why in such hast good *Robin* ?

Robin. I confesse my stay with thee is sweet to mee, but I must spur Cutt the faster for't, to be at home in the morning, I have yet to Lancaster to ride to night, and this my bandileer of bottles, to fill to night, and then halfe a score mile to ride by curriecombe time, i' the morning, or the old man chides *Mal.*

Mal. Hee shall not chide thee, feare it not.

Robin. Pray *Bacchus* I may please him with his wine, which will be the hardest thing to do ; for since hee was last at London and tasted the Divinitie of the Miter, scarce any liquour in Lancashire will go downe with him, sure, sure he will never be a Puritane, he holds so well with the Miter.

Mal. Well *Robert*, I find your love by your haste from me, ile undertake you shal be at Lancaster, & twise as far, & yet at home time enough, and be rul'd by me.

Rob. Thou art a witty rogue, and thinkst to make me believe any thing, because I saw thee make thy broome sweepe the house without hands t'other day.

Mal. You shall see more than that presently, because you shall beleeve me ; you know the house is all a bed here : and I dare not be mist in the morning. Besides, I must be at the wedding of *Lawrence* and *Parnell* to morrow.

Rob. I your old sweet heart *Lawrence* ? Old love will not be forgotten.

Mal. I care not for the losse of him, but if I fit him not hang me : but to the point, if I goe with you to night, and help you to as good wine as your master desires, and you keepe your time with him, you will give me a pinte for my company.

Rob. Thy belly full wench.

Mal. I'le but take up my milk payle and leave it in the field, till our comming backe in the morning, and wee'll away.

Rob. Goe fetch it quickly then.

Mal. No *Robert*, rather than leave your company so long, it shall come to me.

Rob. I would but see that.

The Payle goes.

Mal. Looke yonder, what do you thinke on't.

Rob. Light, it comes; and I do thinke there is so much of the Divell in't as will turne all the milke shall come in't these seven yeares, and make it burne too, till it stinke worse than than the Proverbe of the Bishops foot.

Mal. Looke you sir, heere I have it, will you get up and away.

Rob. My horse is gone, nay prithee *Mal.* thou hast set him away, leave thy Roguerie.

Mal. Looke againe.

Rob. There stands a black long-sided jade: mine was a truss'd gray.

Mal. Yours was too short to carrie double such a journey. Get up I say, you shall have your owne againe i'th morning.

Rob. Nay but, nay but.

Mal. Nay, and you stand butting now, i'le leave you to look your horse. Payle on afore to the field, and staie till I come.

Rob. Come away then, hey for *Lancaster*: stand up.   *Exeunt.*

ACTVS, III.   SCENA, I.

Enter old Seely *and* Ioane *his wife.*

Seely.

Ome away wife, come away, and let us be ready to breake the Cake over the Brides head at her entrance; we will have the honour of it, we that have playd the Steward and Cooke at home, though we loſt Church by't, and ſaw not Parſon *Knit-knot* doe his office, but wee ſhall ſee all the houſe rites perform'd; and—— oh what a day of jollity and tranquility is here towards?

Ioane. You are ſo frolick and ſo cranck now, upon the truce is taken amongſt us, becauſe our wrangling ſhall not wrong the Wedding, but take heed (you were beſt) how ye behave your ſelfe, leſt a day to come may pay for all.

Seel. I feare nothing, and I hope to dye in this humor.

Joan. Oh how hot am I! rather then I would dreſſe ſuch another dinner this twelve moneth, I would wiſh Wedding quite out of this yeares Almanack.

Seel. Ile fetch a Cup of Sack Wife——

Ioan. How brag he is of his liberty, but the holy-day carries it.

Seel. Here, here ſweet-heart, they are long me thinks a comming, the Bels have rung out this halfe houre, harke now the wind brings the found of them fweetly againe.

Ioan. They ring backwards me thinks.

Seel. Ifack they doe, fure the greateſt fire in the Pariſh is in our Kitchin, and there's no harme done yet, no 'tis fome merry conceit of the ſtretch-ropes the Ringers, now they have done, and now the Wedding comes, hearke, the Fidlers and all, now have I liv'd to fee a day, come, take our ſtand, and be ready for the Bride-cake, which we will fo cracke and crumble upon her crowne: o they come, they come.

Enter Muſitians, Lawrence, Parnell, Win. Mal. Spencer, two Country Laſſes, Doughty, Greg. Arthur, Shakton, Bantam, and Whetſtone.

All. Ioy, health, and children to the married paire.

Lawr. & Parn. We thanke you all.

Lawr. So pray come in and fare.

Parn. As well as we and taſte of every cate:

Lawr. With bonny Bridegroome and his lovely mate.

Arth. This begins bravely.

Doug. They agree better then the Bels eene now, 'slid they rung tunably till we were all out of the Church, and then they clatter'd as the divell had beene in the Bellfry: on in the name of Wedlocke, Fidlers on.

Lawr. On with your melody.

Bant. Enter the Gates with joy,
And as you enter play the fack of *Troy*.

The Fidlers paſſe through, and play the battle.

The Spirit appeares.

Ioan. Welcome Bride *Parnell.*

Seel. Bridegroome *Lawrence* eke,
In you before, for we this cake muſt breake.

Exit Lawrence.

Over the Bride——
> *As they lift up the Cake, the Spirit snatches it,*
> *and poures down bran.*

Forgi' me—what's become
O' th' Cake wife!

Ioan. It flipt out of my hand, and is falne into crums I think.

Dought. Crums? the divell of crum is here, but bran, nothing but bran, what prodigie is this?

Parn. Is my beft Brides Cake come to this? o wea warth it.

> *Exit Parn. Seely, Joane, and Maides.*

Whet. How daintily the Brides haire is powder'd with it.

Arth. My haire ftands an end to fee it.

Bant. And mine.

Shak. I was never fo amaz'd!

Dough. What can it meane?

Greg. Pax, I think not on't, 'tis but fome of my Father and Mothers roguery, this is a Law-day with 'em, to doe what they lift.

Whet. I never feare any thing, fo long as my Aunt has but bidden me thinke of her, and fhe'll warrant me.

Dough. Well Gentlemen, let's follow the reft in, and feare nothing yet, the houfe fmels well of good cheere.

Seel. Gentlemen, will it pleafe you draw neere, the guefts are now all come, and the houfe almoft full, meat's taken up.

Dough. We were now comming.

Seel. But fonne *Gregory*, Nephew *Arthur*, and the reft of the young Gentlemen, I fhall take it for a favor if you will (it is an office which very good Gentlemen doe in this Country) accompane the Bridegroome in ferving the meat.

All. With all our hearts.

Seely. Nay neighbor *Doughty*, your yeares fhall excufe you.

Dough. Peugh, I am not fo old but I can carry more meate then I can eate, if the young rafcals coo'd carry their drinke as well, the Country would be quieter——

Knock within, as at drefler.

Seel. Well fare your hearts,—the drefler calls in Gentlemen, *Exeunt Gentlemen.*
'Tis a bufie time, yet will I review the Bill of fare, for this dayes dinner——(*Reades*) for 40. people of the beft quality, 4. mefles of meat; *viz.* a leg of Mutton in plum-broth, a difh of Marrow-bones, a Capon in white-broth, a Surloyne of beefe, a Pig, a Goofe, a Turkie, and two Pyes: for the fecond courfe, to every mefle 4. Chickens in a difh, a couple of Rabbets, Cuftard, Flawn, Florentines, and ftewd pruines,—all very good Country fare, and for my credit,——

Enter Mufitians playing before, Lawrence, Doughty, Arthur, Shakton, Bantam, Whetftone, and Gregory, with difhes: A Spirit (over the doore) does fome action to the difhes as they enter.

The fervice enters, O well fayd Muficke, play up the meat to the Table till all be ferv'd in, Ile fee it pafie in anfwer to my bill.

Dough. Hold up your head Mr. Bridegroome.

Lawr. On afore Fidlers, my doubler cewles in my honds.

Seely. *Imprimus*, a leg of Mutton in plum-broth, —how now Mr. Bridegroome, what carry you?

Lawr. 'Twere hot eene now, but now it's caw'd as a fteane.

Seel. A ftone, 'tis horne man.

Lawr. Aw—— *Exit Fidlers.*

Seely. It was Mutton, but now 'tis the horns on't.

Lawr. Aw where's my Bride—— *Exit.*

Dough. 'Zookes, I brought as good a Surloyne of Beefe from the Drefler as Knife coo'd be put to, and fee——Ile ftay i' this houfe no longer.

Arth. And if this were not a Capon in white broth, I am one i' the Coope.

Shak. All, all's transform'd, looke you what I have!

Bant. And I.

Whet. And I! Yet I feare nothing thank my Aunt.

Greg. I had a Pie that is not open'd yet, Ile fee what's in that—live Birds as true as I live, look where they flye! *Exit Spirit.*

Dough. Witches, live Witches, the houfe is full of witches, if we love our lives let's out on't.

Enter Joane and Win.

Ioan. O husband, O guefts, O fonne, O Gentlemen, fuch a chance in a Kitchin was never heard of, all the meat is flowne out o' the chimney top I thinke, and nothing inftead of it, but Snakes, Batts, Frogs, Beetles, Hornets, and Humble-bees; all the Sallets are turn'd to Iewes-eares, Mufhromes, and Puckfifts; and all the Cuftards into Cowfheards!

Dought. What fhall we doe, dare we ftay any longer?

Arth. Dare we! why not, I defie all Witches, and all their workes; their power on our meat, cannot reach our perfons.

Whet. I fay fo too, and fo my Aunt ever told me, fo long I will feare nothing; be not afrayd Mr. *Doughty.*

Dough. Zookes, I feare nothing living that I can fee more then you, and that's nothing at all, but to thinke of thefe invifible mifchiefes, troubles me I confeffe.

Arth. Sir I will not goe about to over-rule your reafon, but for my part I will not out of a houfe on a Bridall day, till I fee the laft man borne.

Dough. Zookes thou art fo brave a fellow that I I will ftick to thee, and if we come off handfomely,

I am an old Batchelour thou know'ſt, and muſt have an heyre, I like thy ſpirit, where's the Bride? where's the Bridegroome? where's the Muſicke? where be the Laſſes? ha' you any wine i' the houſe, though we make no dinner, lets try if we can make an afternoone.

Ioan. Nay ſir if you pleaſe to ſtay, now that the many are frighted away, I have ſome good cold meates, and halfe a dozen bottles of Wine.

Seel. And I will bid you welcome.

Dough. Say you me ſo, but will not your ſonne be angry, and your daughter chide you.

Greg. Feare not you that ſir, for look you I obey my Father.

Win. And I my Mother.

Ioan. And we are all at this inſtant as well and as ſenſible of our former errors, as you can wiſh us to be.

Dough. Na, if the Witches have but rob'd of your meat, and reſtor'd your reaſon, here has beene no hurt done to day, but this is ſtrange, and as great a wonder as the reſt to me.

Arth. It ſeemes though theſe Hags had power to make the Wedding cheere a *Deceptio viſus*, the former ſtore has ſcap'd 'em.

Dough. I am glad on't, but the divell good 'hem with my Surloyne, I thought to have ſet that by mine owne Trencher——But you have cold meat you ſay?

Joan. Yes Sir.

Dought. And Wine you ſay?

Ioan. Yes ſir.

Dought. I hope the Country wenches and the Fidlers are not gone.

Win. They are all here, and one the merrieſt Wench; that makes all the reſt ſo laugh and tickle.

Seel. Gentlemen will you in?

All. Agreed on all parts.

Dough. If not a Wedding we will make a Wake

on't, and away with the Witch; I feare nothing now you have your wits againe: but look you, hold 'em while you have 'em. *Exeunt.*

Enter Generous, and Robin, with a Paper.

Gener. I confeſſe thou haſt done a Wonder in fetching me ſo good Wine, but my good Servant *Robert*, goe not about to put a Myracle upon me, I will rather beleeve that *Lancaſter* affords this Wine, which I thought impoſſible till I taſted it, then that thou coo'dſt in one night fetch it from *London*.

Rob. I have known when you have held mee for an honeſt fellow, and would have beleev'd me.

Gener. Th' art a Knave to wiſh me to beleeve this, forgi' me, I would have ſworne if thou had'ſt ſtayd but time anſwerable for the journey (to his that flew to *Paris* and back to *London* in a day) it had been the ſame Wine, but it can never fall within the compaſſe of a Chriſtians beleefe, that thou cou'dſt ride above three hundred miles in 8. houres: You were no longer out, and upon one Horſe too, and in the Night too!

Rob. And carry a Wench behind me too, and did ſomething elſe too, but I muſt not ſpeak of her leſt I be divell-torne.

Gen. And fill thy bottles too, and come home halfe drunke too, for ſo thou art, thou wouldſt never a had ſuch a fancy elſe!

Rob. I am ſorry I have ſayd ſo much, and not let *Lancaſter* have the credit o' the Wine.

Gen. O are you ſo! and why have you abus'd me and your ſelfe then all this while, to glorifie the *Myter* in *Fleet-ſtreet*?

Rob. I could ſay ſir, that you might have the better opinion of the Wine, for there are a great many pallats in the Kingdome that can reliſh no Wine, unleſſe it be of ſuch a Taverne, and drawne by ſuch a Drawer——

Gen. I fayd, and I fay againe, if I were within ten mile of *London*, I durſt ſweare that this was *Myter* Wine, and drawn by honeſt *Iacke Paine.*

Rob. Nay then ſir I ſwore, and I ſweare againe, honeſt *Iack Paine* drew it.

Gener. Ha, ha, ha. if I coo'd beleeve there were ſuch a thing as Witchcraft, I ſhould thinke this ſlave were bewitch'd now with an opinion.

Rob. Much good doe you ſir, your Wine and your mirth, and my place for your next Groome, I deſire not to ſtay to be laught out of my opinion.

Gen. Nay be not angry *Robin*, we muſt not part ſo, and how does my honeſt Drawer? ha, ha, ha; and what newes at *London, Robin*? ha, ha, ha; but your ſtay was ſo ſhort 1 think you coo'd heare none, and ſuch your haſte home that you coo'd make none: is't not ſo *Robin*? ha, ha, ha, what a ſtrange fancy has good Wine begot in his head?

Rob. Now will I puſh him over and over with a peece of paper: Yes ſir, I have brought you ſomething from *London*.

Gen. Come on, now let me heare.

Rob. Your honeſt Drawer ſir, conſidering that you conſider'd him well for his good wine——

Gen. What ſhall we heare now?

Rob. Was very carefull to keepe or convay this paper to you, which it ſeemes you dropt in the roome there.

Gener. Bleſſe me! this paper belongs to me indeed, 'tis an acquittance, and all I have to ſhow for the payment of one hundred pound, I tooke great care for't, and coo'd not imagine where or how I might looſe it, but why may not this bee a tricke? this Knave may finde it when I loſt it, and conceale it till now to come over me withall. I will not trouble my thoughts with it further at this time, well *Robin* looke to your buſineſſe, and have a care of my Guelding. *Exit Generous.*

Robin. Yes Sir. I think I have netled him now,

but not as I was netled laſt night, three hundred Miles a Night upon a Rawbon'd Divell, as in my heart it was a Divell, and then a Wench that ſhar'd more o' my backe then the ſayd Divell did o' my Bum, this is ranke riding my Maſters: but why had I ſuch an itch to tell my Maſter of it, and that he ſhould beleeve it; I doe now wiſh that I had not told, and that hee will not beleeve it, for I dare not tell him the meanes: 'Sfoot my Wench and her friends the Fiends, will teare me to pieces if I diſcover her; a notable rogue, ſhe's at the Wedding now, for as good a Mayd as the beſt o' em——O my Miſtreſſe.

Enter Mrs. Generous, with a Bridle.

Mrs. Robin.
Rob. I Miſtreſſe.
Mrs. Quickly good *Robin*, the gray Guelding.
Rob. What other horſe you pleaſe Miſtreſſe.
Mrs. And why not that?
Rob. Truly Miſtreſſe pray pardon me, I muſt be plaine with you, I dare not deliver him you; my maſter has tane notice of the ill caſe you have brought him home in divers times.

Mrs. O is it ſo, and muſt he be made acquainted with my actions by you, and muſt I then be controll'd by him, and now by you; you are a ſawcy Groome.

Rob. You may ſay your pleaſure.
              He turnes from her.
Mrs. No ſir, Ile doe my pleaſure.
              She Bridles him.
Rob. Aw.
Mrs. Horſe, horſe, ſee thou be,
And where I point thee carry me.   *Exeunt Neighing.*

Enter Arthur, Shakſton, and Bantam.

Arth. Was there ever ſuch a medley of mirth, madneſſe, and drunkenneſſe, ſhuffled together.

Shak. Thy Vnckle and Aunt, old Mr. *Seely* and his wife, doe nothing but kiſſe and play together like Monkeyes.

Arth. Yes, they doe over-love one another now.

Bant. And young *Gregory* and his ſiſter doe as much over-doe their obedience now to their Parents.

Arth. And their Parents as much over-doat upon them, they are all as farre beyond their wits now in loving one another, as they were wide of them before in croſſing.

Shak. Yet this is the better madneſſe.

Bant. But the married couple that are both ſo daintily whitled, that now they are both mad to be a bed before Supper-time, and by and by he will, and ſhe wo' not : ſtreight ſhe will and he wo' not, the next minute they both forget they are married, and defie one another.

Arth. My ſides eene ake with laughter.

Shak. But the beſt ſport of all is, the old Batchelour Maſter *Doughty*, that was ſo cautious, & fear'd every thing to be witchcraft, is now wound up to ſuch a confidence that there is no ſuch thing, that hee dares the Divell doe his worſt, and will not out o' the houſe by all perſuaſion, and all for the love of the husbandmans daughter within, *Mal Spencer*.

Arth. There I am in ſome danger, he put me into halfe a beliefe I ſhall be his heire, pray love ſhee be not a witch to charme his love from mee. Of what condition is that wench do'ſt thou know her?

Sha. A little, but *Whetſtone* knowes her better.

Arth. Hang him rogue, he'le belye her, and ſpeak better than ſhe deſerves, for he's in love with her too. I ſaw old *Doughty* give him a box o' the eare for kiſſing her, and he turnd about as he did by thee yeſterday, and ſwore his Aunt ſhould know it.

Bant. Who would ha' thought that impudent rogue would have come among us after ſuch a baffle.

Sha. He told me, hee had complain'd to his Aunt on us, and that fhe would fpeak with us.

Arth. Wee will all to her, to patch vp the bufineffe, for the refpect I beare her husband, noble *Generous*.

Bant. Here he comes.

Enter Whetftone.

Arth. Hearke you Mr. *Byblow*, do you know the laffe within? What do you call her, *Mal Spencer*?

Whet. Sir, what I know i'le keepe to my felfe, a good civile merry harmleffe rogue fhe is, and comes to my Aunt often, and thats all I know by her.

Arth. You doe well to keepe it to your felfe fir.

Whet. And you may do well to queftion her if you dare. For the tefty old coxcombe that will not let her goe out of his hand.

Sha. Take heed, he's at your heels.

Enter Doughty, Mal, and two countrey Laffes.

Dough. Come away Wenches, where are you Gentlemen? Play Fidlers: lets have a dance, ha my little rogue.   *Kiffes Mal.*
Zookes what ayles thy nofe.

Mal. My nofe! Nothing fir.——*turnes about*——
Yet mee thought a flie toucht it. Did you fee any thing?

Dou. No, no, yet I would almoft ha' fworn, I would not have fprite or goblin blaft thy face, for all their kingdome. But hangt there is no fuch thing: Fidlers will you play?

Selengers Round.

Gentlemen will you dance?

All. With all our hearts.

Arth. But ftay wheres this houfhold?
This Family of love? Let's have them into the
   revels.

Dou. Hold a little then.

Sha. Here they come all
In a True-love knot.

Enter Seely, Ioane, Greg, Win.

Greg. O Father twentie times a day is too little to aske you bleſſing.

See. Goe too you are a raſcall: and you houſwife teach your daughter better manners: i'le ſhip you all for New England els.

Bant. The knot's untied, and this is another change.

Ioane. Yes I will teach her manners, or put her out to ſpin two penny tow: ſo you deare husband will but take mee into favor: i'le talke with you dame when the ſtrangers are gone.

Greg. Deare Father.

Win. Deare Mother.

Greg. Win. Deare Father and Mother pardon us but this time.

See. Ioa. Never, and therefore hold your peace.

Dough. Nay thats unreaſonable.

Greg. Win. Oh!—— *Weepe.*

See. But for your ſake i'le forbeare them, and beare with any thing this day.

Arth. Doe you note this? Now they are all worſe than ever they were, in a contrary vaine: What thinke you of Witchcraft now?

Dou. They are all naturall fooles man, I finde it now.
Art thou mad to dreame of Witchcraft?

Arth. He's as much chang'd and bewitcht as they I feare.

Dough. Hey day! Here comes the payre of boyld Lovers in Sorrell ſops.

Enter Lawrence and Parnell.

Lawr. Nay deare hunny, nay hunny, but eance, eance.

Par. Na, na, I han' fwarne, I han' fwarne, not a bit afore bed, and look yeou it's but now dauncing time.

Dough. Come away Bridegroome, wee'll ſtay your ſtomack with a daunce. Now maſters play a good: come my Laſſe wee'l ſhew them how 'tis.

Muſicke. Selengers round.

As they beginne to daunce, they play another tune, then fall into many.

Ar. Ban. Sha. Whether now, hoe?

Dou. Hey day! why you rogues.

Whet. What do's the Divell ride o' your Fiddle-ſtickes.

Dou. You drunken rogues, hold, hold, I ſay, and begin againe ſoberly the beginning of the World.

Muſicke. Every one a ſeverall tune.

Arth. Bant. Shak. Ha, ha, ha, How's this?

Bant. Every one a ſeverall tune.

Dou. This is ſomething towards it. I bad them play the beginning o' the World, and they play, I know not what.

Arth. No 'tis running o' the country ſeverall waies.

But what do you thinke on't. *Muſicke ceaſe.*

Dough. Thinke! I thinke they are drunke. Prithee doe not thou thinke of Witchcraft; for my part, I ſhall as ſoone thinke this maid one, as that theres any in *Lancaſhire*.

Mal. Ha, ha, ha.

Dough. Why do'ſt thou laugh?

Mal. To thinke this Bridegroome ſhould once ha' bin mine, but he ſhall rue it, ile hold him this point on't, and thats all I care for him.

Dough. A witty Rogue.

Whet. I tell you ſir, they ſay ſhee made a payle follow her t'other day up two payre of ſtayres.

Dough. You lying Rafcall.

Arth. O fir forget your anger.

Mal. Looke you Mr. Bridegroome, what my care provides for you.

Lawrence. What, a point?

Mal. Yes put it in your pocket, it may ftand you inftead anon, when all your points be tane away, to truffe up your trinkits, I meane your flopes withall.

Lawr. *Mal* for awd acquaintance I will ma' thy point a point of preferment. It fhan bee the Foreman of a haell Iewrie o' points, and right here will I weare it.

Par. Wy'a, wy'a, awd leove wo no be forgetten, but ay's never be jealous the mare for that.

Arth. Play fidlers any thing.

Dou. I, and lets fee your faces, that you play fairely with us.

Mufitians fhew themfelves above.

Fid. We do fir, as loud as we can poffibly.

Sha. Play out that we may heare you.

Fid. So we do fir, as loud as we can poffibly.

Dough. Doe you heare any thing?

All. Nothing not we fir.

Dough. 'Tis fo, the rogues are brib'd to croffe me, and their Fiddles fhall fuffer, I will breake em as fmall as the Bride cake was to day.

Arth. Looke you fir, they'l fave you a labour, they are doing it themfelves.

Whet. Oh brave Fidlers, there was never better fcuffling for the Tudberry Bull.

Mal. This is mother *Iohnfon* and Gooddy *Dickifons* roguerie, I finde it, but I cannot helpe it, yet I will have muficke: fir theres a Piper without, would be glad to earne money.

Whet. She has fpoke to purpofe, & whether this were witchcraft or not: I have heard my Aunt fay twentie times, that no Witchcraft can take hold of a *Lancaſhire* Bag-pipe, for it ſelfe is able to charme the Divell, ile fetch him.

Dough. Well ſaid, a good boy now; come bride and bridegroome, leave your kiſſing and fooling, and prepare to come into the daunce. Wee'le have a Horne-pipe, and then a poſſet and to bed when you pleaſe. Welcome Piper, blow till thy bagge cracke agen, a luſty Horne-pipe, and all into the daunce, nay young and old.

Daunce. Lawrence and Parnell reele in the daunce. At the end, Mal vaniſhes, and the piper.

All. Bravely performd.

Dou. Stay, wheres my laſſe?

Arth. Ban. Shak. Vaniſht, ſhe and the Piper both vaniſht, no bodie knowes how.

Dou. Now do I plainly perceive again, here has bin nothing but witcherie all this day; therfore into your poſſet, & agree among your ſelves as you can, ile out o' the houſe. And Gentlemen, if you love me or your ſelves, follow me.

Ar. Bant. Sha. Whet. I, I, Away, away.

Exeunt.

See. Now good ſon, wife and daughter, let me intreat you be not angry.

Win. O you are a trim mother are you not?

Ioa. Indeed childe, ile do ſo no more.

Greg. Now ſir, i'le talke with you, your champions are al gon.

Lawr. Weell ſir, and what wun yeou deow than?

Par. Whay, whay, whats here to doe? Come awaw, and whickly, and ſee us into our Brayd Chember, & delicatly ludgd togeder, or wee'l whap you out o' dores ith morne to ſijourne in the common, come away.

All. Wee follow yee. *Exeunt.*

Actvs, IIII. Scæna, I.

Enter Miſtreſſe Generous and Robin.

Now you this gingling bridle, if you see't agen? I wanted but a paire of gingling spurs to make you mend your pace, and put you into a sweat.

Robin. Yes, I have reaſon to know it after my hard journey, they ſay there be light women, but for your owne part, though you be merry. Yet I may be ſorry for your heavineſſe.

Mrs. Gener. I ſee thou art not quite tyr'd by ſhaking of thy ſelfe, 'tis a ſigne that as thou haſt brought mee hither, ſo thou art able to beare mee backe, and ſo you are like good *Robert*. You will not let me have your maſters gelding, you will not. Wel ſir, as you like this journey, ſo deny him to me hereafter.

Rob. You ſay well miſtreſſe, you have jaded me (a pox take you for a jade.) Now I bethinke my ſelfe how damnably did I ride laſt night, and how divelliſhly have I bin rid now.

Mrs. Doe you grumble you groome? Now the bridl's of, I turne thee to grazing, gramercy my good horſe, I have no better provender for thee at this time, thou hadſt beſt like *Æſops* Aſſe to feed upon Thiſtles, of which this place will affoord thee plenty. I am bid to a better banquet, which done, ile take thee up from graſſe, ſpur cutt, and make a ſhort cutt home. Farewell.

Robin. A pox upon your tayle.

Enter all the Witches and Mal, at ſeverall dores.

All. The Lady of the feaſt is come, welcome, welcome.

Mrs. Is all the cheare that was prepared to grace the wedding feaſt, yet come?

Gooddy Dick. Part of it's here.
The other we muſt pull for. But whats hee?

Mrs. My horſe, my horſe, ha, ha, ha.

All. Ha, ha, ha. *Exeunt.*

Rob. My horſe, my horſe, I would I were now ſome country Major, and in authority, to ſee if I would not venter to rowze your Satanicall ſiſterhood: Horſe, horſe, ſee thou be, & where I point thee, cary me: is that the trick on't? the divel himſelfe ſhall be her carrier next if I can ſhun her: & yet my Mr. will not beleeve theres any witches: theres no running away, for I neither know how nor whether, beſides to my thinking, theres a deepe ditch, & a hye quick-ſet about mee, how ſhall I paſſe the time? What place is this? it looks like an old barne: ile peep in at ſome cranny or other, and try if I can ſee what they are doing. Such a bevy of beldames did I never behold; and cramming like ſo many Cormorants: Marry choke you with a miſchiefe.

Gooddy Dickiſon. Whoope, whurre, heres a ſturre, never a cat, never a curre, but that we muſt have this demurre.

Mal. A ſecond courſe.

Mrs. Gen. Pull, and pull hard
For all that hath lately bin prepar'd
For the great wedding feaſt.

Mal. As chiefe.
Of *Doughtyes* Surloine of roſt Beefe.

All. Ha, ha, ha.

Meg. 'Tis come, 'tis come.

Mawd. Where hath it all this while beene?

Meg. Some
Delay hath kept it, now 'tis here,
For bottles next of wine and beere,
The Merchants cellers they ſhall pay for't.

Mrs. Gener. Well,
What ſod or roſt meat more, pray tell.

Good. Dick. Pul for the Poultry, Foule, & Fiſh,
For emptie ſhall not be a diſh.

Robin. A pox take them, muſt only they feed upon hot meat, and I upon nothing but cold ſallads.

Mrs. Gener. This meat is tedious, now ſome Farie,
Fetch what belongs unto the Dairie.

Mal. Thats Butter, Milk, Whey, Curds and Cheeſe,
Wee nothing by the bargaine leeſe.

All. Ha, ha, ha.

Goody Dickiſon. Boy, theres meat for you.

Boy. Thanke you.

Gooddy Dickiſ. And drinke too.

Meg. What Beaſt was by thee hither rid?

Mawd. A Badger nab.

Meg. And I beſtrid
A Porcupine that never prickt.

Mal. The dull ſides of a Beare I kickt.
I know how you rid Lady Nan.

Mrs. Gen. Ha, ha, ha, upon the knave my man.

Rob. A murrein take you, I am ſure my hoofes payd for't.

Boy. Meat lie there, for thou haſt no taſte, and drinke there, for thou haſt no reliſh, for in neither of them is there either ſalt or ſavour.

All. Pull for the poſſet, pull.

Robin. The brides poſſet on my life, nay if they come to their ſpoone meat once, I hope theil breake up their feaſt preſently.

Mrs. Gen. So thoſe that are our waiters nere,
Take hence this Wedding cheere.
We will be lively all, and make this barn our hall.

Gooddy Dick. You our Familiers, come,
In ſpeech let all be dumbe,
And to cloſe up our Feaſt,
To welcome every geſt
A merry round let's daunce.

Meg. Some Muſicke then ith aire

The Witches of Lancashire. 221

Whilest thus by paire and paire,
We nimbly foote it; strike. *Musick.*
   Mal. We are obeyd.
   Sprite. And we hels ministers shall lend our aid.

Dance and Song together. In the time of which the Boy speakes.

   Boy. Now whilest they are in their jollitie, and do not mind me, ile steale away, and shift for my selfe, though I lose my life for't. *Exit.*
   Meg. Enough, enough, now part,
To see the brides vext heart,
The bridegroomes too and all,
That vomit up their gall
For lacke o'th wedding chere.
   Gooddy Dickison. But stay, wheres the *Boy*, looke out, if he escape us, we are all betrayed.
   Meg. No following further, yonder horsemen come,
In vaine is our pursuit, let's breake up court.
   Gooddy Dickison. Where shall we next met?
   Mawd. At Mill.
   Meg. But when?
   Mrs. At Night.
   Meg. To horse, to horse.
   2. Where's my *Mamilian*.
   1. And my *Incubus*. *Robin stands amaz'd at this.*
   3. My Tyger to bestri'd.
   Mal. My Puggie.
   Mrs. Gen. My horse.
   All. Away, away,
The night we have Feasted, now comes on the day.
   Mrs. Come sirrah, stoope your head like a tame jade,
Whil'st I put on your Bridle.
   Rob. I pray Mistresse ride me as you would be rid.
   Mrs. That's at full speed.

Rob. Nay then Ile try Conclufions.
A great noyfe within at their parting.
Mare Mare, fee thou be,
And where I point thee carry me. *Exeunt.*

Enter Mr. Generous, making him ready.

Gen. I fee what Man is loath to entertaine,
Offers it felfe to him moft frequently,
And that which we moft covet to embrace,
Doth feldome court us, and proves moft averfe;
For I, that never coo'd conceive a thought
Of this my woman worthy a rebuke,
(As one that in her youth bore her fo fairely
That fhe was taken for a feeming Saint)
To render me fuch juft occafion,
That I fhould now diftruft her in her age;
Diftruft! I cannot, that would bring me in
The poore afperfion of fond jealoufie;
Which even from our firft meeting I abhorr'd.
The Gentile fafhion fometimes we obferve
To funder beds; but moft in thefe hot monthes
Iune, Iuly, Auguft, fo we did laft night.
Now I (as ever tender of her health)
And therefore rifing early as I ufe,
Entring her Chamber to beftow on her
A cuftom'd Vifite; finde the Pillow fwell'd,
Vnbruis'd with any weight, the fheets unruffled,
The Curtaines neither drawne, nor bed layd down;
Which fhowes, fhe flept not in my houfe to night.
Should there be any contract betwixt her
And this my Groome, to abufe my honeft truft;
I fhould not take it well, but for all this
Yet cannot I be jealous. *Robin*——

Enter Robin.

Gen. Is my horfe fafe, lufty, and in good plight?
What, feeds he well?

Rob. Yes fir, he's broad buttock'd and full flanck'd, he doth not bate an ace of his flefh.

Gen. When was he rid laft?

Rob. Not fir fince you backt him.

Gen. Sirrah, take heed I finde you not a Knave, Have you not lent him to your Miftreffe late? So late as this laft Night?

Rob. Who I fir, may I dye fir, if you finde me in a lye fir.

Gen. Then I fhall finde him where I left him laft.

Robin. No doubt Sir.

Gener. Give me the Key o'th Stable.

Robin. There Sir.

Gen. Sirrah, your Miftreffe was abroad all night, Nor is fhe yet come home, if there I finde him not, I fhall finde thee, what to this prefent houre I never did fufpect; and I muft tell thee Will not be to thy profit. *Exit.*

Rob. Well fir, finde what you can, him you fhall finde, and what you finde elfe; it may be for that, inftead of Gramercy horfe, you may fay Gramercy *Robin*; you will beleeve there are no Witches! had I not been late brideled, I coo'd have fayd more, but I hope fhe is ty'd to the racke that will confeffe fomething, and though not fo much as I know, yet no more then I dare juftifie——

Enter Generous.

Have you found your Gelding fir?

Gen. Yes, I have.

Rob. I hope not fpurr'd, nor put into a fweat, you may fee by his plump belly and fleeke legs he hath not bin fore travail'd.

Gener. Y'are a fawcy Groome to receive horfes Into my Stable, and not aske me leave. Is't for my profit to buy Hay and Oates For every ftrangers jades?

Rob. I hope fir you finde none feeding there but

your owne, if there be any you fufpect, they have nothing to chanipe on, but the Bridle.

Gener. Sirrah, whofe jade is that ty'd to the Racke?

Rob. The Mare you meane fir?

Gener. Yes, that old Mare.

Rob. Old doe you call her? You fhall finde the marke ftill in her mouth, when the Bridle is out of it? I can affure you 'tis your owne Beaft.

Gen. A beaft thou art to tell me fo, hath the wine
Not yet left working? not the *Myter* wine?
That made thee to beleeve Witchcraft?
I'rithee perfwade me,
To be a drunken Sot like to thy felfe;
And not to know mine owne.

Rob. Ile not perfwade you to any thing, you will beleeve nothing but what you fee, I fay the Beaft is your owne, and you have the moft right to keepe her, fhee hath coft you more the currying, then all the Combs in your Stable are worth. You have paid for her Provender this twentie yeares and upwards, and furnifht her with all the Caparifons that fhe hath worne, of my Knowledge, and becaufe fhe hath been ridden hard the laft Night, doe you renounce her now?

Gener. Sirrah, I feare fome ftolne jade of your owne
That you would have me keepe.

Rob. I am fure I found her no jade the laft time I rid her, fhe carried me the beft part of a hundred Miles in leffe then a quarter of an houre.

Gener. The divell fhe did!

Robin. Yes fo I fay, either the divell or fhe did; an't pleafe you walke in and take off her Bridle, and then tell me who hath more right to her, you or I.

Gen. Well *Robert*, for this once Ile play the Groome,

The Witches of Lancashire.

And doe your office for you. *Exit.*

Rob. I pray doe Sir, but take heed left when the Bridle is out of her mouth, fhe put it not into yours; if fhe doe, you are a gone man: if fhe but fay once— Horfe, horfe, fee thou be.
Be you rid (if you pleafe) for me.

Enter Mr. Generous, and Mrs. Generous, he with a Bridle.

Gener. My blood is turn'd to Ice, and my all vitals
Have ceas'd their working! dull ftupidity
Surprifeth me at once, and hath arrefted
That vigorous agitation; Which till now
Expreft a life within me: I me thinks
Am a meere Marble ftatue, and no man;
Vnweave my age O time, to my firft thread;
Let me loofe fiftie yeares in ignorance fpent:
That being made an infant once againe,
I may begin to know, what? or where am I
To be thus loft in wonder.

Mrs. Gen. Sir.

Gen. Amazement ftill purfues me, how am I chang'd
Or brought ere I can underftand my felfe,
Into this new World.

Rob. You will beleeve no Witches?

Gen. This makes me beleeve all, I any thing;
And that my felfe am nothing: prithee *Robin*
Lay me to my felfe open, what art thou,
Or this new transform'd Creature?

Rob. I am *Robin*, and this your wife, my Mrs.

Gen. Tell me the Earth
Shall leave it's feat, and mount to kiffe the Moone;
Or that the Moone enamour'd of the Earth,
Shall leave her fpheare, to ftoope to us thus low.
What? what's this in my hand, that at an inftant

Can from a foure leg'd Creature, make a thing
So like a wife?

   Rob. A Bridle, a jugling Bridle Sir.

   Gage. A Bridle, hence inchantment,
A Viper were more safe within my hand
Then this charm'd Engine.

                          Casts it away. Robin takes it up.

   Rob. Take heed Sir what you do, if you cast it hence, and she catch it up, we that are here now, may be rid as far as the *Indies* within these few houres, Mistresse down of your Mares bones, or your Marybones whether you please, and confesse your selfe to be what you are; and that's in plaine *English* a Witch, a grand notorious Witch.

   Gen. A Witch! my wife a Witch!

   Rob. So it appeares by the storie.

   Gener. The more I strive to unwinde
My selfe from this *Meander*, I the more
Therein am intricated; prithee woman
Art thou a Witch?

   Mrs. It cannot be deny'd,
I am such a curst Creature.

   Gen. Keep aloofe,
And doe not come too nearme, O my trust;
Have I since first I understood my selfe,
Bin of my soule so charie, still to studie
What best was for it's health, to renounce all
The workes of that black Fiend with my best force
And hath that Serpent twin'd me so about,
That I must lye so often and so long
With a Divell in my bosome!

   Mrs. Pardon sir.

   Gen. Pardon! Can such a thing as that be hop'd?
Lift up thine eyes (lost woman) to yon Hils;
It must be thence expected: look not down
Vnto that horrid dwelling, which thou hast sought
At such deare rate to purchase, prithee tell me,
(For now I can beleeve) art thou a Witch?

Mrs. I am.
Gen. With that word I am thunderſtrooke,
And know not what to anſwer, yet reſolve me
Haſt thou made any contract with that Fiend
The Enemy of Mankind?
Mrs. O I have.
Gen. What? and how farre?
Mrs. I have promis'd him my foule.
Gen. Ten thouſand times better thy Body had
Bin promis'd to the Stake, I and mine too,
Then ſuch a compact ever had bin made. Oh——
Rob. What cheere ſir, ſhow your ſelfe a man, though ſhe appear'd ſo late a Beaſt; Miſtreſſe confeſſe all, better here than in a worſe place, out with it.
Gen. Reſolve me, how farre doth that contract ſtretch?
Mrs. What intereſt in this Soule, my ſelfe coo'd claime
I freely gave him, but his part that made it
I ſtill reſerve, not being mine to give.
Gen. O cunning Divell, fooliſh woman know
Where he can clayme but the leaſt little part,
He will uſurpe the whole; th'art a loſt woman.
Mrs. I hope not ſo.
Gen. Why haſt thou any hope?
Mrs. Yes Sir I have.
Gen. Make it appeare to me.
Mrs. I hope I never bargain'd for that fire,
Further then penitent teares have power to quench.
Gen. I would ſee ſome of them.
Mrs. You behold them now.
(If you looke on me with charitable eyes)
Tinctur'd in blood, blood iſſuing from the heart,
Sir I am ſorry; when I looke towards Heaven
I beg a gracious Pardon; when on you
Me thinkes your Native goodneſſe ſhould not be
Leſſe pittifull than they: 'gainſt both I have err'd,
From both I beg attonement.

Gener. May I prefum't?

Mrs. I kneele to both your Mercies.

Gener. Know'ft thou what a Witch is?

Mrs. Alas, None better,
Or after mature recollection can be
More fad to thinke on't.

Gen. Tell me, are thofe teares
As full of true hearted penitence,
As mine of forrow, to behold what ftate
What defperate ftate th'art falne in.

Mrs. Sir they are.

Gen. Rife, and as I doe, fo heaven pardon me;
We all offend, but from fuch falling off,
Defend us. Well, I doe remember wife,
When I firft tooke thee, 'twas for good and bad;
O change thy bad to good, that I may keep thee,
As then we paft our faiths, till Death us fever.
I will not aggravate thy griefe too much,
By Needles iteration: *Robin* hereafter
Forget thou haft a tongue, if the leaft Syllable
Of what hath paft be rumour'd, you loofe me;
But if I finde you faithfull, you gaine me ever.

Rob. A match fir, you fhall finde me as mute as if
I had the Bridle ftill in my mouth.

Gen. O woman thou had'ft need to weepe thy felfe
Into a fountaine, fuch a penitent fpring
As may have power to quench invifible flames
In which my eyes fhall ayde; too little all,
If not too little, all's forgiven, forgot;
Only thus much remember, thou had'ft extermin'd
Thy felfe out of the bleft fociety
Of Saints and Angels, but on thy repentance
I take thee to my Bofome, once againe,
My wife, fifter, and daughter: faddle my Gelding,
Some bufineffe that may hold me for two dayes
Calls me afide. *Exeunt.*

Rob. I fhall Sir, well now my Miftreffe hath promis'd to give over her Witchery, I hope though I ftill

continue her man, yet she will make me no more her journey-man; to prevent which the first thing I doe shall be to burne the Bridle, and then away with the Witch. *Exit.*

Enter Arthur and Doughty.

Arth. Sir you have done a right noble courtesie, which deserves a memory, as long as the name of friendship can beare mention.

Dough. What I have done, I ha' done, if it be well, 'tis well, I doe not like the bouncing of good Offices, if the little care I have taken shall doe these poore people good, I have my end in't, and so my reward.

Enter Bantam.

Bant. Now Gentlemen, you seeme very serious.

Arth. 'Tis true we are so, but you are welcome to the knowledge of our affayres.

Bant. How does thine Vncle and Aunt, *Gregory* and his sister, the Families of *Seelyes* agree yet, can you tell?

Arth. That is the businesse, the *Seely* houshold is divided now.

Bant. How so I pray?

Arth. You know, and cannot but with pitty know
Their miserable condition, how
The good old couple were abus'd, and how
The young abus'd themselves; if we may say
That any of them are their selves at all
Which sure we cannot, nor approve them fit
To be their owne disposers, that would give
The governance of such a house and living
Into their Vassailes hands, to thrust them out on't
Without or Law or order, this consider'd
This Gentleman and my selfe have taken home

By faire entreaty, the old folkes to his houſe,
The young to mine, untill ſome wholeſome order
By the judicious of the Common-wealth,
Shall for their perſons and eſtate be taken.

Bant. But what becomes of *Lawrence* and his *Parnell?*
The luſty couple, what doe they now?

Dough. Alas poore folks, they are as farre to ſeeke of how they doe, or what they doe, or what they ſhould doe, as any of the reſt, they are all growne *Ideots*, and till ſome of theſe damnable jades, with their divelliſh deviſes bee found out, to diſcharme them, no remedy can be found, I mean to lay the Country for their Hagſhips, and if I can anticipate the purpoſe, of their grand Mr. Divell to confound 'em before their leaſe be out, be ſure ile do't.

A ſhout within.

Cry. A Skimington, a Skimmington, a Skimington.

Dough. Whats the matter now, is Hell broke looſe?

Enter Mr. Shakſtone.

Arth. *Tom Shakſtone*, how now, canſt tell the newes?

Sha. The news, ye heare it up i'th aire, do you not?

Within. A Skimington, a Skimington, a Skimington.

Sha. Hearke ye, do you not heare it? theres a Skimington, towards gentlemen.

Dou. Ware Wedlocke hoe.

Bant. At whoſe ſuit I prithee is Don Skimington come to towne.

Sha. Ile tell you gentlemen, ſince you have taken home old *Seely* and his wife to your houſe, and you their ſon and daughter to yours, the houſe-keepers

Lawrence, and his late bride *Parnell* are fallen out by themselves.

Arth. How prithee?

Sha. The quarell began they say upon the wedding night, and in the bride bed.

Bant. For want of bedstaves?

Sha. No but a better implement it seemes the bridegroome was unprovided of, a homely tale to tell.

Dou. Now out upon her shee has a greedy worme in her, I have heard the fellow complain'd on, for an over mickle man among the maids.

Arth. Is his haste to goe to bed at afternoone come to this now?

Dough. Witchery, witchery, more witcherie still flat and plaine witchery. Now do I thinke upon the codpeece point the young jade gave him at the wedding: shee is a witch, and that was a charme, if there be any in the World.

Arth. A ligatory point.

Bant. Alas poore *Lawrence*.

Sha. He's comming to make his mone to you about it, and she too, since you have taken their masters & mistresses to your care, you must do them right too.

Dough. Marry but ile not undertake her at these yeares, if lusty *Lawrence* cannot do't.

Bant. But has she beaten him?

Sha. Grievously broke his head in I know not how many places: of which the hoydens have taken notice, and will have a Skimmington on horse-backe presently. Looke ye, here comes both plaintiffe and defendant.

Enter Lawrence and Parnell.

Dough. How now *Lawrence*, what has thy wedlock brought thee already to thy night-cap?

Lawr. Yie gadwat sir, I ware wadded but aw to seun.

Par. Han yeou reefon to complayne or ay trow yeou gaffer Downought? Wa warth the day that ever I wadded a Downought.

Ar. Ban. Sha. Nay hold *Parnel* hold.

Dough. We have heard enough of your valour already, wee know you have beaten him, let that fuffice.

Parn. Ware ever poore mayden betrayed as ay ware unto a fwagbellied Carle that cannot aw waw that cannot.

Dou. What faies fhe?

Dou. I know not, fhe catterwawles I think. *Parnel* be patient good *Parnell*, and a little modeft too, 'tis not amiffe, wee know not the relifh of every eare that heares vs, lets talke within our felves. Whats the defect? Whats the impediment? *Lawrence* has had a lufty name among the Batchellors.

Par. What he ware when he ware a Batchelor, I know better than the beft maid ith tawne. I wad I had not.

Ar. Ba. Sha. Peace *Parnell*.

Par. 'Tware that, that coffen'd me, he has not now as he had than?

Ar. Ba. Sha. Peace good *Parnell*.

Parn. For then he could, but now he connot, he connot.

Ar. B. Sha. Fie *Parnel* fie.

Par. I fay agean and agean, hee connot, he connot.

Ar. Ba. Sha. Alas poore *Parnel*.

Par. I am not a bit the better for him fin wye ware wad. *Cries.*

Dou. Heres good ftuffe for a jurie of women to paffe upon.

Arth. But *Parnel*, why have you beaten him fo grievoufly? What would you have him doe in this cafe?

Dou. He's out of a doing cafe it feemes.

Par. Marry fir, and beat him will I into his grave,

or backe to the Prieſt, and be unwadded agone, for I wonot bee baund to lig with him and live with him, the laiſe of an honeſt woman for aw the layves good i' *Loncoſhire*.

Dou. An honeſt woman : thats a good mind *Parnel.* What ſay you to this *Lawrence?*

Law. Keepe her of o'me, and I ſhan teln yeou, and ſhe be by I am no body : But keep her off and ſearch me, let me be ſearcht as never witch was ſearcht, and finde ony thing mor or laſſe upo me than a ſufficient mon ſhold have, and let me me be honckt by't.

Art. Do you heare this *Parnell?*

Par. Ah leear, leear, deell tacke the leear, troiſt yee and hong yee.

Dou. Alaſſe it is too plaine, the poore fellow is bewitcht.
Heres a plaine *Maleficium verſus hanc* now.

Ar. And ſo is ſhe bewitcht too into this immodeſty.

Ban. She would never talke ſo elſe.

Law. I prayn yeow gi' me the lere o' that Latine ſir.

Dough. The meaning is, you muſt get halfe a dozen baſtards Within this twelvemoneth, and that will mend your next mariage.

Law. And I thought it would ma' *Parnel*, love me i'd be ſure on't, and gang about it now right.

Sha. Y'are ſoone provided it ſeems for ſuch a journey.

Dou. Beſt tarry till thy head be whole *Lawrence*.

Pa. Nay, nay, ay's white caſten away ent I be unwadded agen : And then ine undertack to find 3 better husbands in a bean cod.

Sha. Hearke gentlemen, the ſhew is comming.

Ar. What ſhall we ſtay & ſee't.

Ban. O by all means Gent.

Dou. 'Tis beſt to have theſe away firſt.

Par. Nay mary ſhan yeou not ſir, I heare yeou

well enogh, & I con the meaning o' the fhow well enogh, & I ftay not the fhow & fee not the fhow, & ma' one i' the fhow, let me be honckt up for a fhow ile ware them to mel or ma with a woman that mels or mae's with a teftril a longie, a dowlittle lofell that connot, & if I skim not their skimingtons cockskeam for't, ma that warplin boggle me a week lonker, & thats a curfe eno' for any wife I tro.

Dough. Agreed, perhaps 'twill mend the fport.

Enter drum (beating before) a Skimington, and his wife on a horfe; Divers country rufticks (as they paffe) Par. (puls Skimington of the horfe: and Law. Skimingtons wife: they beat em. Drum beats alar. horfe comes away: The hoydens at firft oppofe the Gentlemen: who draw: the clownes vaile bonnet, (make a ring Par. and Skim. fight.

Dou. Beat drum alarum.
Enough, enough, here my mafters: now patch up your fhew if you can, and catch your horfe again, and when you have done drinke that.

Rabble. Thanke your worfhip.   *Exeunt fhout.*

Par. Lat'hem as they laik this gang a proceffion with their aydoll Skimington agean.

Arth. Parnel, thou didft bravely.

Parn. I am fure I han drawne blood o' theyr aydoll.

Law. And I thinke I tickled his waife.

Par. Yie to be fure, yeou bene eane of the owd ticklers.
But with what con yeou tell?

Law. Yieu with her owne ladel.

Par. Yie marry a ladell is fomething.

Dou. Come you have both done well, goe in to my houfe, fee your old mafter and miftreffe, while I travell a courfe to make yee all well againe, I will now a witch hunting.

Par. Na courfe for hus but to be unwadded agone.

The Witches of Lancashire.

Arth. Sha. Bant. Wee are for *Whet.* and his Aunt you know.
Dou. Farewell, farewell.   *Exeunt.*

Enter Mrs. Generous, and Mal. Spencer.

Welcome, welcome, my girle, what hath thy puggy
Yet fuckt upon thy pretty duggy?
  Mal. All's well at home, and abroad too.
What ere I bid my Pug, hee'l doo. You fent for
    mee?
  Mrs. I did.
  Mal. And why?
  Mrs. Wench ile tell thee, thou and I
Will walk a little, how doth *Meg*?
And her Mamillion.
  Mal Of one leg
Shee's growne lame.
  Mrs. Becaufe the beaft
Did miffe us laft *Goodfriday* Feaft,
I geft as much.
  Mal. But *All-Saints* night
She met though fhe did halt downe right.
  Mrs. Dickifon and *Hargrave* prithee tel,
How do they?
  Mal. All about us well.
But Puggy whifperd in mine eare
That you of late were put in feare.
  Mrs. The flave my man.
  Mal. Who *Robin*?
  Mrs. Hee.
  Mal. My Sweet-heart?
  Mrs. Such a tricke ferv'd me.
  Mal. About the bridle, now alacke.
  Mrs. The villain brought me to the rack.
Tyed was I both to rack and manger.
  Mal. But thence how fcap't you?
  Mrs. Without danger,
I thank my fpirit.
  Mal. I but than

How pacified was your good man?

Mrs. Some paſſionate words mixt with forc't
tears
Did ſo inchant his eyes and eares
I made my peace, with promiſe never
To doe the like ; but once and ever
A Witch thou know'ſt. Now underſtand
New buſineſſe wee tooke in hand.
My Husband packt out of the towne
Know that the houſe, and all's our owne.

Enter Whetſtone.

Whet. Naunt, is this your promiſe Naunt? (What *Mal*! How doeſt thou *Mal*?) You told mee you would put a tricke upon theſe Gentlemen, whom you made mee invite to ſupper, who abuſed and called me baſtard. (And when ſhall I get one upon thee my ſweet Rogue?) And that you would doe I know not what; for you would not tell mee what you would doe. (And ſhall you and I never have any doing together) ſupper is done, and the table ready to withdraw: And I am riſen the earlieſt from the boord, and yet for ought I can ſee I am never a whit the neerer. What not one kiſſe at parting *Mal*?

Mrs. Well Cozen this is all you have to do:
Retire the Gallants to ſome privat roome,
Where call for wine, and junckets what you pleaſe,
Then thou ſhalt need to do no other thing
Than what this note directs thee, obſerve that
And trouble me no farther.

Whet. Very good, I like this beginning well : for where they ſleighted me before, they ſhall finde me a man of note. *Exit.*

Mal. Of this the meaning.

Mrs. Marry Laſſe
To bring a new conceit to paſſe.
Thy Spirit I muſt borrow more,

To fill the number three or foure;
Whom we will ufe to no great harm,
Only affift me with thy charme.
This night wee'l celebrate to fport:
'Tis all for mirth, we mean no hurt.

Mal. My Spirit and my felfe command;
Mamillion, & the reft at hand,
Shall all affift.

Mrs. Withdraw then, quicke,
Now gallants, ther's for you a trick. *Exeunt.*

Enter Whetftone, Arthur, Shakstone, Bantam.

Whet. Heer's a more privat roome gentlemen, free from the noife of the Hall. Here we may talke, and throw the chamber out of the cafements. Some wine and a fhort banquet.

Enter with a Banquet, Wine, and two Tapers.

Whet. So now leave us.

Arth. Wee are much bound to you mafter *Whetftone* for this great entertainment: I fee you command the houfe in the abfence of your vnkle.

Whet. Yes, I thanke my Aunt; for though I be but a daily gueft yet I can be welcome to her at midnight.

Shak. How fhall we paffe the time?

Bant. In fome difcourfe.

Whet. But no fuch difcourfe as we had laft, I befeech you.

Bant. Now mafter *Whetftone* you refleᶜt on me.
'Tis true, at our laft meeting fome few words
Then paft my lips, which I could wifh forgot:
I thinke I call'd you Baftard.

Whet. I thinke fo too; but whats that amongft friends, for I would faine know which amongft you all knowes his owne father.

Bant. You are merrie with your friends, good

maſter *By-Blow*, and wee are gueſts here in your Vnckles houſe, and therefore priviledged.

Enter Miſtreſſe Generous, Mal and Spirits.

Whet. I preſume you had no more priviledge in your getting than I. But tell me gentlemen, is there any man here amongſt you, that hath a minde to ſee his father?

Bant. Why, who ſhall ſhew him?

Whet. Thats all one; if any man here deſire it, let him but ſpeake the word, and 'tis ſufficient.

Bant. Why, I would ſee my father.

Miſtreſſe Gener. Strike. *Muſique.*

Enter a Pedant dauncing to the muſique; the ſtrain don, he points at Bantam, & looks full in his face.

Whet. Doe you know him that lookes ſo full in your face?

Bant. Yes well, a pedant in my fathers houſe. Who beeing young, taught me my A, B, C.

Whet. In his houſe, that goes for your father you would ſay: For know one morning, when your mothers husband rid early to have a *Niſi prius* tryed at *Lancaſter* Syzes, hee crept into his warme place, lay cloſe by her ſide, and then were you got. Then come, your heeles and tayle together, and kneele unto your own deare father.

All. Ha, ha, ha.

Bant. I am abuſed.

Whet. Why laugh you Gentlemen? It may be more mens caſes than his or mine.

Bant. To be thus geer'd.

Arth. Come, take it as a jeſt. For I preſume 'twas meant no otherwiſe.

Whet. Would either of you two now ſee his father in earneſt.

Shak. Yes, canſt thou ſhew me mine ?
Mrs. Gen. Strike.

Enter a nimble Taylor dauncing, uſing the ſame poſture to Shakſtone.

Whet. . Hee lookes on you, ſpeake, doe yon know him ?
Shak. Yes, he was my mothers Taylor, I remember him ever ſince I was a childe.
Whet. Who when hee came to take meaſure of her upper parts had more minde to the lower, whileſt the good man was in the fields hunting, he was at home whoring.
Then, ſince no better comfort can be had,
Come downe, come downe, aske bleſſiing of your dad.
All. Ha, ha, ha.
Bont. This cannot be indur'd.
Arth. It is plaine Witchcraft.
Nay ſince we are all bid unto one feaſt,
Lets fare alike, come ſhew me mine too.
Mrs. Gener. Strike.

Enter Robin with a ſwitch and a Currycombe, he points at Arthur.

Whet. He points at you.
Arth. What then ?
Whet. You know him.
Arth. Yes, *Robin* the groome belonging to this houſe.
Whet. And never ſerved your father ?
Arth. In's youth I thinke he did.
Whet. Who when your ſuppoſed father had buſineſſe at the Lord Preſidents Court in Yorke, ſtood for his Atturney at home, & ſo it ſeems you were got by deputy : what all a mort ? if you will have but a little patience, ſtay & you ſhall ſee mine too :

And knew I show you him the rather,
To finde who hath the best man to his Father.
    Mrs. Strike——

   Musicke. Enter a Gallant, as before to him.

Whet. Now Gentlemen make me your President, learne your duties, and doe as I doe——A blessing Dad.
    Bant. Come, come, let's home, we'l finde some other time,
When to dispute of these things——
    Whet. Nay Gent. no parting in spleene, since we have begun in mirth, let's not end in melancholy; you see there are more By-blowes than beare the name; It is growne a great kindred in the Kingdome. Come, come, all friends; Let's into the Cellar and conclude our Revels in a lusty health.
    Shak. I faine would strike, but cannot.
    Bank. Some strange fate holds me.
    Arth. Here then all anger end,
Let none be mad at what they cannot mend.
                                                  Exeunt.
    Mal. Now say what's next?
    Mrs. I'th' Mill there lyes
A Souldier yet with unscratcht eyes,
Summon the Sister-hood together
For we with all our Spirits will thither;
And such a Catterwalling keepe,
That he in vaine shall thinke to sleepe.
Call *Meg*, and *Doll*, *Tib*, *Nab*, and *Iug*,
Let none appeare without her Pug.
We'l try our utmost Art and skill.
To fright the stout Knave in the Mill.   *Exeunt.*

ACTVS, V. SCENA I.

Enter Doughty, Miller, Boy in a Cap.

Doughty.

Thou art a brave Boy, the honour of thy Country; thy Statue ſhall be ſet up in braſſe upon the Market Croſſe in *Lancaſter*, I bleſſe the time that I anſwered at the Font for thee: 'Zookes did I ever thinke that a Godſon of mine ſhould have fought hand to fiſt with the Divell!

Mil. He was ever an unhappy Boy Sir, and like enough to grow acquainted with him; and friends may fall out ſometimes.

Dought. Thou art a dogged Sire, and doeſt not know the vertue of my Godſonne, my ſonne now; he ſhall be thy ſonne no longer: he and I will worry all the Witches in *Lancaſhire*.

Mil. You were beſt take heed though.

Dough. I care not, though we leave not above three untainted women in the Pariſh, we'll doe it.

Mil. Doe what you pleaſe Sir, there's the Boy ſtout enough to juſtifie anything he has ſayd. Now 'tis out, he ſhould be my Sonne ſtill by that: Though he was at Death's dore before he would reveale anything, the damnable jades had ſo threatned him, and as ſoone as ever he had told he mended.

Dought. 'Tis well he did ſo, **we** will ſo ſwing them in twopenny halters Boy.

Mil. For my part I have no reaſon to hinder any

thing that may root them all out; I have tasted enough of their mischiefe, witnesse my usage i' the Mill, which could be nothing but their Roguerie. One night in my sleepe they set me a stride stark naked a top of my Mill, a bitter cold night too; 'twas daylight before I waked, and I durst never speake of it to this houre, because I thought it impossible to be beleeved.

Dought. Villanous Hags!

Mil. And all last Summer, my Wife could not make a bit of butter.

Dough. It would not come, would it?

Mill. No Sir, we could not make it come, though she and I both together, churn'd almost our harts out, and nothing would come, but all ran into thin waterish geere: the Pigges would not drinke it.

Dought. Is't possible?

Mil. None but one, and he ran out of his wits upon't, till we bound his head, and layd him a sleepe, but he has had a wry mouth ever since.

Dought. That the Divell should put in their hearts to delight in such Villanies! I have sought about these two dayes, and heard of a hundred such mischievous tricks, though none mortall, but could not finde whom to mistrust for a Witch till now this boy, this happy boy informes me.

Mil. And they should neere have been sought for me if their affrightments and divellish devices, had not brought my Boy into such a sicknesse; Whereupon indeed I thought good to acquaint your worship, and bring the Boy unto you being his Godfather, and as you now stick not to say his Father.

Dought. After you I thanke you Gossip. But my Boy thou hast satisfied me in their names, and thy knowledge of the women, their turning into shapes, their dog-trickes, and their horse trickes, and their great Feast in the Barne (a pox take them with my Surloyne, I say still.)· But a little more of thy combat with the Divell, I prithee; he came to thee like a Boy thou sayest, about thine owne bignesse?

Boy. Yes Sir, and he asked me where I dwelt, and what my name was.

Dough. Ah Rogue!

Boy. But it was in a quarrelſome way; Whereupon I was as ſtout, and ask'd him who made him an examiner ?

Dough. Ah good Boy.

Mil. In that he was my Sonne.

Boy. He told me he would know or beat it out of me,
And I told him he ſhould not, and bid him doe his worſt;
And to't we went.

Dough. In that he was my ſonne againe, ha boy; I ſee him at it now.

Boy. We fought a quarter of an houre, till his ſharpe nailes made my eares bleed.

Dough. O the grand Divell pare 'em.

Boy. I wondred to finde him ſo ſtrong in my hands, ſeeming but of mine owne age and bigneſſe, till I looking downe, perceived he had clubb'd cloven feet like Oxe feet : but his face was as young as mine.

Dovgh. A pox, but by his feet, he may be the Club-footed Horſe-courſers father, for all his young lookes.

Boy. But I was afraid of his feet, and ran from him towards a light that I ſaw, and when I came to it, it was one of the Witches in white upon a Bridge, that ſcar'd me backe againe, and then met me the Boy againe, and he ſtrucke me and layd mee for dead.

Mil. Till I wondring at his ſtay, went out and found him in the Trance; ſince which time, he has beene haunted and frighted with Goblins, 40. times; and never durſt tell any thing (as I ſayd) becauſe the Hags had ſo threatned him till in his ſicknes he revealed it to his mother.

Dough. And ſhe told no body but folkes on't.

VVell Gossip *Gretty*, as thou art a Miller, and a close thiefe, now let us keepe it as close as we may till we take 'hem, and see them handsomly hanged o' the way : Ha my little Cuffe-divell, thou art a made man. Come, away with me. *Exeunt.*

Enter Souldier.

Soul. These two nights I have slept well and heard no noise
Of Cats, or Rats ; most sure the fellow dream't,
And scratcht himselfe in 's sleep. I have traveld' Desarts,
Beheld Wolves, Beares, and Lyons : Indeed what not ?
Of horrid shape ; And shall I be afrayd
Of Cats in mine owne Country ? I can never
Grow so Mouse-hearted. It is now a Calme
And no winde stirring, I can beare no sayle ;
Then best lye downe to sleepe. Nay rest by me
Good *Morglay*, my Comrague and Bedfellow
That never fayl'd me yet ; I know thou did'st not.
If I be wak'd, see thou be stirring too ;
Then come a *Gib* as big as *Ascapart*
We'l make him play at Leap-frog. A brave Souldiers lodging,
The floore my Bed, a Milstone for my Pillow,
The Sayles for Curtaines. So good night.
Lyes downe.

Enter Mrs. Generous, Mall, *all the Witches and their Spirits* (*at severall dores.*)

Mrs. Is *Nab* come ?
Mal. Yes.
Mrs. Where's *Jug* ?
Mal. On horseback yet,
Now lighting from her Broome-staffe.
Mrs. But where's *Peg* ?

Mal. Entred the Mill already.
Mrs. Is he faſt ?
Mal. As fenceleſſe as a Dormouſe.
Mrs. Then to work, to work my pretty Lap-
  lands
Pinch, here, ſcratch,
Doe that within, without we'l keep the watch.

The Witches retire : the Spirits come about him with a dreadfull noiſe ; he ſtarts.

Sold. Am I in Hell, then have among'ſt you
  divels ;
This ſide, and that ſide, what behinde, before ?
Ile keep my face unſcratch'd diſpight you all :
What, doe you pinch in private, clawes I feele
But can ſee nothing, nothing pinch me thus ?
Have at you then, I and have at you ſtill ;
And ſtil have at you.

Beates them off, followes them in, and Enters againe.

One of them I have pay'd,
In leaping out oth' hole a foot or eare
Or ſomething I have light on. What all gone ?
All quiet ? not a Cat that's heard to mew ?
Nay then Ile try to take another nap,
Though I ſleepe with mine eyes open.   *Exit.*

Enter Mr. *Generous, and Robin.*

Gen. *Robin*, the laſt night that I lodg'd at home
My Wife (if thou remembreſt) lay abroad,
But no words of that.
  Rob. You have taught me ſilence.
  Gen. I roſe thus early much before my houre,
To take her in her bed ; 'Tis yet not five :
The Sunne ſcarce up. Thoſe horſes take and lead
  'em

Into the Stable, fee them rubb'd and dreſt,
We have rid hard. Now in the interim I
Will ſtep and fee how my new Miller fares,
Or whether he ſlept better in his charge,
Than thoſe which did precede him.
 Rob. Sir I ſhall.
 Gen. But one thing more—— *Whiſpers.*

Enter Arthur.

 Arth. Now from the laſt nights witchcraft we are freed,
And I that had not power to cleare my ſelfe
From baſe aſperſion, am at liberty
For vow'd revenge : I cannot be at peace
(The night-ſpell being took of) till I have met
With noble Mr. *Generous* : in whoſe ſearch
The beſt part of this morning I have ſpent,
His wife now I ſuſpect.
 Rob. By your leave Sir.
 Arth. O y'are well met, pray tell me how long is't
Since you were firſt my Father?
 Rob. Be patient I befeech you, what doe you meane Sir?
 Arth. But that I honour
Thy Maſter, to whoſe goodneſſe I am bound,
And ſtill muſt remaine thankfull, I ſhould prove
Worſe then a Murderer, a meere Paricide
By killing thee my Father.
 Rob. I your Father? he was a man I alwayes lov'd
And honour'd. He bred me.
 Arth. And you begot me? oh you us'd me finely laſt night?
 Gen. Pray what's the matter Sir?
 Arth. My worthy friend, but that I honour you
As one to whom I am ſo much oblig'd,
This Villaine could not ſtirre a foot from hence

Till perisht by my sword.
  Gener. How hath he wrong'd you?
Be of a milder temper I intreat,
Relate what and when done?
  Arth. You may command me,
If aske me what wrongs, know this Groome pretends
He hath strumpeted my mother, if when, blaz'd
Last night at midnight. If you aske me further
Where, in your owne house; when he pointed to me
As had I been his Bastard.
  Rob. I doe this? I am a horse agen if I got you,
Master, why Master.
  Gen. I know you Mr. *Arthur*, for a Gentleman
Of faire endowments, a most solid braine,
And setled understanding. Why this fellow
These two dayes was scarce sundred from my side,
And for the last night I am most assur'd
He slept within my Chamber, 12. miles off,
We have nere parted since.
  Arth. You tell me wonders.
Since all your words to me are Oracles,
And such as I most constantly beleeve.
But Sir, shall I be bold and plaine withall,
I am suspitious all's not well at home;
I dare proceed no farther without leave,
Yet there is something lodged within my breast
Which I am loath to utter.
  Gen. Keepe it there,
I pray doe a season (O my feares)
No doubt ere long my tongue may be the Key
To open that your secret: Get you gone sir
And doe as I commanded.
  Rob. I shall Sir. Father quoth he
I should be proud indeed of such a sonne. *Exit.*
  Gen. Please you now walk with me to my Mill, I faine would see

How my bold Soldier speeds.   It is a place
Hath beene much troubled.

Enter Soldier.

 Arth. I shall waite on you.—See he appeares.
 Gen. Good morrow Soldier.
 Sold. A bad night I have had
A murrin take your Mill-sprights.
 Gen. Prithee tell me, hast thou bin frighted then?
 Sold. How frighted Sir,
A Doungcart full of Divels coo'd not do't.
But I have bin so nipt, and pull'd, and pinch'd,
By a company of Hell-cats.
 Arth. Fairies sure.
 Sold. Rather foule fiends, Fairies have no such clawes;
Yet I have kept my face whole thanks my Semiter,
My trusty Bilbo, but for which I vow,
I had been torne to pieces.   But I thinke
I met with some of them.   One I am sure
I have sent limping hence.
 Gen. Didst thou fasten upon any?
 Sold. Fast or loose, most sure I made them flye,
And skip out of the Port-holes.   But the last
I made her squeake, she had forgot to mew,
I spoyl'd her Catter-wawling.
 Arth. Let's see thy sword.
 Sold. To look on, not to part with from my hand,
'Tis not the Soldiers custome.
 Arth. Sir, I observe 'tis bloody towards the point.
 Sold. If all the rest scape scot-free, yet I am sure
There's one hath payd the reckoning.
 Gen. Looke well about,
Perhaps there may be seene some tract of bloud.
       Lookes about and findes the hand.

   Sold. What's here ? is't poſſible Cats ſhould have hands
And rings upon their fingers.
   Arth. Moſt prodigious.
   Gen. Reach me that hand.
   Sold. There's that of the three I can beſt ſpare.
   Gen. Amazement upon wonder, can this be ;
I needs muſt know't by moſt infallible markes.
Is this the hand once plighted holy vowes,
And this the ring that bound them ? doth this laſt age
Afford what former never durſt beleeve ?
O how have I offended thoſe high powers ?
That my great incredulity ſhould merit
A puniſhment ſo grievous, and to happen
Vnder mine owne roofe, mine own bed, my boſome.
   Arth. Know you the hand Sir ?
   Gen. Yes and too well can reade it.
Good Maſter *Arthur* beare me company
Vnto my houſe, in the ſociety
Of good men there's great ſolace.
   Arth. Sir Ile waite on you.
   Gen. And Soldier do not leave me, lock thy Mill,
I have imployment for thee.
   Sold. I ſhall ſir, I think I have tickled ſome of your Tenants at will, that thought to revell here rent-free ; the beſt is if one of the parties ſhall deny the deed, we have their hand to ſhew.   *Exeunt.*

   A Bed thruſt out, Mrs. Gener. in't ; Whetſtone,
          Mall Spencer by her.

   Whet. Why Aunt, deere Aunt, honey Aunt, how doe you, how fare you, cheere you, how is't with you ! you have bin a luſty woman in your time, but now you look as if you could not doe with all.
   Mrs. Good *Mal* let him not trouble me.
   Mal. Fie Mr. *Whetſtone* you keep ſuch a noiſe in

the chamber that your Aunt is defirous to take a little reft and cannot.

Whet. In my Vncles abfence who but I fhould comfort my Aunt,
Am not I of the Bloud, am not I next of Kin?
Why Aunt?

Mrs. Gen. Good Nephew leave me.

Whet. The Divell fhall leave you ere ile forfake you, Aunt, you know, *Sic* is *So*, and being fo ficke doe you thinke ile leave you, what know I but this Bed may prove your death-bed, and then I hope you will remember me, that is, remember me in your Will.—(*Knocke within.*) Who's that knocks with fuch authority. Ten to one my Vncles come to towne.

Mrs. Gen. It it be fo, excufe my weaknes to him, fay I can fpeake with none.

Mal. I will, and fcape him if I can; by this accident all muft come out, and here's no ftay for me—(*Knock again*) Againe, ftay you here with your Aunt, and ile goe let in your Vncle.

Whet. Doe good *Mal*, and how, and how fweet Aunt?

Enter Mr. Gener., Mal, Arthur, Soldier, and Robin.

Gen. Y'are well met here, I am told you oft frequent
This houfe as my Wives choyfe companion,
Yet have I feldome feene you.

Mal. Pray, by your leave Sir,
Your wife is taken with a fuddaine qualme
She hath fent me for a Doctor.

Gen. But that labour ile fave you, Soldier take her to your charge.
And now where's this ficke woman.

Whet. O Vncle you come in good time, my Aunt is fo fuddainly taken as if fhe were ready to give up the fpirit.

Gen. 'Tis almoſt time ſhe did, ſpeake how is't wife
My Nephew tels me you were tooke laſt night
With a ſhrewd ſickneſſe, which this Mayde confirmes.
Mrs. Yes ſir, but now deſire no company.
Noyſe troubles me, and I would gladly ſleepe.
Gener. In company there's comfort, prithee wife
Lend me thy hand, and let me feele thy pulſe,
Perhaps ſome Feaver, by their beating I
May gueſſe at thy diſeaſe.
Mrs. Gen. My hand, 'tis there.
Gen. A dangerous ſicknes, and I feare t death,
'Tis oddes you will not ſcape it. Take that backe
And let me prove the t' other, if perhaps
I there can finde more comfort.
Mrs. Gen. I pray excuſe me.
Gener. I muſt not be deny'd,
Sick folkes are peeviſh, and muſt be ore-rul'd, and ſo ſhall you.
Mrs. Gen. Alas I have not ſtrength to lift it up.
Gener. If not thy hand Wife, ſhew me but thy wriſt,
And ſee how this will match it, here's a Teſtate
That cannot be out-fac'd.
Mrs. Gener. I am undone.
Whet. Hath my Aunt bin playing at handee dandee, nay then if the game goe this way I feare ſhe'l have the worſt hand on't.
Arth. 'Tis now apparant
How all the laſt nights buſineſſe came about,
In this my late ſuſpicion, is confirm'd.
Gen. My heart hath bled more for thy curſt relapſe
Than drops hath iſſu'd from thy wounded arme.
But wherefore ſhould I preach to one paſt hope?
Or where the divell himſelfe claimes right in all,
Seeke the leaſt part or intereſt? Leave your Bed,

Vp, make you ready; I muſt deliver you
Into the hand of Iuſtice. O deare friend
It is in vaine to gueſſe at this my griefe
'Tis ſo inundant. Soldier take away that young
But old in miſchiefe.
And being of theſe *Apoſtat*'s rid ſo well,
Ile ſee my houſe no more be made a Hell.
Away with them. *Exeunt.*

Enter Bantam, and Shakſton.

Ban. Ile out o' the Country, and as foone live in *Lapland* as *Lancaſhire* hereafter.

Shak. What for a falſe illuſive apparition? I hope the divell is not able to perſwade thee thou art a Baſtard.

Bant. No, but I am afflicted to thinke that the divell ſhould have power to put ſuch a trick upon us, to countenance a Raſcal, that is one.

Shak. I hope *Arthur* has taken a courſe with his Vncle about him by this time, who would have thought ſuch a foole as hee could have beene a Witch?

Bant. Why doe you thinke there's any wiſe folks of the quality; Can any but fooles be drawne into a Covenant with the greateſt enemy of mankind? yet I cannot thinke that *Whetſtone* is the Witch? The young Queane that was at the Wedding was i'th houſe yee know.

Enter Lawrence and Parnell, in their firſt Habits.

Shak. See *Lawrence* and *Parnell* civilly accorded againe it ſeems, and accoutred as they were wont to be when they had their wits.

Law. Bleſt be the houre I ſay may hunny, may ſweet *Pall*, that Ay's becom'd thaine agone, and thou's becom'd maine agone, and may this ea kiſſe ma us tway become both eane for ever and a day.

Parn. Yie marry *Lall*, and thus ſhadden it be, there is nought getten by fawing out, we mun faw in or we get nought.

Bant. The world's well mended here; we cannot but rejoyce to ſee this, *Lawrence*.

Lawr. And you been welcome to it Gentlemen.

Parn. And we been glad we han it for you.

Shak. And I proteſt I am glad to ſee it.

Parn. And thus ſhan yeou ſee't till our deeing houre.
Ween eon leove now for a laife time, the Dewle ſhonot ha the poore to put us to peeces agone.

Bant. Why now all's right and ſtraight and as it ſhould be.

Lawr. Yie marry that is it, the good houre be bleſſed for it, that put the wit into may head, to have a miſtruſt of that peſtilent Codpeece-point, that the witched worch *Mal Spencer* go me, ah woe worth her, that were it that made aw ſo nought.

Bant. & Shak. Is 't poſſible?

Parn. Yie marry it were an Inchauntment, and about an houre ſince it come intill our hearts to doe, what yeou thinke, and we did it.

Bant. What *Parnell*?

Parn. Marry we take the 'point, and we caſten the point into the fire, and the point ſpitter'd and ſpatter'd in the fire, like an it were (love bleſſe us) a laive thing in the faire; and it hopet and skippet, and riggled, and frisket in the faire, and crept about laike a worme in the faire, that it were warke enough for us both with all the Chimney tooles to keepe it into the faire, and it ſtinket in the faire, worſen than ony brimſtone in the faire.

Bant. This is wonderfull as all the reſt.

Lawr. It wolld ha ſcar'd ony that hadden their wits till a ſeen't, and we werne mad eont it were deone.

Parn. And this were not above an houre fine, and you cannot devaife how we han lov'd t' on t' other by now, yeou woud een bliffe your feln to fee't.

Lawr. Yie an han pit on our working geere, to fwinke and ferve our Mafter and Maiftreffe like intill painfull fervants agone, as we fhudden.

Bant. 'Tis wondrous well.

Shak. And are they well agen?

Parn. Yie and weel's laike heane bliffe them, they are awas weel becom'd as none ill had ever beene aneaft 'hem; Lo ye, lo ye, as they come.

Enter Seely, Ioane, Gregory, and Win.

Greg. Sir, if a contrite heart ftrucke through with fence
Of it's fharpe errors, bleeding with remorfe
The blacke polluted ftaine it had conceived
Of foule unnaturall difobedience
May yet by your faire mercy finde Remiffion;
You fhall upraife a Sonne out o' the gulph
Of horrour and defpaire, unto a bliffe
That fhall for ever crowne your goodneffe, and
Inftructive in my after life to ferve you,
In all the duties that befit a fonne.

Seel. Enough, enough, good boy, 'tis moft apparant
We all have had our errors, and as plainly
It now appearfe, our judgments, yea our reafon
Was poyfon'd by fome violent infection,
Quite contrary to Nature.

Bant. This founds well.

Seely. I feare it was by Witchcraft: for I now
(Bleft be the power that wrought the happy means
Of my delivery) remember that
Some 3. months fince I croft a wayward woman
(One that I now fufpect) for bearing with
A moft unfeemly difobedience,
In an untoward ill-bred fonne of hers,

When with an ill looke and an hollow voyce
She mutter'd out thefe words. Perhaps ere long
Thy felfe fhalt be obedient to thy fonne.
She has play'd her pranke it feemes.

Greg. Sir I have heard, that Witches apprehended under hands of lawfull authority, doe loofe their power;
And all their fpells are inftantly diffolv'd.

Seel. If it be fo, then at this happy houre,
The Witch is tane that over us had power.

Joane. Enough Childe, thou art mine and all is well.

Win. Long may you live the well-fpring of my bliffe,
And may my duty and my fruitfull Prayers,
Draw a perpetuall ftreame of bleffings from you.

Seely. Gentlemen welcome to my beft friends houfe,
You know the unhappy caufe that drew me hether.

Bant. And cannot but rejoyce to fee the remedy fo neere at hand.

Enter Doughty, Miller, and boy.

Dought. Come Goffip, come Boy——Gentlemen you are come to the braveft difcovery——Mr. *Seely* and the reft, how is't with you? you look reafonable well me thinkes.

Seely. Sir, we doe find that we have reafon enough to thank you for your Neighbourly and pious care of us.

Doughty. Is all fo well with you already? goe to, will you know a reafon for't Gentlemen: I have catcht a whole Kennel of Witches. It feemes their Witch is one of 'hem, and fo they are difcharm'd, they are all in Officers hands, and they will touch here with two or three of them for a little private parley, before they goe to the Iuftices. Mafter *Generous* is comming hither too, with a fupply that you dreame not of, and your Nephew *Arthur*.

Bant. You are beholden Sir to Mafter *Generous* in behalfe of your Nephew for faving his land from forfeiture in time of your diftraction.

Seely. I will acknowledge it moft thankfully.

Shak. See he comes.

Enter Mr. Generous, Mrs. Generous, Arthur, Whet-stone, Mal, Soldier, and Robin.

Seel. O Mr. *Generous*, the noble favour you have fhew'd
My Nephew for ever bindes me to you.

Gener. I pittyed then your mifery, and now
Have nothing left but to bewayle mine owne
In this unhappy woman.

Seel. Good Miftreffe *Generous*——

Arth. Make a full ftop there Sir, fides, fides, make fides,
You know her not as I doe, ftand aloofe there Miftreffe with your darling Witch, your Nephew too if you pleafe, becaufe though he be no witch, he is a wel-willer to the infernal fcience.

Gener. I utterly difcard him in her blood
And all the good that I intended him
I will conferre upon this vertuous Gentleman.

Whet. Well Sir, though you be no Vnckle, yet mine Aunt's mine Aunt, and fhall be to her dying day.

Doug. And that will be about a day after next Sizes I take it.

Enter Witches, Conftable, and Officers.

O here comes more o' your Naunts, Naunt *Dickenfon* & Naunt *Hargrave*, ods fifh and your Granny *Johnfon* too; we want but a good fire to entertaine 'em.

Arth. See how they lay their heads together?

Witches charme together.

Gill. No fuccour.
Maud. No reliefe.
Peg. No comfort!
All. *Mawfy*, my *Mawfy*, gentle *Mawfy* come.
Maud. Come my fweet *Puckling*.
Peg. My *Mamilion*.
Arth. What doe they fay?
Bant. They call their Spirits I thinke.
Dough. Now a fhame take you for a fardell of fooles, have you knowne fo many of the Divels tricks, and can be ignorant of that common feate of the old Iugler; that is, to leave you all to the Law, when you are once feized on by the tallons of Authority? .Ile undertake this little *Demigorgon* Conftable with thefe Common-wealth Characters upon his ftaffe here, is able in fpite of all your bugs-words, to ftave off the grand Divell for doing any of you good till you come to his Kingdome to him, and there take what you can finde.

Arth. But Gentlemen, fhall we try if we can by examination get from them fomething that may abbreviate the caufe unto the wifer in Commiffion for the peace before wee carry them before 'em.

Gen. & Seel. Let it be fo.

Dought. Well fay, ftand out Boy, ftand out Miller, ftand out *Robin*, ftand out Soldier, and lay your accufation upon 'em.

Bant. Speake Boy doe you know thefe Creatures, women I dare not call 'em?

Boy. Yes Sir, and faw them all in the Barne together, and many more at their Feaft and Witchery.

Rob. And fo did I, by a Divellifh token, I was rid thither, though I rid home againe as faft without fwitch or fpur.

Mill. I was ill handled by them in the Mill.

Sold. And I fliced off a Cats foot there, that is fince a hand, who ever wants it.

Seel. How I and all my family have fuffered you all know.

Lawr. And how I were betwitcht my *Pall.* here knowes.

Parn. Yie *Lall*, and the Witch I knaw, an I prayen yeou goe me but leave to fcrat her well-favorely.

Bant. Hold *Parnell.*

Parn. Yeou can blame no honeft woman, I trow, to fcrat for the thing fhe leoves.

Mal. Ha, ha, ha.

Dough. Doe you laugh Gentlewoman? what fay you to all thefe matters?

Mrs. Gen. I will fay nothing, but what you know you know,
And as the law fhall finde me let it take me.

Gil. And fo fay I.

Mawd. And I.

Mal. And I, other confeffion you get none from us.

Arth. What fay you Granny?

Peg. *Mamilion*, ho *Mamilion*, *Mamilion*.

Arth. Who's that you call?

Peg. My friend, my Sweet-heart, my *Mamilion*.

Witches. You are not mad?

Dought. Ah ha, that's her Divell, her *Incubus* I warrant; take her off from the reft they'l hurt her. Come hether poore old woman. Ile dandle a Witch a little, thou wilt fpeake, and tell the truth, and fhalt have favour doubt not. Say art not thou a Witch?

They ftorme.

Peg. 'Tis folly to diffemble yie fir, I am one.

Dought. And that *Mamilion* which thou call'ft upon
Is thy familiar Divell is't not? Nay prithee fpeake.

Peg. Yes Sir.

Dough. That's a good woman, how long haft had's acquaintance, ha?

Peg. A matter of fixe yeares Sir.

Dough. A pretty matter. What was he like a man?

Peg. Yes when I pleas'd.

Dought. And then he lay with thee, did he not fometimes ?

Peg. Tis folly to diffemble; twice a Weeke he never fail'd me.

Dough. Humh—and how ? and how a little ? was he a good Bedfellow ?

Peg. Tis folly to fpeake worfe of him than he is.

Dough. I truft me is't. Give the Divell his due.

Peg. He pleas'd me well Sir, like a proper man.

Dought. There was fweet coupling.

Peg. Onely his flefh felt cold.

Arth. He wanted his great fires about him that he has at home.

Dough. Peace, and did he weare good clothes ?

Peg. Gentleman like, but blacke blacke points and all.

Dought. I, very like his points were blacke enough. But come we'l trifle w' yee no longer. Now fhall you all to the Iuftices, and let them take order with you till the Sizes, and then let Law take his courfe, and *Vivat Rex.* Mr. *Generous* I am forry for your caufe of forrow, we fhall not have your company ?

Gener. No fir, my Prayers for her foules recovery Shall not be wanting to her, but mine eyes
Muft never fee her more.

Rob. *Mal,* adiew fweet *Mal,* ride your next journey with the company you have there.

Mal. Well Rogue I may live to ride in a Coach before I come to the Gallowes yet.

Rob. And Mrs. the horfe that ftayes for you rides better with a Halter than your gingling bridle.

Exeunt Gen. & Robin.

Dought. Mr. *Seely* I rejoyce for your families attonement.

Seel. And I praife heaven for you that were the means to it.

Dough. On afore Drovers with your untoward Cattell. *Exeunt severally.*

Bant. Why doe not you follow Mr. *By-blow.* I thanke your Aunt for the tricke she would have father'd us withall.

What. Well Sir, mine Aunt's mine Aunt, and for that trick I will not leave her till I see her doe a worse.

Baut. Y'are a kinde Kinsman. *Exeunt.*

Flourish.

FINIS.

Song. II. Act.

Come Mawfy, *come* Puckling,
And come my fweet Suckling,
　My pretty Mamillion, *my Ioy*,
Fall each to his Duggy,
While kindly we huggie,
　As tender as Nurfe over Boy.
　　Then suck our blouds freely, and with it be jolly,
　　While merrily we fing, hey Trolly Lolly.

We'l dandle and clip yee,
We'l ftroke yee, and leape yee,
　And all that we have is your due;
The feates you doe for us,
And thofe which you ftore us
　Withall, tyes us onely to you.
　　Then suck our blouds freely, and with it be jolly,
　　While merrily we fing, hey Trolly Lolly.

THE EPILOGVE.

Now while the Witches muſt expect their due
By lawfull Iuſtice, we appeale to you
For favourable cenſure; what their crime
May bring upon 'em, ripenes yet of time
Has not reveal'd. Perhaps great Mercy may
After juſt condemnation give them day
Of longer life. We repreſent as much
As they have done, before Lawes hand did touch
Vpon their guilt ; But dare not hold it fit,
That we for Iuſtices and Iudges fit,
And perſonate their grave wiſedomes on the Stage
Whom we are bound to honour ; No, the Age
Allowes it not. Therefore unto the Lawes
We can but bring the Witches and their cauſe,
And there we leave 'em, as their Divels did,
Should we goe further with 'em ? Wit forbid ;
What of their ſtorie, further ſhall enſue,
We muſt referre to time, our ſelves to you.

Londons Ius Honorarium.

Exprest in sundry Triumphs, pagiants, and shews:
At the Initiation or Entrance of the Right Honourable
George Whitmore, into the Maioralty of the famous and
farre renouned City of London..

All the charge and expence of the laborious proiects, and obiects both by Water and Land, being the
sole vndertaking of the Right Worshipfull, the
society of the Habburdashers.

Redeunt spectacula.

Printed at *London* by NICHOLAS OKES. 1631.

§⊷ To the Right Honourable, *George* Whitmore, Lord Maior of this renowned *Metrapolis, London.*

Right Honorable,

IT was the speech of a Learned and grave Philosopher the Tutor and Counseler to the Emperour *Gratianus, Pulcrius multo parari, quam creari nobilem.* More faire and famous it is to be made, then to be borne Noble, For that Honour is to be most Honored, which is purchast by merrit, not crept into by descent: For you; whose goodnesse, hath made you thus great, I make my affectionate presentment of this annuall Celebration, concerning which : (without flattery be it spoken) there is nothing so much as mentioned (much less enforced) in this your *Ius honorarium*, which rather commeth not short, then any way exceedeth the hope and expectation which is now vpon you, and therefore worthily was your so free Election, (without either emulation, or competitorship conferd vpon you, since of you it may be vndeniably spoken: that none euer in your place was more sufficient or able, any cause whatsoeuer shall be brought before you, more truly to discerne; being apprehended more aduisedly to dispose, being digested, more maturely to despatch. After this short tender of my seruice vnto you, I humbly take my leaue, with this sentence borrowed from *Seneca: Decet timeri Magistratum, at plus diligi.*

                Your Lordships in all
                  obseruance,

                Thomas Heywood.

ᔧ To the Right Worſhipfull *Samuell Cranmer*, and *Henry Pratt*, the two Sheriffs of the Honourable Citty of *London, Lately Elected.*

Right Worſhipfull,

*He cheife Magiſtrats next vnto the Lord Maior, are the two ſheriffes, the name* Sheriffe *implyeth as much as the Reeue and Gouernour of a Shcire, for* Reeue : *is* Graue Count *or* Earle (*for ſo ſaith Maſter* Verſtigan :) *and theſe, were of like authority with the* Cenſors, *who were reputed in the prime and beſt ranke amongſt the Magiſtrates of* Rome ? *They were ſo cal'd a* Ceſſendo, *of ceaſing, for they ſet a rate vpon euery mans eſtate : regiſtring their names, and placing them in a fit century : A ſecond part of their Office conſiſted in the reforming of maners, as hauing power to inquire into euery mans life and carriage. The Embleame of which Authority was their* Tirgula cenſoria *borne before them : they are (by others) reſembled to the* Tribunes *of*

the people, and thefe are cal'd Sacro Sancti, *whofe perfons might not be iniured, nor their names any way fcandaliz'd, for whofoeuer was proued to be a delinquent in either, was held to be* Homo facer; *an excommunicated perfon, and hee that flew him was not liable vnto any Iudgement: their Houfes ſtand open continually, not onely for Hofpitality, but for a Sanctuary to all fuch as were diftreſt: neither was it lawfull for them to be abfent from the Colledge one whole day together, during their Yeare. Thus you fee how neere the Dignities of this Citty, come neere to thefe in* Rome, *when it was moſt flouriſhing. The firſt* Sheriffes *that bore the name and office in this* Citty, *were* Peter Duke, *and* Thomas Neale, *Anno* 1209. *The nouiſſimi, now in prefent* Samuell Cranmer *and* Henry Pratt. *Anno* 1631. *To whom I direct this ſhort Remembrance.*

Your Worſhips euer

Attendant,

Thomas Heywood.

LONDONS

Ius Honorarium.

Hen *Rome* was erected: at the firſt eſtabliſhing of a common weale, *Romulus* the founder of it, inſtituted a prime officer to gouerne the Citty, who was cald *præfectus vrbis, i.e.* the præfect of the City, whoſe vncontroulable authority, had power, not onely to examine, but to determine, all cauſes & controuerſies, & to ſit vpon, and cenſure all delinquents, whether their offences were capitall or criminall: *Intra centiſſimum lapidem*, within an hundred miles of the City, in proceſſe of time the *Tarquins* being expeld, & the prime foueraignty remaining in the conſuls. They (by reaſon of their forraigne imployments) hauing no leaſure to adminiſter Iuſtice at home, created two cheife officers, the one they cald *prætor vrbanus*, or *Maior*, the other *peregrinus*: The firſt had his iuriſdiction, in and ouer the Citty, the other excerciſed his authority meerely vpon ſtrangers.

The name *Prætor* is deriued from *Præſcendo* or *Præeundo*, from priority of place, which as a learned Roman Author writs, had abſolute power ouer all publique aud priuat affaires, to make new Lawes, and abolifh old, without controwle, or contradiction: His authority growing to that height, that whatfoeuer he decreed or cenfured in publique, was cald *Ius Honorarium*, the firft on whome this dignity was conferd in *Rome*, was *fpur* : *furius Camillus*, the fonne of *Marcus* : And the firft *Prætor* or Lord Maior appointed to the Gouernment of the Honorable Citty of *London*, was *Henry Fitz Allwin*, aduaunced to that Dignity, by King *Iohn*, Anno. 1210. fo much for the Honor and Antiquity of the name and place, I proceede to the fhowes.

Vpon the water.

Are two craggy Rockes, plac'd directly oppofit, of that diftance that the Barges may paffe betwixt them : thefe are full of monfters, as Serpents, Snakes, Dragons, &c. fome fpitting Fier, others vomiting water, in the bafes thereof, nothing to be feene, but the fad relicks of fhipwracke in broken Barkes and fplit Veffels, &c. The one is cald *Silla*, the other *Charibdis*, which is fcituate directly againft *Meffana* ; *Scilla* againft *Rhegium* : and what foever fhippe that paffeth thefe Seas, it it keepe not the middle Channell, it is either wrackt upon the one, or deuoured by the other ; *Medio tutifsimus ibit*. Vpon thefe Rocks are placed the *Syrens*, excellent both in voyce and Inftrument : They are three in number, *Telfipio, Iligi, Aglaofi*; or as others will have them called, *Parthenope*, skilfull in muficke ; *Leucofia*, upon the winde Inftrument; *Ligni*, upon the Harpe. The morrall intended by the Poets, that whofoever fhall lend an attentive eare to their muficke, is in great danger to perifh ; but he that can warily avoyd it by ftopping his eares' againft their inchantment, fhall not onely fecure themfelves, but bee their ruine : this was made good in *Vliffes* the fpeaker, who by his wifedome and pollicy not onely preserved himselfe and his people, but was the cause that they from the rocks cast themselves headlong into the Sea. In him is personated a wise and discreete Magistrate.

            Vlisses *his speech.*

BEhold *great Magistrate, on either hand*
   Sands, shelves, and Syrtes, and upon them stand
Two dangerous rocks, your safety to ingage,
Boasting of nought save shipwrake spoyle and strage.
This Sylla, *that* Charibdis, (*dangerous both*)
Plac't in the way you rowe to take your oath.
   Yet though a thousand monsters yawne and gape
To ingurdge and swallow you, ther's way to scape;
Vlisses *by his wisedome found it, steare*
You by his Compasse, and the way lyes cleare,
Will you know how? looke upward then; and sayle
By the signe Libra, *that Celestiall scale,*
In which (some write) the Sunne at his creation
First shone; and is to these times a relation
Of Divine Justice: It in justice shind,
Doe you so (Lora) and be like it divind.
   Keepe the even Channell, and be neither swayde,
To the right hand nor left, and so evade
Malicious envie (never out of action,)
Smooth visadgd flattery, and blacke mouthd detraction,
Sedition, whisprings, murmuring, private hate,
All ambushing, the godlike Magistrate.
   About these rockes and quicksands Syrens *haunt,*
One singes connivence, th' other would inchaunt
With partiall sentence; and a third ascribes,
In pleasing tunes, a right to gifts and bribes;
Sweetning the eare, and every other fence,
That place, and office, may with these dispence.
But though their tones be sweete, and shrill their
   notes,

They come from foule brests, and impostum'd throats,
Sea monsters they be stiled, but much (nay more,
'Tis to be doubted,) they frequent the shoare.
   Yet like Vlisses, *doe but stop your eare*
To their inchantments, with an heart sincere;
They fayling to indanger your estate,
Will from the rocks themselves precipitate.
   Proceede then in your blest Inauguration,
And celebrate this Annual Ovation;
Whilst you nor this way, nor to that way leane,
But shunne th' extreames, to keepe the golden meane.
This glorious City, Europs *chiefest minion,*
Most happy in so great a Kings dominion:
Into whose charge this day doth you invest,
Shall her in you, and you in her make blest.

The first show by land.

THe first show by Land, (presented in *Pauls* Church yard, is a greene and pleasant Hill, adorned with all the Flowers of the spring, upon which is erected a faire and flourishing tree, furnished with variety of faire and pleasant fruite, under which tree, and in the most eminent place of the Hill, sitteth a woman of beautiful aspect, apparrelled like Summer: Her motto, *Civitas bene Gubernata. i.* a Citty well governed. Her Attendants (or rather Associats) are three Damsels habited according to their qualitie, and representing the three Theologicall vertues, *Faith, Hope,* and *Charity*: Amongst the leaves and fruits of this Tree, are inscerted diverse labels with severall sentences expressing the causes which make Cities to flourish and prosper: As, *The feare of God, Religious zeale, a Wise Magistrate, Obedience to rulers, Vnity, Plaine and faithfull dealing,* with others of the like nature. At the foot of the Hill sitteth old Time, and by him his daughter Truth, with this infcription; *Veritas eſt Temporis Filia, i.* Truth is the Daughter of Time; which Time fpeaketh as followeth.

Tymes fpeech.

Non nova funt femper, & quod fuit Ante relictum eſt fit que quod haud fuerat, &c.

IF Time *(fome fay) have bin here
oft in view
Yet not the fame, old* Time *is each day
new,
Who doth the future lockt up houres inlarge,
To welcome you to this great Cities charge.*
Time, *who hath brought you hither (grave and great)
To inaugure you, in your Prætorium feate:
Thus much with griefe doth of him felfe profeſſe
Nothing's more precious, and efteemed leſſe.
Yet you have made great ufe of me, to afpire
This eminence, by defert, when in full quire
Avees and Acclamations, with loud voyce,
Meete you on all fides, and with* Time *re'oyce.
This Hill, that Nimph apparreld like the Spring,
Thefe Graces that attend her, (every thing)
As fruitful trees, greene plants, flowers of choife fmell,
All Emblems of a City governd well;
Which muſt be now your charge. The Labels here
Mixt with the leaves will ſhew what fruit they
beare:*
The feare *of* God, *a* Magiftrate difcreete,
Iuftice *and* Equity: *when with thefe meete,*
Obedience unto Rulers, Vnity,
Plaine *and* juft dealing, Zeale, *and* Induftry:
*In fuch bleſt fymptoms where thefe ſhall agree,
Cities, ſhall like perpetuall Summers bee.
You are now Generall, doe but bravely lead,
And (doubtleſſe) all will march, as you ſhall tread:
You are the Captaine, doe but bravely ſtand
To oppofe vice, fee, all this goodly band
Now in their City Liveries will apply
Themfelves to follow, where your Colours fly.
You are the chiefe, defend my daughter* Truth,

And then both Health and Poverty, Age and Youth,
Will follow this your Standard, to oppofe
Errour, Sedition, Hate, (the common foes.)
  But pardon Time *(grave Lord) who fpeaks to thee,*
As well what thou now art, as ought to be.

Then Time maketh a paufe, and taking up a leave-leffe & withered branch, thus proceedeth.

See you this withered branch, by Time *o're growne*
A Cities Symbole, ruind, and trod downe.
A Tree that bare bad fruit ; Diffimulation,
Pride, Malice, Envy, Atheifme, Supplantation,
Ill Government, Prophannes, Fraud, Oppreffion,
Neglect of vertue, Freedome to tranfgreffion,
Obedience, *here with power did difagree,*
All which faire London *be ftill farre from thee.*

The fecond fhow by land. The fecond fhow by Land, is prefented in the upper part of Cheapfide, which is a Chariot; The two beafts that are placed before it, are a Lyon paffant, and a white Vnicorne in the fame pofture, on whofe backs are feated two Ladies, the one reprefenting *Iuftice* upon the Lyon, the other *Mercy* upon the Vnicorne. The motto which *Iuftice* beareth, is *Rebelles protero* ; the infcription which *Mercy* carrieth, is *Imbelles protego* : Herein is intimated, that by thefe types and fymboles of Honour (reprefented in thefe noble beafts belonging to his Majeftie) all other inferiour magiftracies and governments either in Common weales, or private Societies, receive both being and fupportance.

The prime Lady feated in the firft and moft eminent place of the Chariot, reprefenteth *London*, behinde whom, and on either fide, diverfe others of the chiefe Cities of the Kingdome take place : As *Weftminfter, Yorke, Briftoll, Oxford, Lincolne, Exeter*, &c. All thefe are to be diftnguifhed by their feverall Efcutchons ; to them *London* being Speaker, directeth he firft part of her fpeech as followeth.

London the speaker. *You noble Cities of this generous Isle,*
May these my two each Ladies ever smile.
(Iustice, and mercy) on you. You we know
Are come to grace this our triumphant show.
And of your curtesy, the hand to kisse
Of London, this faire lands Metropolis.
Why sister Cittyes sit you thus amazd?
Ist to behold above you, windows glas'd
With Diamonds 'sted of glasse? Starres hither sent,
This day to deck our lower Firmament?
Is it to see my numerous Children round
Incompasse me? So that no place is found.
In all my large streets empty? My yssue spred
In number more then stones whereon they tread.
To see my Temples, Houses, even all places,
With people covered, as if Tyl'd with faces?
Will you know whence proceedes this faire increase,
This ioy? the fruits of a continued peace,
The way to thrive; to prosper in each calling,
The weake, and shrinking states, to keepe from falling,
Behold; my motto shall all this display,

Serve and obey: the Motto of the Worshp. Company of the Habberd.

Reade and observe it well: Serve and obay.

Obedience *though it humbly doth begin,*
It soone augments unto a Magazin
Of plenty, in all Citties 'tis the ground,
And doth like harmony in musicke found:
Nations and Common weales, by it alone
Flourish: It incorporates, many into one,
And makes vnanimous peace content and joy,
Which pride, doth still Insidiate to destroy.
And you grave Lord, on whom right honour calls.
Both borne and bred i' th circuit of my wals,
By vertue and example, have made plaine,
How others may like eminence attaine.
Persist in this blest concord, may we long,
That Citties to this City may still throng,

To view my annuall tryumphs, and so grace,
Those honored Pretors *that supply this place.*

Next after the Chariot, are borne the two rocks, *Sylla* and *Caribdis*, which before were prefented upon the water: upon the top of the one ftands a Sea Lyon vpon the other a Meare-maide or *Sea-Nimphe*, the *Sirens* and *Monfters*, beeing in continuall agitation and motion, fome breathing fire, others fpowting water, I fhall not neede to fpend much time in the Defcription of them, the worke being fufficiently able to Commend it felfe.

The third fhew by Land Prefented neere vnto the great Crofle in Cheape-fide, beareth the title of the *Palace* of *Honour*: A faire and curious ftructure archt and Tarreft aboue, on the Top of which ftandeth *Honour*, a Glorious prefens, and richtly habited, fhee in her fpeech directed to the right Honorable: the Lord Maior, difcouers all the true and direct wayes to attaine vnto her as, firft:

A King: Eyther by fucceffion or Election.
A Souldier, by valour and martiall Difcipline.
A Churchman by Learning and degrees in fcooles.
A Statesman by Trauell and Language, &c.
A Lord Maior by Commerce and Trafficke both by Sea and Land, by the Inriching of the Kingdome, and Honour of our Nation.

The Palace of Honour is thus governed
    Induftry *Controwler*, his Word
      Negotior
   Charity *Steward*, the Word
     Miferior.
   Liberality *Trefurer*, the Word
     Largior.
 Innocence and } *Henchmen*, the words,
 Deuotion
   Patior : *Precor.*

And fo of the reft, and according to this Pallace of *Honour* is facioned not onely the management of the whole *Citty* in generall : but the Houfe and Family of the *Lord Maior* in particular.

Before in the Front of this pallace is feated Saint *Katherin*, the Lady and Patroneffe of this Worfhipfull Society of whom I will giue you this fhort Character, the name it felfe imports in the Originall, *Omnis ruina*, which (as fome interpret it) is as much as to fay, the fall and ruin of all the workes of the Diuell : Others deriue the word from *Catena*, a Chaine wherein all cheife Vertues and Graces are concatinated and link't together, fo much for her name.

For her birth, fhee was lineally defcended from the Roman Emperours, the daughter of *Coftus* the fonne of *Conftantine* which *Coftus* was Crowned King of *Armenia*, for *Conftantine* hauing conquered that King dome, grew Inamored of the Kings Daughter by whom he had Iffue, this *Coftus* who after fucceeded his Grand Father.

Conftantine after the death of his firft Wife made an expedition from *Roome*, and hauing Conquered this Kingdome of Great Britaine : he tooke to his Second Wife *Helena*, which *Helena* was fhe that found the Croffe vpon which the Sauiour of the World was Crucified, &c.

Coftus Dying whilft *Katherine* was yet young, and fhee being all that Time liuing in *Famogofta*, (a cheife City) becaufe fhee was there Proclaimed and Crowned was called *Queene* of *Famogofta*, fhe liued and dyed a Virgin and a *Martyr* vnder the Tiranny of *Maxentius*, whofe Empreffe, with many other great and eminent perfons fhe had before conuerted to the Faith. So much for her character. Her fpeech to the Lord Maior as followeth.

I Katherine, *long fince Sainted for true piety,*
 The Lady patroneffe of this Society,
A queene, a Virgin, and a Martir : All
My Attributes : Inuite you to this Hall

Cald Honours pallace: nor is this my Wheele,
Blind Fortunes Embleame, fhe that makes to reele;
Kingdomes and Common weales, all turning round,
Some to aduance, and others to Confound:
 Mine is the Wheele of Faith, (*all wayes in motion*)
Stedfaſt in Hope, *and Conſtant in Deuotion.*
It imitates the Spheres fwift agitation,
Orbicularly, ſtill mouing to Saluation:
That's to the Primus motor: *from whom Flowes,*
All Goodneſſe, Vertue: There, true Honour growes.
 Which: If you will attaine t' muſt be your care,
(*Graue Magiſtrate*) *Inſtated as you are,*
To keepe this Curoular action, in your charge,
To Curbe th' opreſſor, the oppreſt to inlarge;
To be the Widdowes Husband, th' Orphants Father,
The blindmans eye, the lame mans foot: fo gather
A treaſure beyond valew, by your place;
(*More then Earths Honour,*) *trew Cœleſtiall grace,*
Ayme firſt at that: what other Honors be,
Honour Her felfe can beſt Inſtruct thats fhee.

At that word fhee poynteth vpward to a Glorious prefens which perfonates *Honor* in the top of the pallace, who thus fecondeth *Saint Katherens Speech*.

Honours Speech.

The way to me though not debard,
Yet it is dificult and hard.
If Kings arrive to my profection
Tis by Succeſſion, or Election
When Fortitude *doth Action grace,*
The Souldier then with me takes place
When Stooddy, Knowledge and degree
Makes Scollers *Eminent heere with mee;*
They 'are lifted with the Honored: and
The Trauilar, *when many a land*

He hath 'peirſt for language, and much knowes
A great reſpected ſtateſman growes.
  So you, and ſuch as you (Graue Lord)
Who weare this Scarlet, vſe that Sword
Collar, and Cap of Maintenance.
Theſe are no things, that come by chance
Or got by ſleeping but auerſe
From theſe I am gain'd : by care, Commerce,
The hazarding of Goods, and men
To Pyrats Rocks, ſhelues, Tempeſt, when ?
You through a Wilderneſſe of Seas,
Dangers of wrack, Surpriſe, Defeaſe
Make new deſcoueryes, for a laſting ſtory
Of this our Kingdomes fame and Nations glory
Thus is that Collar, and your Scarlet worne,
And for ſuch cauſe, the Sworde before you Borne.
They are the emblems of your Power, and heere
Though curb'd within the Limmet of one yeare,
Yet manadge as they ought by your Indeuour,
Shall make your name (as now) Honored for euer.
Vnto which Pallace of peace, reſt and bliſſe,
Supply of all things, where nought wanting is
Would theſe that ſhall ſucceede you know the way ?
Tis plaine, God, the King Serue *and* Obay.

I cannot heare forget that in the preſentment of my papers to the Maſter, Wardens, & Committies of this Right Worſhipfull Company of the Haberdaſhers (at whoſe ſole expence and charges all the publick Triumphes of this dayes Solemnity both by water and land, were Celebrated) nothing here deuiſed or expreſſed was any way forraigne vnto them, but of all theſe my conceptions, they were as able to Iudge, as ready to Heare, and to direct as well as to Cenſure ; nether was there any dificulty which needed a comment, but as ſoone known as ſhowne, and apprehended as read : which makes me now confident of the beſt ranke of the Cittiſens : That as to the Honour and ſtrength both of the Citty and Kingdome in generall, they excerciſe

Armes in publicke, fo to the benefit of their Iudgements, and inriching of their knowledge, they neglect not the ftuddy of arts, and practife of literature in priuate, fo that of them it may be truly faid they are, *Tam Mercurio quam Marte periti*: I proceede now to the laft Speech at night in which *Vliſſes* at the taking leaue of his Lordſhip at his Gate, vfeth this ſhort Commemoration, of all that hath been included in the former pageants, poynting to them in order, the manner thereof thus.

Night growes, Inuiting you to reſt, prepare
To riſe to morrow to a whole Yeares care,
Enuy ſtill waites on Honour, *then prouide*
Vliſſes *Wiſdome may be ſtill your guide*
To ſtere you through all dangers : Husband Time
That this day brings you to a place ſublime,
By the Supporture of his daughter Truth
This Ancient Citty *in her priſtine Youth,*
Your ſword may reeſtabliſh : and ſo bring
Her ſtill to floriſh; like that laſting Spring
That London *in whoſe Circuit you were bred*
And borne therein, to be the Cheife and Head
Drawne by theſe two beaſts in an Equall line
May in your Mercy *and your* Iuſtice *ſhine.*
So Honour *who this day did you Inuite*
Vnto Her palace bids you thus Good Night,
No following day but adde to your Renowne
And this your Charge, with numerous Bleſſings crowne.

I have forborne to fpend much paper in needeleſſe and Inpertinent deciphering the worke, or explaining the habits of the perfons, as being freely expofed to the publicke view of all the Spectators. The maine fhow, being performed by the moſt excellent in that kind, Maiſter *Gerard Chriſtmas* hath expreſt his Modals to be exquifite (as hauing fpared nei-ther Coſt nor care, either in the Figures or ornaments. I fhall not neede to point vnto them to fay, this is a Lyon, and that an Vnicorne, &c. For of this Artift, I may bouldly and freely thus much fpeake, though many about the towne may enuie their worke, yet with all their indeuor they fhall not be able to compare with their worth. I Conclude with *Plautus in ſticho* : *Nam curiofus eſt nemo qui non fit malevolus.*

FINIS.

Londini Sinus Salutis,

OR,

Londons *Harbour of Health, and Happineſſe.*

Expreſſed in ſundry Triumphs, Pageants and Showes; at the Initiation of the Right Honorable,

CHRISTOPHER CLETHROWE,

Into the Maioralty of the farre Renowned City London.

All the Charges and Expences of this preſent Ovation; being the ſole undertaking of the Right Worſhipfull Company of the *Ironmongers.*

The 29. of October, Anno Salutis. 1635.

Written by Thomas Heywood.

——*Redeunt Spectacula,*——

Printed at *London* by *Robert Raworth.* 1635.

TO THE RIGHT
Honorable, *Chriſtopher Clethrowe*,
Lord Maior of this Renowned
Metropolis, LONDON,

RIGHT HONOURABLE,

*T is one of* Erasmus *his undeniable Apothegms, that there is no Citie can bee ſo ſtrongly immur'd or Defenc'd, but may bee either by Engins defaced, by Enemies inuaded, or by Treaſon ſurprized*; but the Counſells and Decrees of a wiſe Magiſtrate, are in-expugnable. Time, and your Merit, have call'd you to this Office and Honor : As all eyes are upon you, ſo all hearts are towards you ; *never was any more freely voyc't in his Election, and therfore none more hopefull in expectation*: your Abilitie, *what you can doe, is known*; your purpoſe, *what you intend,* you have amply delivered; your purpoſe, *what you* intend, you have amply delivered ; onely the Performance remaines : *In which, there is no queſtion, but that you will* accommodate all your future Proceedings to theſe three heads : Pro Rege, pro Lege, pro Grege ; *for as you are a Magiſtrate, ſo you are a Iudge*: A calling, both of Truſt, and Trouble : *Of* Truſt; becauſe all ſuch as ſit in Iudicature, are Perſons ordained by GOD, to examine Cauſes diſcreetely ; Heare both Parties Conſiderately,

and Cenſure all matters unpartially: *For* Iuſtice *is the Badge of* Vertue, *the ſtaffe of* Peace, *and the maintainance of* Honor. *Of* Trouble; *becauſe in no part of your Time; during your regency, neither in publicke, or private, forraine, or domeſtick things, whether you meditate alone, or conuerſe with others, you ſhall find the leaſt vacancie, which remembers me of that which* Dion *witneſſeth of one* Similis, *who living long in great Place and Authoritie under the Emperour* Adrian, *after much intreaty, got leave to retire himſelfe into the Countrey, where after ſeaven contented yeeres expiring, hee cauſed this Epitaph to be Inſculpt upon his tombe*: Similis hic jacet, cujus ætas multorum fuit annorum. Septem tamen Duntaxat, Annos vixit. Lanctantius *further teacheth us, that it is moſt requiſite, in all ſuch as have charge in the Common Weale, under their Prince and Governour, ſo to know the bownds of their Calling, and underſtand the full effects of their dutie, that by executing* Iuſtice, *they may be feared, and by ſhewing* Mercy, *bee loved*: *I conclude all in this ſhort ſentence*, Non, quid Ipſe velis, ſed quod lex & Religio Cogat, Cogita, *Ever ſubmitting my ſelfe to your better Iudgement, and remaining, to your Lordſhip moſt obſequious.*

THO. HEYWOOD.

LONDONS
SINVS SALVTIS.

 shall not neede to borrow my Induction from the Antiquitie of this Famous *Metropolis*, nor to enter into a large difcourfe, of the noble Magiftracy and government thereof; being Arguments already granted, and therefore unneceffary to be difputed: and yet I hold it not altogether Impertinent to remember fome few things of remarke, which have happened in the Prætorfhips of the Right Honourable, the Lord Maiors of this Renowned Citie, who have beene Free of the Right Worfhipfull Company of the *Iron-mongers*.

In the year 1409, RICHARD MARLOE, of the fame Fraternitie, bearing the Sword, there was a Show prefented by the Parifh *Clerkes* of *London*, at a place called *Skinners Well*, and now *Clerken Well*, which was of matter from the Creation of the World; and lafted for the fpace of Eight Intyre dayes: EDWARD the *Fourth* (then King) being prefent with his Queene, and the greateft part of his Nobilitie, which RICHARD MARLOE, was after Inaugurated Into the fame Honor, *Anno* 1417. In the yeere 1566. Sir CHRISTOPHER DRAPER, being Lord Maior, King IAMES, of late and moft Sacred memory, was borne the Sixth day of *June*, *Anno* 1569. In Sir ALEXANDER AVE-

NONS Maioralty, was the fuppreffion of the Rebells in the *North*, *Anno* 1581. Sir FRANCIS HARVEY being Mayor, was the *French Mounfiers* comming over into *England*, and his Royall entertainement by Queene ELIZABETH, *Anno* 1607. Sir THOMAS CAMBEL being Invefted into the fame Honor: All the like Showes and Triumphs belonging unto the folemnitie of this day, which for fome yeeres, had beene omitted and neglected, were by a fpeciall commandement from his Majeftie, King IAMES, againe retained, and have beene till this prefent day continued; whom fince hath fucceeded in the fame Honor, Sir IAMES CAMBEL, his Sonne, a worthy Senator of this Citie, yet living. (The laft of this worthy and Worfhipfull Company, who hath fate in that feate of Iuftice) now this day fucceeded by the Right Honourable, CHRISTOPHER CLETHROWE: but I leave all circumftances, and come to the Showes, now in prefent Agitation.

The firft Showe by Water:

IS an Artificiall Moddell, partly fafhioned like a Rock, and beautified with fundry varieties, and rarities, in all which Art (in Imitating) ftriveth to exceed Nature: The Decorements that adorne the Structure, I omit, and defcend to the Perfons that furnifh it, which are the Three Cæleftiall Goddeffes, *Iuno, Pallas, Venus*: In *Iuno*, is figured Power and State; In *Pallas* or *Minerua*, Arms and Arts; In *Venus*, Beautie and Love: The firft beft knowne by her *Peacocks*; the fecond by her *Owles*; the third by her *Swans* & *Turtles*, who is alfo attended by her Sonne *Cupid*, in whom is Emblem'd *Love;* by whom fome have thought, the Vniverfe to have beene Created, becaufe of the Beautie, Glory, and Flourifhing forme thereof, as alfo, that *Love* (though pictured young) yet in Age exceeds all things: But *Venus*, becaufe borne of the Seas, I hold moft proper to fpeake upon the Waters: Thefe Three Goddeffes are sent from *Jupiter*, with severall Presents, to honour this dayes Triumphs, and him to whom they are devoted; *Iuno* brings Power, *Pallas* Wisedome, *Venus* Love; whose Speech is as followeth:

Venus the Speaker.

THe Three *Cœlestiall goddesses this day*
    Descend (*Grave* Prætor) *to prepare your way*
To your new Oath, and Honor : Iove, *whose station*
Is still above, hath sent to this Ovation
And glorious Triumph, Vs : Iuno *the great*
And Potent Queene ; *who to your Iurall seat,*
Brings State and Power : Pallas, *who from* Ioves *brain*
Derives her selfe, and from the highest straine
Of all the other gods, claimes her descent,
Her Divine Wisedome, doth this day present.
  But I, Emergent Venus, *Loves faire Queene,*
Borne of the Seas ; *and therefore best beseene*
To speake upon the Waters, bring a gift,
Priz'd equally with theirs ; *that which shall lift*
You up on voyces, and from the low frame
Of sordid Earth, give you (*above*) *a name* :
From iust affections. and pure thoughts, Love *springs,*
And these are Impt with no Icarian *wings,*
But Plumes Immortall, such as Angels beare,
To fixe your Name in an eternall spheare.
  Which to attaine ; *Take* Iuno *for your guide,*
Maintaine her Peacocks riches, not her pride ;
Who to prove all Earths glory is but vaine,
Lookes but upon her feete, and flaggs her traine.
  Obserue next Pallas *Owles, and from them take*
This notion ; *you must watch even as they wake* :
For all such as the management of state
Shall undergoe, rise earlie, and bed late,
So Wisedome is begot ; *from Wisedome Love,*
(*Sweete Child of such a Parent*) *may't then prove* :
That as this day you doe attract the eyes,

And expectation of the great, and wise,
So in the happy progreſſe of your yeere,
You may their hearts and ſoules to you Indeere:
From Love, *your Waters paſſage vnderſtand,*
But Power *and* Wiſedome *wellcoms you on land.*

THe next Modell by Land, which was onely ſhowne upon the Water, is one of the twelue Cæleſtiall ſignes: *Sagitarius* called *Croton*; hee, before he was tranſlated into the Heavens, was ſaid to bee the Sonne of *Pan*, and the Nimph *Euphemes*, and in his Infancy, was *Conlacteus Muſarum. i.* Hee ſuckt of the ſame breſt with the *Muſes*, his mother being their Nurſe and dwelt in *Helicon*; hee was Famous for his skill in Archerie, wonderous ſwift of foote, and when the Nine *Siſters* ſung to their ſeverall inſtruments of Muſick, his cuſtome was to dance before them in ſundry active figures and poſtures. For which, and other indowments, knowne to be eminent in, hee was at their requeſt to *Iupiter* tranſlated amongſt the ſtarres, in the plat-forme, on which hee is borne: at the foure corners, are ſeated foure other dignified with the like Conſtellations: *Virgo*, beſt knowne by the name of *Aſtrea* and *Iuſta*, the daughter of *Iupiter*, and *Themis*; and for her Iuſtice and Integritie, thither transferr'd, and numbred amongſt the Twelue: Next *Ariadne*, beſt knowne amongſt the *Aſtrologians*, by the name of *Corona*, the Crowne, which was ſaid to bee forged by *Vulcan* in *Lemnos*, the materialls thereof were Gold, and *Indian* Gemmes, of extraordinary ſplendor, which ſhee lending to *Theſeus* at that time when her Father *Minos* had expos'd him to the *Minotaure*, by the luſter thereof, hee paſſed freely through the darkneſſe of the Laborinth: Some ſay, it was firſt given her by *Liberpater*, or *Bacchus*, the Sonne of *Iupiter* and *Semele*, and was the price of her Virginitie: but howſoever, ſhee being moſt ingratefully forſaken by *Theſeus*, in the Ile of *Naxos*; was there found by *Bacchus*, who having

Sagitarius.

Virgo.

Ariadne.

Londons Sinus Salutis.

espoused her with great solemnitie, caused her after her death, with this Crowne to bee Inuested in the Firmament. The Third, *Cassiopeia*, Cassiopeia. the wife of *Cepheus*, who preferring her owne beautie before the *Nereides*, who were the daughters of *Neptune*, was for that insolence, doom'd to be bownd in a chayre, hand and foote, and so placed amongst the spheares, where shee remaines Conspicuous, in Thirteene Starres. The Fourth, is *Andro-* *meda*, the Daughter of *Cepheus* and *Cassio-* Andromeda. *peia*, who by the wrath of *Neptune*, being chain'd unto a Rocke, and ready to bee devoured by a Sea Monster, was delivered thence by *Perseus*, the Sonne of *Iupiter*, and *Danaæ*, to whom being after married, was call'd *Persa*, and Stellified by *Minerua* : The Speaker is an *Astrologian*.

¶ The Speech followeth :

Late risen in the Heaven is Sagitary,
(*With you, great Lora*) *who doth about him carry*
Fifteene bright Starres, most Influent, and these all
Appearing in the Circle hiemall :
His Bow deuided in that beaten roade,
Call'd Galaxia, *where the gods haue troade*
So oft ; that looke upon it in the night,
When all the rest's dull, that alone shines bright :
(*As you now at this instant :*) *Hee fifteene*
Starres, did I say ? How you then ; who betweene
Your landing and repose, by power divine,
Have full Three-score, about your state to shine :
For every Company's *a Starre this day,*
Visible to all, and over these you sway :
But twelue in chiefe ; and those wee must confesse,
Of greater lustre made, to guide the lesse :
All enioy one like Freedome, all are Free,
And all (Great Prætor) *to bee rul'd by thee :*
Commanding all the rest, who in thy spheare,
Now rising, art to shine a compleate yeere.

*You may obserue his Bow still ready bent,
In which there is a perfect Emblem ment
Of Divine Iustice: Th' Arrow, with a Starre
Headed, Implies, that her power reacheth farre;
And no oppofure, fraude, violence, or rape,
Can (when shee aimes to strike) her vengeance scape;
Yet though the string be drawne up to his eare,
(As alwayes prest) hee rather seemes with feare
To threat, then punish, and though hee can still
Let loose his shafts, hee seldome shoots to kill.
  Obserue it well, the Morrall doth imply,
All Iustice should be mixt with lenitie,
So, Imitate the gods, since them wee know,
Apt still to Mercie, but to vengeance flow:
And the Cœlestiall bodies, though they trade
Above, yet were for our example made.
As oft as man sinnes, should Ioue punnish vice,
His Quiver would be emptied in a trice,
And man-kind, at once perish: O mixe them
Mercy with Iustice, Interweave againe
Iustice with Mercy; so shall you in your state,
Not Starres alone, but the gods Imitate:
So shall your Terrene body, in the end,
All the Cœlestiall bodies farre transcend,
And deckt with better lights then those you see
Above the spheares, shine to eternitie.*

THe Third Plat-forme, is contrived onely for Pastime, to please the vulgar, and therefore deserves no further Charractar, then a plaine nomination, as devised onely to please the eye, but no way to feast the eare: and so I leave it to proceede to the next.

THe Fourth Moddell, is a Castle munified with sundry Peeces of Ordnance; and Accomodated with all such Persons as are needfull for the defence of such a Citadell: the Gunner being ready to give fire upon all occasions; as for the curious Art in the contriving thereof, I make no queſtion but the worke it ſelfe is ſufficiently able to commend the Workeman, being knowne to be an excellent Artiſt, of which, the ſpectatours may beſt cenſure ; I will onely deliver unto you a word or two concerning the preſenter, which is *Mars*.

Mars. Hee is ſtyled the third amongſt the gods, becauſe hee ſtands in that degree amongſt the Planets : and is ſaid to be the ſonne of *Iupiter* ; ſome write that *Bellona* was his Nurſſe, others that ſhe was his Mother, and ſome his ſiſter. Yet none of theſe improper, for *Ennio* which is *Bellona*, implies no more then an incouragement of the minde to hardineſſe and valour in all Skyrmiſhes and Battailes. He His ſundry is alſo cal'd *Ares* which ſignifieth Dammage Denominations. or detriment, and *Mavors* quaſi *Mares vorans*, of devouring of men ; and by the *Gentiles*, had the Denomination of the god of Battailes. He was antiently figured an angry man ſitting in a Chariot, armed with a ſheild and other weapons, both offenſiue, and defenſiue. Vpon his head a plumed Helmet, his ſword mounted vpon his thigh, hee held in one hand a whip, in the other, the Raines, being drawne in his Chariot by wylde and vntam'd Horſes. Before him was portraied a Wolfe devouring a Lambe, the Wolfe being the beaſt particularly offered vpon his ſhrine, and becauſe the two *Romane* Twinnes the firſt founders of *Rome*, ROMVLVS and REMVS, were fained to be the ſonnes of *Mars* (of which the one ſlewe the other) therefore ROMVLVS is figured vpon his Chariot as the vnnatural ſurvivor. The *Athenians* were the firſt that ever ſacrificed to this god of Warre, which Celebration was call'd *Ekaton pephomena* for whoſoever had ſlaine an Hundred of the publike Enemies, was bownd to ſacrifice a man vpon his Altar, ſituate in the Ile *Lemnos*, but after the bloodineſſe, and inhumanitie thereof, diſpleaſing the *Athenians*, they changed that cuſtome, and in ſtead of a man, offered a gelded Hogge, which they call'd *Nefrendes* : *Varro* writes, that amongst the *Romans*, SICINNIVS DENTATVS, having fought one hundered and Ten severall Duells, and being Victor in them all, receiving Forty five wounds, whose skarres were visible upon his body, all before, and none backward: Hee was for his Valour, honoured with Twenty five severall Crownes, and received moreover, an Hundred and Forty golden Bracelets; and was the first amongst the *Romanes*, that ever made oblation to this Deity: *Mars* sitting in the front of the Tower, speakes as followeth.

The *Speech* of Mars.

BEllipotent Mars *is from his spheare come downe,*
To heighten these brave Triumphs of Renowne,
Seated *in this mur'd Citadel, defenc'd* A Peece goes off.
With Bullets wrapt in Fire, and Cloudes condenst.
  The Tormentary Art, *not long since found,*
Which shatters Towers, & by which Ships are drown'd,
I bring along; to let you understand
These guard your safety, both by Sea, and Land.
  O, *when I late saw from mine orbe Divine,*
So many Sonnes of Mars, *amongst you, shine*
In compleat Arms, *Plum'd Casks, and Ensigns spred*
By such brave Captaines, *and* Commanders *led*:
No Souldier, but his Posture to the life,
Acting to'th Musick of the Drum and Fyffe,
Some practising small Bombards, some the great,
Whose very thunder, rowsd mee from my seate:
This Peacefull Citie, *I much prayf'd, whose power*
Could to a Campe, *it selfe change in an houre*:
Proceed in your brave Practise; whilst I tell
Wherein your Iron *and* Steele *doth most excell.*
  Without these Metalls, *Nature could produce*
Nothing that is conducefull to mans use:
The Plow, *without the* Coulter *and the* Share,
Could make no Furrows, and those Graines that are
Vpon them throwne, were lost to them that sowe them,
Without the Sickle, *or the* Sythe *to mowe them*:

The Gardeners Art, *would ceafe to be a trade,*
If take from him the Matocke, *and the* Spade.
In Denns and Caves wee fhould be forc'd to dwell,
Were there no Axes *made, that* Timber *fell* :
Nor on the Seas could wee have Shipps *to fayle,*
Without the Sawe, *the* Hammer, *and the* Nayle :
Aske thofe that take in Angling *moft delight,*
Without the baited Hooke, *no fifh will bite.*
The Iron Crowe *turnes up the* Indian *mould,*
Trenching the Earth untill they dig out Gold.
If with the Iron *the* Adamant *fhould contend,*
There fhould be no more Compaffe, *but an end*
Of all Difcovery : *Even the Horfe wee ride*
Vnfhod, *would founder, who takes greateft pride,*
When the moft curb'd, *and playing with the* bit,
Hee fnewes the ground, and doth the Spurre *forgit.*
There is no Art, *Craft*, *Faculty*, *or Trade*,
Without it, can fubfift : *Your* Sword *is made*
Of thefe mixt Metalls (*Sir*) Iuftice *would ceafe,*
If (*as in Warre*) *it were not us'd in Peace* :
Power makes it yours, your wifedome now direct you ;
Whilft Peace fwayes heere, Mars *fhall abroad protect*
  you.

THe fpeech being ended, the Ordnance goeth off from the Caftle; and now I come to the fift and laft.

Heere I might enter into large difcourfe, concerning the commodioufneffe of *Iron* and *Steele*, and to fpeake of *Tuball Cain*, who made the firft *Forge*, and found out the vfe of thefe Metalls : as alfo *Vulcan* the deified Smith and of his *Cyclopean Hammers* with which hee was faid to have beaten out *Ioves* Thunderboults, with other fixions to the like purpofe, thefe having before been expofed to the publick view vpon occafion of the like folemnity, & knowing withall that *Cibus his coctus*, relifheth not the quefie ftomackes of thefe times. I therefore purpofly omit them proceeding to the laft Pageants, ftyled *Sinus falutis*, firft the

Boofome, or harbour of Health and Happineffe. The fculpture being adorned with eight feveral perfons, reprefenting fuch vertues as are neceffary to bee imbraced by all fuch Majeftrates, who after their ftormy and tempeftuous progreffe through all judicature caufes incident to their places, feeke to anchor in that fafe and fecure Port fo ftyled.

Every Magiftrate is a minifter vnder God, appointed by his divine ordinance to that calling to be a protector of the Church, a preferuer of difcipline and Peace, confonant with his lawes, the lawes of nature, and the land, which hee ought faithfully to execute, with corporall punifhment, correcting the proud and difobedient, and againft all unjuft oppreffors, defending the conformable and humble. The firft vertue adorning the ftructure is ftiled *Fortitudo togata*, which gowned Fortitude is thus defined.

<small>Fortitudo togata.</small>

A conftancy of minde perfevering in honeft purpofe rightly undertaken and according to his place and calling, tollerating private injuries for lawdable caufe, difpifing pleafures, corrupt guifts, detraction, and the like: and thefe meerly for vertues fake and preferring the publike good before his owne private gaine, &c. Of which *Fabritius* was a noble prefident, who refufing the gold fent him by *Pyrhus* was no whit affrighted with the terror of his Elephants; to fpeake or act any thing againft the dignity of the Republicke. Of whom *Eutropius* reports, *Pyrhus* to have faid: the Sunne is more eafie to bee altered in his courfe, then this *Fabritius* to be removed from his honefty.

<small>Manfuetudo.</small>

Manfuetudo, or gentleneffe is a vertue mediating wrath and fuppreffing all defire of revenge and remitting offences, for publicke concords fake, which notably appeared in *Pericles*, who when one had bitterly rayled on him, for fpace of one whole after noone, in the open market place: night comming, hee caufed his fervants to light him to his houfe with Torches.

Londons Sinus Salutis.

Candor, or fincerity is when without fimulation we
Candor. our felues fpeake, and with no diffidence fufpect the good meaning of others : wifhing all juft men well, rejoycing at theire profperity, and commifferating their difafter : It is reported of *Trajanus* the Emperour, that when *Sura Licinius* one of the Tribunes, was accufed unto him, to have Infidiated his life, not queftioning the faith of fo knowne a friend ; the fame night, un-invited, fupt with him privately in his houfe, and the Table being with-drawne, trufted himfelfe to be trim'd by *Sura's* Barbar.

Patientia Phylofophica. *Patientia Philofophica*, Is a Vertue obedient unto reafon, in bearing wrongs, and fuffering adverfities ; it moderates griefe, and bridles nature, fo that it never rebells againft Iuftice, Modefty, Conftancy, or any other vertue ; *Xenophon* ports *Cyrus* and *Agefolanus* to be of fuch Philofophical patience, that in their height of determination in all their actions, and fpeech, they appeared to all men affable, and offenceleffe.

Placabilitas. Placabilitie is a vertue, having corefpondence with that which I before ftil'd *Manfuctudo*, or Gentleneffe ; *Philofuchia*, or ftudy of Peace, and Concord, is when a Magiftrate thinks Humbly of himfelfe, moderating his owne anger, and bearing with the Infirmities of others, pardoning Injuries, and maintaining unitie, being provident that all unneceflary controverfie bee aton'd, leaft the publike Peace and Vnitie of the Church, or Commonweale be difturbed, or hindred ; of which Vertue, *Abraham* was a moft Imitable Prefident, who, though in Authoritie, Wifedome, and age, hee had, Prioritie before *Lot*, yet not-with-ftanding, gave place to him ; only for Concords fake.

Humanitie, which the *Greekes* call *Ethos*, Is Iuftice, coupled with Gentleneffe, Equitie, Vp-
Humanitas. right-life, Affabilitie, and the like, for which are remark't, *Alexander*, *Cyrus*, *Octavius Cæfar*, &c. It hath alfo beene obferued amongft Schollars (In which

number I may Catalogue your Lordſhip), that the more learned they have beene, they have ſhewed themſelues the more humane, and humble.

<small>Nemeſis ſive Zealus.</small> The laſt is *Nemeſis*, or Zeale, which is an ardent love of Gods glory, of Iuſtice, Pietie, Sanctitie, &c. With an earneſt Indignation againſt whatſoever is evill, ſupporting the Religious, and ſeverely puniſhing the wicked, and refractory. *Phinees zelo Inflammatus Confodit ſcortatorem, &c.* So much to Illuſtrate the Perſons, I come now to the Speech.

HEE that is call'd to bee a Majeſtrate,
    A Guide, a Ruler, or a Candidate,
Muſt of ſo great a burden know the weight;
But firſt the ſtepps that mount him to that height:
Shall I direct you then, what ſayle to beare?
(Like a good Pilot) and what courſe to ſteare:
(Your pardon, Great Sir) daring to deſcry
A paſſage, which you better know then I.
  There is a double Fortitude, *both Crown'd*
With merited Palme; one Gunn'd, the other Gown'd:
The Souldier claymes the firſt, as his by due,
The next, the Civill Sword, now borne by you:
By which, as great a glory you ſhall win
In Peace, *as hee in* Warre, *by curbing ſinne,*
And cheriſhing vertue; In the ſecond place,
Stands Gentleneſſe, *and* Mercy, *O what grace*
Hath Peace, *with* Pitty *mixt?* Metalls *beſt feele,*
When Iron *is well Incorporate with* Steele:
A body ſo calcin'd to publike uſe,
As to ſupport Right, and ſuppreſſe abuſe:
Sinceritie *may chalenge the third claſſe,*
Next Patience, *which by ſuffering, doth ſurpaſſe*
All other Vertues: Placability,
Study of Concord, *and* Fidelity;
Laſt, holy Zeale, *and that doth crowne the reſt:*
All theſe being harbour'd in your honour'd breſt,
Shall (maugre ſhelues and rocks) your paſſage cleare,

And bring you to the Port, *to which you fteare :*
You are the Citties Chiefe, *the Prime, the Sole,*
In expectation : like the ftedfaft Pole :
Proove conftant in your Courfe, be ftill the fame,
*So let your Sword (tutch'd with Truth's Adamant)
  aime*
In your yeeres compaffe, that to all mens view
(Skilfull in ftearage) it may ftill goe true :
  So, thofe that were before you, and rul'd well,
  Equall you fhall, although not Antecell.

THere remaines the Speech at Night, which is onely a Sumnary, or reiteration of the former Showes, Applied to the taking leave of his Lordfhip, and to commend him to his reft : *Mars* being the Speaker.

¶ The Speech at Night.

PHœbus *his Steedes hath ftabled in the* Weft,
  And Night (fucceeding Day) inuites to reft :
The three Cœleftiall Queenes, fent from above,
Leaving with you their Power, *their* Wifdom, Love
Now take their leaves : The Centaure *doth beftow*
On you his Iuftice, *with his fhaft, and bowe,*
Who to your beft repofe, bequeath's you heere,
To mount himfelfe againe unto his fpheare :
The Night being come, he cannot well be mift :
For without him, his Orbe cannot fubfift :
Neither can mine : Now muft my Starre difplay
It's Luminous Rays, being borrowed thence this day,
To waite upon your Triumphs, and fhall ftill
Protect you, and your weighty charge, untill
Hee, which fhall all your upright Actions bleffe,
Conduct you to your Port of Happineffe.

THefe Frames, Modells, and Structures, were Fafhioned, Wrought, and Perfected, by the Two Artifts, IOHN, and MATHIAS CHRISMAS ; Succeffors to their Father, Mr. GERALD CHRISMAS, late difceafed, as well in the Exquifite performance of his qualititie, as in his true finceritie, and honefty; of whom I may confidently fpeake, as no man could out-vie him in thefe Workes, which hee underwent, fo none could outmatch him in his word, For any thing hee undertooke; concerning whom I make no fcruple, thus Ingenioufly to conclude: *Ars patris, in fili·is etiam, poft fata viget.*

FINIS.

Londini Speculum: or,

Londons Mirror, Expreſt in ſundry *Triumphs, Pageants,* and *Showes,* at the Initiation of the right Honorable *Richard Fenn,* into the Mairolty of the Famous and farre renowned City *LONDON.*

All the Charge and Expence of theſe laborious projects both by Water and Land, being the ſole undertaking of the Right Worſhipful Company of the *Habberdaſhers.*

Written by Tho. Heywood.

Imprinted at *London* by *I. Okes* dwelling in little *St. Barthtolmews.* 1637.

To the Right Honour-
able *Richard Fenn*, Lord
Maior of this Renowned
Metropolis LONDON.

Right Honourable:

Xcufe (I intreate) this my boldneffe, which proceedeth rather from *Cuftome* in others, then *Curiofity* in my *Selfe*, in prefuming to prompt your *Memory* in fome things tending to the *greatnes* of your high *place* and *Calling*; You are now entred into one of the moft famous *Mairolties* of the *Chriftian World*. You are alfo cald *Fathers*, *Patrons* of the *Afflicted*, and *Procurators of the Publicke good*. And whatfoever hath reference to the true confideration of *Juftice* and *Mercy*, may be *Analogically* conferd upon pyous and iuft *Magiftrates*.

And for the *Antiquity* of your yearely *Government*, I read that the *Athenians* elected theirs *Annually*: and for no longer continuance: And fo of the *Carthagians*, the *Thebans*, &c. And the *Roman* Senate held, that continued *Magiftracy* was in fome

The Epistle Dedicatory.

respects unprofitable to the *Weale-publicke*, against which there was an *Act* in the Lawes of the twelve Tables. And it is thus concluded by the Learned, that the Dominion of the *greatest Magistrates* which are *Kings* and *Princes*, ought to be perpetuall; but of the lesse which be *Prætors*, *Censors*, and the like, only *Ambulatory* and *Annuall*. I conclude with that saying of a wise man, Prime Officers ought to Rule by Good Lawes, and commendable Example, Iudge by *Providence*, *Wisdome* and *Iustice*, and Defend by *Prowes*, *Care* and *Vigilancy*: These things I can but Dictate, of which your *Lordship* knoweth best how to Dispose: ever (as now) remayning your Honors

Humble servant,

Thomas Heywood.

Londini Speculum,

OR,

Londons Mirrour.

LL Triumphes have their Titles, and fo this, according to the nature thereof, beareth a name: It is called *Londini* Κατόπτρον, that is, *Speculum*, more plainly, *Londons Mirrour*, neither altogether unproperly fo termed, fince fhe in her felfe may not onely perfpicuoufly behold her owne vertues, but all forraigne Cities by her, how to correct their vices.

Her Antiquity fhe deriveth from *Brute*, lineally difcended from *Æneas*, the fonne of *Anchifes* and *Venus*, and by him erected, about the yeare of the world two thoufand eight hundred fifty five: before the Nativity of our bleffed Saviour, one thoufand one hundred and eight: firft cald by him *Trinovantum*, or *Troy-novant*, *New Troy*, to continue the remembancer of the old, and after, in the proceſſe of time *Caier Lud*, that is, *Luds Towne*, of King *Lud*, who not onely greatly repaired the City, but increaſed it with goodly and gorgeous buildings; in the Weſt part whereof, he built a ſtrong gate, which hee called after his owne name *Lud-gate*, and ſo from *Luds Towne*, by contraction of the word and *dialect* uſed in thoſe times, it came ſince to be called *London*.

I will not inſiſt to ſpeake of the name of *Maior*, which implyeth as much as *the greater*, or more prime perſon; ſuch were the *Prætors*, or *Præfecti* in *Rome*, neither were the *Dictators* any more, till *Julius Cæſar* aiming at the Imperiall Purple, was not content with that annuall *honour*, which was to paſſe ſucceſſively from one to another, but he cauſed himſelfe to be Elected *Perpetuus Dictator*, which was in effect no leſſe than Emperor.

And for the name of *Elder-man*, or *Alder-man*, it is ſo ancient, that learned Maſter *Cambden* in his *Britan*, remembreth unto us, that in the daies of Royal King *Edgar*, a noble Earle, and of the Royall blood, whoſe name was *Alwin*, was in ſuch favour with the King, that he was ſtiled *Healf Kunning*, or halfe King, and had the ſtile of Alderman of all *England*: This man was the firſt founder of a famous Monaſtery in the Iſle of *Ely*, where his body lies interred, upon whoſe Tombe was an inſcription in *Latin*, which I have, *verbatim*, thus turned into *Engliſh*, Here reſteth Alwin, *couzen to King* Edgar, *Alderman of all* England, *and of this Holy Abbey the miraculous founder*. And ſo much (being tide to a briefe diſcourſe) may ſerve for the Antiquity of London, and the Titles for *Maior* or *Alderman*.

I come now to the *Speculum*, or *Mirrour*. *Plutarch* tels us, *That a glaſſe in which a man or woman behold their faces, is of no eſtimation or value (though the frame thereof be never ſo richly deckt with gold & gemmes, unleſſe it repreſent unto us the true figure and obiect. Moreover, that ſuch are fooliſh and flattering glaſſes, which make a ſad face to looke pleaſant, or a merry countenance melancholy: but a perfect and a true Chriſtall, without any falſity or flattery, rendreth every obiect its true forme, and proper figure, diſtinguiſhing a ſmile from a wrinkle; and ſuch are the meanes many times to bridle our refractory affections: for who being in a violent rage, would be pleaſed that his ſervant ſhould bring him a glaſſe wherein hee might be hold thetorvity and ſtrange alteration of his countenance? Minerva playing upon a Pipe, was mockt by a Satyre in theſe words.*

> Non te decet forma iſtæc, pone fiſtulas,
> Et Arma capeſſe componens recte genus.

> That viſage miſ-becomes, thy Pipe
> Caſt from thee, Warlike dame,
> Take unto thee thy wonted Armes,
> And keepe thy Cheekes in frame.

But though ſhe deſpiſed his Councell for the preſent, when after, playing upon the ſame Pipe, in which ſhe ſo much delighted, ſhee beheld in a river ſuch a change in her face, ſhee caſt it from her, and broke it aſunder, as knowing that the ſweetnes of her muſick could not countervaile or recompence that deformity which it put upon her countenance, and therefore I have purpoſed ſo true and exact a Mirrour, that in it may be diſcovered as well that which beautifies the governour, as deformes the government.

One thing more is neceſſitouſly to be added, and then I fall upon the ſhowes in preſent agitation: namely, that the fellowſhip of the Merchant Adventurers of *England* were firſt truſted with the ſole venting of the manufacture of Cloth out of this kingdome, & have for above this 4 hundred years traded in a priviledged, & wel governed courſe, in *Germany*, the *Low Countries*, &c., and have beene the chiefe meanes to raiſe the manufacture of all wollen commodities to that height in which it now exifteth, which is the moſt famous ſtaple of the Land, and whereby the poore in all Countries are plentifully maintained: and of this Company his Lordſhip is free; as alſo of the *Levant*, or *Turkey*, and of the *Eaſt India* Company, whoſe trading hath beene, and is in theſe forraine adventures: alſo who ſpent many yeares and a great part of his youth in other Countries.

Now the firſt ſhow by water is preſented by *St. Katherine*, of whom I will give you this ſhort Character: *She was the daughter of King* Coſtus, *and had the generall title of Queene of* Famogoſta, *becauſe crowned in that City, being lineally diſcended from the* Roman *Emperors, who as ſhe lived a Virgin ſo ſhe dyed a Martyr, under the Tyrant* Maxentius, *whoſe Empreſſe with divers other eminent perſons ſhe had before converted to the Faith: ſhe rideth on a Scallop, which is part of his Lordſhips Coate of Armes, drawne in a Sea-Chariot, by two Sea-horſes with divers other adornments to beautifie the peece: the Art of which, the eye may better diſcover, than my pen deſcribe, and why ſhe being a Princeſſe, and Patroneſſe of this Company of the Haberdaſhers, who onely ruled on the Land, ſhould at this time appeare upon the water, and without any iuſt taxation, to make that cleare, ſhee thus delivereth her ſelfe.*

St. Katherines *ſpeech by Water.*

Great *Prætor*, and grave Senators, ſhe craves
A free admittance on theſe curled waves,
Who doth from long antiquity profeſſe
Her ſelfe to be your gratious Patroneſſe:
Oft have I on a paſſant Lyon ſate,
And through your populous ſtreets beene borne in ſtate:
Oft have I grac't your Triumphes on the ſhore,
But on the Waters was not ſeene before.
Will you the reaſon know why it doth fall,
That I thus change my Element? you ſhall:

When *Triton* with his pearly trumpets blew
A ftreperous blaft, to fummon all the crew
Of Marine gods and goddeffes to appeare,
(As the annuall cuftome is) and meet you here:
As they were then in councell to debate,
What honour they might adde unto the ftate
Of this Inauguration; there appear'd
God *Mercury*, who would from *Jove* be heard:
His *Caducæus* filence might command;
Whilft all attentive were to underftand
The tenor of his meffage: who thus fpake.

The Sire of gods, with what you undertake
Is highly pleas'd, and greatly doth commend
That faire defigne and purpofe you intend;
But he beheld a Machine from an high,
Which at firft fight daz'd his immortall eye;
A royall Arke, whofe bright and glorious beams
Rivall the Sunnes, ready to proove your ftreames:
A veffell of fuch beauty, burthen, ftate,
That all the high Powers were amaz'd thereat;
So beautified, fo munified, fo clad,
As might an eight to the feaven wonders adde:
Which muft be now your charge; 'twas *Joves* owne motion,
That all of you attend her to the *Ocean*.

This notwithftanding, fuch was their great care,
(To fhew that o're you they indulgent are)
That *Neptune* from his Chariot bad me chufe
Two of his beft Sea-horfes, to excufe
His inforc't abfence: *Thames* (whofe breaft doth fwell
Still with that glorious burthen) bad me tell,
That *Joves* command fhall be no fooner done,
But every Tide he'le on your errands runne
From hence to the Lands end, and thence againe
Backe, to conveigh your trafficke from the Maine:
My meffage thus delivered; now proceed
To take your oath; there is no further need

Of my affiftance: who on Land will meete you,
And with the ftate of greater Triumphes greete you.

Thefe few following Lines may, (and not impertinently) be added unto *Jupiters* meffage, delivered by *Mercury*, which though too long for the Bardge, may perhaps not fhew lame in the booke, as being leffe troublefome to the Reader than the Rower.

Dance in thy raine-bow colours *Protæus*, change
Thy felfe to thoufand figures, 'tis not ftrange
With thee, thou old Sea-prophet, throng the feas
With *Phorcus* Daughters, the *Nereides*,
And all the blew-hair'd Nymphes, in number more,
Than Barkes that float, or Pibbles on the fhore:
Take *Æolus* along to fill her failes
With profperous windes, and keepe within his gailes
Tempeftuous gufts: which was no fooner faid,
But done: for all the Marine gods obey'd.

The fecond fhow, but the firft by Land, is prefented by the great *Philofopher Pythagoras, Samius*, the fonne of *Menarchus*; which being outwardly *Sphericall* and *Orbicular*, yet being opened it quadrates it felfe iuft into fo many *Angles* as there be Scepters, over which his Sacred Maiefty beareth title: namely, *England, Scotland, France*, and *Ireland*, concerning which number of *foure*, I thus Read: *Pythagoras* and his *Schollers*, who taught in his fchooles, that *Ten* was the nature and foule of all number; one Reafon which he gave (to omit the reft) was, becaufe all nations, as well civill as barbarous, can tell no farther than to the *Denary*, which is *Ten*, and then returne in their account unto the *Monady*, that is one: For example, from *Tenne* wee proceed to *Eleven* and *Twelve*, which is no more than *Ten* and *One*, *Ten* and *Two*, and fo of the reft, till the number rife to an infinite.

Againe hee affirmeth, that the ftrength and vertue of all number confifteth in the *quarternion*; for begin-

ning with *one, two, three,* and *foure,* put them together
and they make *ten*; he faith further, that the nature of
number confifteth in *ten,* and the faculty of number
is comprized in *foure*: in which refpect the *Pythago-
reans* exprefſe their holy oath in the *quaternion,*
which they cal'd τετρακτιν, as may appear in thefe
words.

Per tibi noſtræ animæ præbentem tetrada Iuro,
Naturæ fontemque & firmamenta perennis.

For they held the foule of man to fubfift in that number, proportionating it into thefe *foure* Faculties, *Mens,*
Scientia, Opinio, Senfus, the *Mind, Knowledge, Opi-*
nion, and *Sence,* and therefore according to that number *Pythagoras* frames his *Speech,* alluding to thofe
four Kingdomes over which his Maiefty beareth
title.

The *Speech* of the fecond Show, delivered in *Paules* Church-yard.

Sacred's the number foure, *Philofophers fay,*
 And beares an happy Omen; as this day
It may appeare: foure *Elements confpire,*
Namely, the Water, Earth, the Aire, and Fire,
To make up man: the colours in him bred
Are alfo foure, *White, Pallid, Blacke, and red:*
Of foure *Complexions he exifteth foly,*
Flegmaticke, Sanguine, Choler, Melancholy.
His meate foure *feverall digeftions gaines,*
In Stomacke, Liver, Members, and the Veines.
Foure *qualities cald* primæ *within lie,*
Which are thus titled, Hot, Cold, Moift, and Drie.
He acts his whole life on this earthy ftage,
In Child-hood, Youth, Man-hood, Decripit age.
The very day that doth afford him light,
Is Morning, the Meridian, Evening, Night.
Foure *feafons ftill fucceffively appeare,*

Which put together make a compleat yeare.
The earth, with all the Kingdomes therein guided,
Is into foure *distinguish'd parts devided.*
The foure *Windes from the Worlds* foure *quarters blow,*
Eurus, Favonius, Auster, Aquilo.
All Morall vertues we in foure *include,*
As Prudence, Iustice, Temperance, Fortitude.
Court, City, Campe, and Countrey, the foure *C C C s ;*
Which represent to us the foure *degrees,*
Requir'd in every faire and flourishing Land,
Substract but one a Kingdome cannot stand.
Foure Colonels *are in this City knowne,*
Of which you, honoured Sir, have long beene one :
And those foure Crownes, *(for so the high Powers please)*
Embleme the Kings foure *Scepters, and* foure *Seas.*
The fift (1) Imperiall Arch above, *proclaimes*
That glorious Crowne, *at which his* Highnesse *aimes.*
Thus is our round Globe *squared, figuring his power,*
And yours beneath Him, in the number foure.

The third Show.

THe third Pageant or Show meerly consisteth of Anticke gesticulations, dances, and other Mimicke postures, devised onely for the vulgar, who are better delighted with that which pleaseth the eye, than contenteth the eare, in which we imitate *Custome*, which alwaies carrieth with it excuse : neither are they altogether to be vilefied by the most supercilious, and censorious, especially in such a confluence, where all Degrees, Ages, and Sexes are assembled, every of them looking to bee presented with some fancy or other, according to their expectations and humours : Since grave and wise men have beene of opinion, that it is convenient, nay necessitous, upon the like occasions, to mixe *seria*

---

(1) Quinta perennis.

iocis; for what better can set off matter, than when it is interlaced with mirth? From that I proceede to the fourth.

The fourth Show.

IT beareth the Title of an *Imperiall* Fort : nor is it compulsive, that here I should argue what a Fort is, a Skonce, or a Cittadall, nor what a Counterskarfe, or halfe Moone, &c. is; nor what the opposures or defences are: my purpose is onely to expresse my selfe thus farre, that this Fort which is stil'd *Imperiall*, defenc'd with men and officers, suiting their functions and places proper to such a muniment; doth in the morall include his Majesties royall chamber, which is the City of *London*, for to that onely purpose was the project intended.

The Speaker is *Bellona*, whom some held to be the Daughter, some the Sister, others the Nurse of *Mars* the god of Warre; neither in any of these is any impropriety, or ought that is dissonant from authority, because *Enyo*, which is *Bellona*, implyeth that which putteth spirit and courage into an army. &c. Antiquity called her *Duellona*, that is, the goddesse of warre, to whom their Priests sacrificed their owne blood, and before whose Temple the *Fœcialis* set a speare against some prime pillar thereof, when any publicke warre was to be denounced: Shee was most honoured of the *Thracians*, the *Scithians*, and those wild and barbarous nations, upon whose Altars they used to sacrifice a Vulture, which is a ravenous bird, used to prey upon dead carcasses, and assemble themselves in great flocks after any fought battaile: but this Discourse may to some appeare impertinent to the project in hand, and therefore I thus proceed to her speech.

Bellonaes *Speech upon the* Imperiall *Fort.*

THis *Structure (honour'd* Sir) *doth title beare*
 Of an Imperiall Fort, *apt for that spheare*
In which you now moove, borrowing all her grace,

As well from your owne perſon as your place;
For you have paſt through all the degrees that tended
Vnto that height which you have now aſcended.

   You have beene in this City *('tis knowne well)*
A Souldier, Captaine, *and a* Colonell.
And now in times faire progreſſe, to crowne all,
Of this Metropolis *chiefe Generall.*
You, of this Embleme, which this day we bring,
To repreſent the Chamber of the King,
Are the prime governour: a Royall Fort,
And ſtrongly ſcited, as not built for ſport,
But for example and defence: a Tower
Supported by no leſſe than Soveraigne power:
The Theologicke *vertues, the three* Graces,
And Charities *have here their ſeverall places.*
Here Piety, *true* Zeale, *ſtudy of* Peace,   <small>Concordia</small>
(By which ſmall mites to Magozines *increaſe)* <small>parva res</small>
<small>Creſcunt,</small>
Have reſidence: now oppoſite there are   <small>is the Motto</small>
To theſe, and with them at continuall warre, <small>of the Com-</small>
<small>pany of the</small>
Pride, Arrogance, Sloath, Vanity, Preſtigion, <small>right Wor-</small>
Prophaneſſe, the contempt of true Religion,   <small>ſhipfull</small>
<small>Habber-</small>
With thouſands more, who aſſiduatly waite   <small>daſhers.</small>
This your Imperiall Fort *to inſidiate.*

   You may obſerve i'th muſicke of your Bels
Like found in Triumphes, *and for funerall knels;*
Marriage and death to them appeare all one,
Masking nor mourning cannot change their tone:
With our Fort *'tis not ſo, whoſe faire pretence, is*
To comply with the nature of offences,
Errors; *ſhe knowes in low termes how to chide*
Great faults, with greater noiſe are terrifi'd:
But ſhe can load her Cannons, *and ſpeake loud*
To encounter with the arrogant and proud:
Whats further in your Prætorſhip *aſsign'd,*
You, in your Londons Mirrour *there may find.*

The fifth show, cald Londons Mirrour.

THis beareth the title of the whole Triumphe; of Glasses pertinent to this our purpose, there bee severall sorts, as *Opticke, Perspective, Prospective, Multiplying, &c.* The presenter is *Visus*, or Sight; for what the minde is to the soule, the same is the eye to the body, being the most precious part thereof. Sight is the most soveraigne sence, the first of five, which directeth man to the studdy & search of knowledge & wisedome; the eyes are placed in the head as in a Citadel, to be watch-towers and Centinels for the safety, and guiders and conducters for the sollace of the body.

We read that one *Marcus Varro* was sir-named *Strabo*, for the excellency and quicknesse of his sight, who from *Libæum*, a Province in *Scicilia*, could distinguish and give an exact account of all such ships as came out of the haven of *Carthage*, which two places some hold to be more than an hundred *Italian* leagues distant: indeed no man can better estimate the vertue and value of the sight, than he that is made blinde and wants it, neither could I devise a more apt Speaker to present this *Mirrour*, than the sence of the sight, without which, the purest Christall is of no use at all.

The Pageant it selfe is decored with glasses of all sorts: the persons upon or about it are beautifull Children, every one of them expressing their natures and conditions in the impresaes of their shields, eight of the prime of which suiting with the quality of the *Optick* sence, beare these severall Inscriptions: *Aspice, Despice, Conspice, Prospice, Perspice, Inspice, Circumspice, Respice:*

Οψσις, or *Opsis* the Speaker.

BEhold me Sight, *of the five sences prime;*
(*Now best complying with the place and time*)
Presenting Londons Mirrour, *and this Glasse*

Shewes not alone what she is, or once was,
But that the spacious Vniverse might see
In her, what their great Cities ought to be;
That every forraigne Magistrate from hence
Might learne how to dispose his Opticke *sence.*

    Aspice *saith, Looke toward and upon*
Desartfull men whom this Age frowneth on.
And Despice *cast downe thy powerfull eye*
On the poore wretch that doth beneath thee lye.
Then Conspice *take counsell first and pause*
With meditation, ere thou iudge a cause.
Prospice *bids looke afarre off, and view*
(Before conclude) what dangers may insue.
Perspice *wils, in sifting doubts, then scan*
The nature of the matter with the man.
Let every cause be searcht, and duely sought,
Saith Inspice, *ere thou determinst ought.*
Circumspice *saith, looke about to immure*
So great a charge, that all within be sure.
Considerate Respice *inioynes thee last,*
To cast thine eyes backe upon all things past.

    For Londons *selfe, if they shall first begin*
To examine her without, and then within,
What Architectures, Palaces, what Bowers,
What Citadels, what turrets, and what towers?
Who in her age, grew pregnant, brought a bed
Of a New Towne, *and late delivered*
Of such a burthen, as in few yeares space,
Can almost speake all tongues, (to her more grace.)
Then her Cathedrals, Temples *new reparing,*
An act of true devotion, no man sparing
His helping hand; and many, 'tis well knowne,
To further Gods house have forgot their owne.

    Vnto her outward shape I doe not prize her,
But let them come within to anatomize her.
Her Prætor, *scarlet Senate, Liveries,*
The ordering of her brave societies:
Divine Astræa *here in equall scale*
Doth ballance Iustice, Truth *needes not looke pale,*

Londons Mirrour.

Nor poverty deiected, th' Orphants cause,
And Widowes plea finde helpe ; no Jubtile clause
Can make demurre in sentence : a faire hearing,
And upright doome in every Court appearing :
   Still to preserve her so, be't your indeavour,
   And she in you ; you her shall live for ever.

I come now to the Linvoy, or last Speech, when his Lordship, after his dayes long and tedious trouble, retireth himselfe to his rest at night, in which *Pythagoras* the Speaker briefly runs over the passages of the Pageant before expressed, after this manner.

The Speech at Night.

WE *to a* Valediction *are confin'd,*
   (Right Honoured) *and intreat You beare in minde*
What was this Day presented : Your *chiefe* Saint
A Martyr *once of the* Church militant,
But now of the tryumphant, *bids You spare*
Your selfe this Night : for to a World of Care
You are ingag'd to morrow, which must last
Till the whole progresse of Your Yeere *be past.*
The Spheare-like Globe quadrated, lets You know,
What Pro-Rex *doth to the foure Scepters owe.*
Your Military honours, (*in your Dayes*
Of lesse command) *th'* Imperiall Fort *displayes,*
And Londons Mirrour, *that all men may see*
What Magistrates *have beene, and ought to be.*
Set is the Sunne *long since, and now the Light*
Quite fayling us, Thrice Honourd Sir, *good Night.*

For the Artists, and directors of these Pageants and showes, *John Christmas* and *Mathias*, the two Sonnes of *Gerard*, their now deceased Father, a knowne Master in all those Sciences he profest : I can say no more but thus, that proportioning their Workes according to the limits of the gates through which they were to paffe, being ty'de not to exceede one Inch either in height, or breadth: My Opinion is, that few Workemen about the Towne can paralell them, much leffe exceede them. But if any fhall either out of Curiofity or malice taxe their ability, in this kind of Art, I referre them to the Carving of his Majefties *Great Ship* lately built at *Woolwitch*, which Worke alone is able both to fatisfie *Emulation*, and qualifie *Envie*.

FINIS.

NOTES AND ILLUSTRATIONS.

PAGE 1.
THE ENGLISH TRAVELLER.

Reprinted in the Sixth Volume of Dilke's *Old Plays* (1816).

Of the *English Traveller* the story, as far as it relates to Young Lionel and Reignald, is (as Langbaine observes) borrowed from the *Mortellaria* of Plautus. Indeed, so considerable a part of the play is closely copied from that performance, that it is curious Heywood did not think it necessary to acknowledge the obligation.

The *English Traveller*, it may be added further, is not the only drama which has been very deeply indebted to the *Mortellaria*. The *Intriguing Chambermaid* of Fielding is evidently founded upon it: and the entertainment given by the rakish son, the old man's return from a voyage, the project of the knavish servant to prevent the father's surprising the company that were carousing in his house by making him believe it was haunted, and his pretending that the young gentleman had purchased another in the room of it, are all introduced with little variation from the original. And these observations apply as closely to *The English Traveller*, as to the *Intriguing Chambermaid*.

PAGE 16.
Drinke Whig *and sowre Milke*.

"Whig" was formed from the whey of milk after the cheese curd had been separated from it by runnet, a second and inferior curd being separated from the whey by an acid mixture; the remainder, after a slight fermentation, was called *whig*, and drunk by the poorer classes instead of small beer.

PAGE 26.
Alfareffe.

Alfarez, or *alfares*, feems to have been a fubordinate officer (an enfign, fays Reed). Don Juan, in Maffinger's *Rule a Wife and have a Wife*, fays, Leon had been recommended to him as his "Alferez."

Ib.
rebellings.

Qy. "*Ravelines?*"

PAGE 28.
In the height of their caroufing, all their braines
Warmd with the heate of wine, &c.

"This piece of pleafant exaggeration," fays Charles Lamb, "(which, for its life and humour might have been told, or acted, by Petruchio himfelf) gave rife to the title of Cowley's Latin play, *Naufragium Ioculare*, and furnifhed the idea of the beft fcene in it."

Hazlitt confiders this account of fhipwreck by drink "the moft fplendid paffage in Heywood's comedies."

PAGE 48.
Pollute the Nuptiall bed with Michall *finne.*

The word "michall," or "mechal," has been already explained.

Mr. Dilke, not being able to underftand it, fubftituted "mickle," though he confeffed himfelf "not altogether fatisfied with the alteration"!

PAGE 63.
What braue cann'd poafts; Who knowes but heere,
In time, Sir, you may keepe your Shreualtie.

It appears from many of our old writers, that it was cuftomary for the fheriff to have pofts in front of his houfe, ornamented in fome particular way, probably for the purpofe of pointing out his refidence, or, as Warburton conjectures, "that the King's proclamations, and other public acts, might be affixed thereon by way of publication."

PAGE 65.
Chauelah.

A corruption of *Qui va là?*

PAGE 167.
THE LATE LANCASHIRE WITCHES.

In 1633 Pendle Foreſt again became the ſcene of pretended witchcrafts : and from various circumſtances the trial which took place then has acquired even greater notoriety than that which preceded it twenty years before. The particulars are ſubſtantially compriſed in the *Examination of Edmund Robinſon* (1) ſon of Edm. Robinſon, of Pendle Foreſt, Maſon, taken at Padiham, before Richard Shuttleworth and John Starkie, Eſqs., two of his Majeſty's juſtices of the peace, within the county of Lancaſter, 10th February, 1633.

Heywood and Brome, in their play, *The late Lancaſhire Witches,* follow the terms of this depoſition very cloſely. It is very probable that they had ſeen and converſed with the boy, to whom, when taken up to London, there was a great reſort of company. The Lancaſhire dialect, as given in this play, and by no means unfaithfully, was perhaps derived from converſations with ſome of the actors in this drama of real life—a drama quite as extraordinary as any that Heywood's imagination ever bodied forth from the world of fiction.

Alice Nutter (concerning whom ſee *The Wonderfull Diſcoverie of Witches in the Countie of Lancaſter by Thomas Potts,* 1613) (2) was doubtleſs the original of the ſtory of which Heywood availed himſelf in the *The late Lancaſhire Witches*—a ſtory frequently noticed by the writers of the ſeventeenth century—that the wife of a Lancaſhire country gentleman had been detected in

---

(1) This examination (which is too long to be given here) is printed *in extenſo* in Whitaker's *Whalley,* p. 213 ; Webſter's *Diſplaying of Witchcraft,* p. 347 ; and Baines's *Lancaſhire,* vol. i. p. 604.

(2) Reprinted for the Chetham Society (*Remains Hiſtorical and Literary, Vol. VI.*) in 1845, with an Introduction and Notes by James Croſſley, Eſq.; to which we are mainly indebted for the information given above.

practifing witchcraft and unlawful arts, and had been condemned and executed. " In that play there can be little hefitation in afcribing to Heywood the fcenes in which Mr. Generous and his wife are the interlocutors, and to Brome the fubordinate and farcical portions. It is a very unequal performance, but not deftitute of thofe fine touches, which Heywood is never without, in the characters of Englifh country gentlemen and the pathos of domeftic tragedy."—CROSSLEY (*ubi fuprà*) : Introduction, lxv—lxx. ; Notes, pp. 34—38.

There is a reprint of this play by Mr. Halliwell, thus entitled: " The Poetry of Witchcraft illuftrated by Copies of the Plays on the Lancafhire Witches by Heywood and Shadwell. Brixton Hill : Printed for Private Circulation only, 1853."

Mr. Harrifon Ainfworth has written a romance on the fubject of *The Lancafhire Witches.*

PAGE 262.

Londons Ius Honorarium.

An exact reprint from the only copy known to be extant o this pageant, kindly placed at our difpofal by H. Huth, Efq., of whofe invaluable library it is one of the many pricelefs treafures.

Heywood alfo wrote the pageants for 1632 and 1633 : to thefe we have not fucceeded in obtaining accefs ; but we are enabled to give fome account of them extracted from an interefting book publifhed fome thirty years ago by the Percy Society. (2).

That of 1632 is entitled : " Londini Artium et Scientiarum Scaturigo, Londons Fountain of Arts and Sciences ; expreft in fundrie Triumphes, Pageants and Shews, at the Initiation of the Right Honorable Nich. Raynton, in the Majoralty of the famous and far-renowned City of London. All the charge and Expenfe of the Laborious Projects, both by Sea and Land, being the fole Undertaking and Charge of the Right Worfhipfull Company of Haberdafhers. Written by Thomas Heywood. Lond. 1632."

The Pageant of 1633 is entitled :—" Londini Emporia, or London's

---

(2) Lord Mayor's Pageants : being Collections towards a hiftory of thefe Annual Celebrations. By F. W. Fairholt. Lond. (Percy Society), Part I., 1843.

Mercatura: expreſt in ſundry triumphs, pageants, and ſhowes, at the inauguration of the Right Honorable Ralph Freeman into the Maioralty of the famous and farre-renowned citty London. All the charge and expenſe of the laborious proiects, both by water and land being the ſole undertaking of the Right Worſhipfull Company of the Cloath-workers. Written by Thomas Heywood. *Redeunt Spectacula.* Printed at London by Nicholas Okes. 1633."

The pamphlet opens with the praiſe of merchantmen, detailing "the eight offices of piety in a merchant required:—" 1. Rectitude of conſcience; 2. Abſence of equivocation; 3. Honeſty in bargaining; 4. Juſtice; 5. Humility; 6. Charity to the poor; 7. Abſence of Avarice; 8. A renunciation of "all care and trouble of mind, which may hinder divine contemplation." Of courſe—"all theſe things defireable being knowne to be eminent in your lordſhip," Heywood tells us, "was the maine inducement to entitle this preſent ſhow by this apt denomination *Londoni Emporia.*"

The firſt pageant is exhibited on the water; "which is a ſea-chariot, beautified and adorned with ſhel-fiſhes of ſundry faſhion and ſplendour." It is drawn by two griffins; upon them are ſeated two figures bearing pendants, "upon which are portrayed the armes of the two ſheriffes now in place." Thames rides in the chariot, ſurrounded by water nymphs, and appears to arouſe from a ſleep, as the mayor's barge approaches. He addreſſes him in a ſpeech, which contains an alluſion to the "clenſing of the river at this time by ſundry water engines," in theſe ſtrange words:—

"Can Thameſis himſelf ſo far forget?
But 'tis long ſince Tame and Iſis met,
That 'tis not rare; for we two are groune old,
And being rivers, ſubiect to take cold;
Forc't with extremity of paine to grone,
As troubled with the gravell and the ſtone,
(Whole ſhelves are in our raines) but (Fates ſo pleaſe)
By artiſts' helpe wee late have got ſome eaſe.
Thanks to our patriots!"

After explaining the pageant and its myſtic alluſions, he ends:—

"But why ſhould I, though beſt of Neptunes' ſons,

> (Whofe ftreame almoft by your permiffion runnes)
> Inftruct him who can teach? fince the laft yeare,
> Till this day, never ran my tides fo cleare
> As now they doe, were never fo become
> With barges, enfignes, trumpets, fyfe and drum,
> Methinkes you make mee young againe to view,
> Old cuftomes kept, and (in them) all things new."

The firft fhow by land is placed in St. Paul's Churchyard. It is the trade-pageant of the company.—The fhepherd and fheep, with his dog guarding them from the ever-watchful wolf. He fits "upon a dyall, to which his fheep-hooke is the gnomon," and he explains this, in his fpeech to the mayor.—

> "As I, fo you muft on a dyall fit,
> Which hath no gnomon but my ftaffe to it,
> And fuch your fword is now, your wakefull eye
> Muft ftill be ope, to watch where you can fpy
> The ravenous woolfe, to preffe, and blocke the way,
> Leaft hee on any of your flocke fhould prey.
>
> . . . . .
>
> And that your charge fo carefully be borne,
> That they be neuer *but in feafon* fhorne."

The fecond pageant "is a fhip, moft proper to the trade of merchant-adventurers," with Mercury as pilot, who addreffes the mayor in a fpeech alluding to his own large mercantile occupation, and its confequent beneficial effects to the country.

"The third fhow by land, is a modell devifed to humour the throng, who come rather to fee than to heare: and without fome fuch intruded anti-maske, many who carry their ears in their eyes, will not fticke to fay, *I will not give a pinne for the Show*. Since therefore it confifts only in motion, agitation, and action, and thefe (expreffed to the life) being apparently vifible to all, in vaine fhould I imploy a fpeaker, where I prefuppofe all his words would be drown'd in noyfe and laughter. I therefore paffe to the fourth and laft."

"Which is a curious and neately framed architect, beautified with many proper and becoming ornaments: bearing the title of the Bower of Bliffe; an embleme of that future happineffe which not onely all juft and upright magiftrates, but every good man, of what condition or quality foever, in the courfe of his life efpecially aimeth at." Herein are feated Prudence, Temperance, Juftice and Fortitude, and "the three theologicall vertues, Faith, Hope and Charity, as handmaides attending to conduct all fuch pious and religious magiftrates the way to the celeftiall bower of bliffe." Prudence defcribes and defcants upon all in a moral fpeech, in which fhe delares it

"Aptly may be titled *Freeman's* bower."

"The fpeech at night" alludes "to the twelve celeftiall fignes, which may aptly be applied unto the twelve moneths during the lord mayor's goverment." The entire fpeech runs thus :—

" Sleepe may you foundly fir, to morrow preft
To a yeares trouble, for this one nights reft,
In which may ftarres and planets all confpire,
To warme you fo by their celeftiall fire ;
Aries whofe Gold Fleece Greece doth fo renowne,
May both inrich you, and this glorious toune,
That *Taurus* in your ftrength may fo appeare,
You this great weight may on your fhoulders beare ;
That the two *Twins*, the mother's bleft increafe,
May in this citty ftill continue peace.
That *Cancer* who incites to hate and fpleene,
May not in your faire government be feene,
That *Leo* waiting on your iudgement feate,
May moderate his rage and fcorching heate ;
That the celeftial *Maide* may you aduife,
Virgins and orphans ftill to patronize ;
And rather then your juftice heere fhould faile,
Libra no more be feene with golden fcale ;
And that the *Scorpions* fting may be fo charm'd,
The poore may not be wrong'd nor innocent harm'd.
That *Chiron's* bent bow fo may guide your will,
You may ftill aime, but neuer fhoote to kill ;
And *Capricorne* though all things faid to dare,
Though he haue power, yet may have will to fpare ;
That as *Aquarius* doth his water power,
You may your goodnefs on this city fhower :

Pifces, the laſt of twelve, the feet they guide,
From head to foot, O may you fo provide.

It ends with praiſe of " Mr. Gerald Chriſmas," who conſtructed the pageant. Heywood having previouſly returned thanks to the wardens and committee of the Clothworkers company, " for their affability and courtefie, unto myſelfe, being at that time to them all a meere ſtranger, who when I ſent my then unperfect papers, were as able to judge of them, as attentively to heare them ; and rather judicially confidering all things, then nicely carping at any thing."

www.ingramcontent.com/pod-product-compliance
Lightning Source LLC
Chambersburg PA
CBHW030732230426
43667CB00007B/683